Literature and Race in the Democracy of Goods

Bloomsbury Studies in Critical Poetics

Series Editor: Daniel Katz, University of Warwick, UK

Political, social, erotic, and aesthetic—poetry has been a challenge to many of the dominant discourses of our age across the globe. Bloomsbury Studies in Critical Poetics publishes books on modern and contemporary poetry and poetics that explore the intersection of poetry with philosophy, linguistics, psychoanalysis, political and economic theory, protest and liberation movements, as well as other art forms, including prose. With a primary focus on texts written in English but including work from other languages, the series brings together leading and rising scholars from a diverse range of fields for whom poetry has become a vital element of their research.

Titles in the series include:
Affect, Psychoanalysis, and American Poetry, John Steen
City Poems and American Urban Crisis, Nate Mickelson
Lyric Pedagogy and Marxist-Feminism, Samuel Solomon
A Black Arts Poetry Machine, David Grundy
Queer Troublemakers, Prudence Bussey-Chamberlain

Forthcoming titles:
Radical Elegies, Eleanor Perry

Literature and Race in the Democracy of Goods

Reading Contemporary Black and Asian North American Poetry

Christopher Chen

BLOOMSBURY ACADEMIC
LONDON • NEW YORK • OXFORD • NEW DELHI • SYDNEY

BLOOMSBURY ACADEMIC
Bloomsbury Publishing Plc
50 Bedford Square, London, WC1B 3DP, UK
1385 Broadway, New York, NY 10018, USA
29 Earlsfort Terrace, Dublin 2, Ireland

BLOOMSBURY, BLOOMSBURY ACADEMIC and the Diana logo
are trademarks of Bloomsbury Publishing Plc

First published in Great Britain 2022
This paperback edition published 2024

Cover design: Eleanor Rose
Cover image © Studio Parris Wakefield/ Ikon Images

A catalogue record for this book is available from the British Library.

A catalog record for this book is available from the Library of Congress.

ISBN: HB: 978-1-3501-6400-0
PB: 978-1-3502-7880-6
ePDF: 978-1-3501-6401-7
eBook: 978-1-3501-6402-4

Series: Bloomsbury Studies in Critical Poetics

Typeset by Integra Software Services Pvt. Ltd.

Contents

Acknowledgments

Thanks to Daniel Katz, series editor at Bloomsbury, David Avital, Laura Cope, and the external readers for their useful and clarifying comments. Earlier drafts of Chapters 2 and 3, as well as a portion of the Coda, were published in the anthology *Reading Experimental Literature*, edited by Georgina Colby, *boundary 2* (Vol. 46, Issue 4), and post-45 *Contemporaries* cluster on "Poetry's Social Forms," respectively. Thank you to Phillip Brian Harper, Margo Crawford, and Evie Shockley for encouragement and an early opportunity to present work in progress at the 2016 Modern Language Association annual conference. I would also like to thank Myung Mi Kim for the opportunity to present work in progress at the 2017 "Poetics Plus" Series at the Buffalo Poetics Program. I am grateful for the institutional support provided by the University of California at Santa Cruz Humanities Institute Research Fellowship. Thanks also to the University of Sussex Asa Briggs Fellowship for giving me the chance to enter into conversation with Natalia Cecire, Samuel Solomon, Sara Crangle, Amy De'Ath, Sean O'Brien, and Seb Franklin.

I'm indebted to friends, advisors, teachers, colleagues, and reading group participants near and far for lively conversations about the relationship between race, capitalism, and/or contemporary literature. Thank you Colleen Lye, Chris Nealon, Lyn Hejinian, Sau-Ling Wong, Juliana Spahr, Joshua Clover, Margaret Ronda, Jasper Bernes, Claudia Rankine, Wendy Trevino, Brigitte Johnson, Oki Sogumi, Chris O'Kane, Beverly Best, Tongo Eisen-Martin, Chika Okoye, Melissa Mack, Andrew Wilson, Michelle Koerner, Lara Durback, Ben Furstenberg, Angela Hume Lewandowski, Madeline Lane-McKinley, Kyle Lane-McKinley, Jackie Wang, Bhanu Kapil, David Buuck, David Lau, Hugo Garcia Manriquez, Melanie Gilligan, Roger Reeves, Daniel Borzutzky, Trisha Low, Neil Larsen, Dennis Terry, George Ciccariello-Maher, Zhivka Valiavicharska, Zachary Levenson, Daniel Marcus, Christopher Daniels, John Gould, Cathy Park Hong, Francesca Manning, Tara Fickle, Neal Shirley, Saralee Stafford, Hunter Bivens, Jo Isaacson, Brian Whitener, and Dan Nemser.

I would also like to acknowledge the support of the UC Santa Cruz Literature Department, and in particular the staff and faculty who provided invaluable assistance in navigating the institution. Thank you Carla Freccero, Jody Greene,

Susan Gillman, Kim Lau, Juan Poblete, Kirstin Gruesz, Sharon Kinoshita, Chris Connery, Dorian Bell, Sean Keilen, Bali Sahota, Vilashini Cooppan, Tyrus Miller, Deanna Shemek, Sylvanna Falcon, Nathaniel Deutsch, Amy Tessier, Stephanie Casher, Heidi Flores, Julie Hannah Brower, and Janina Larenas. I'd also like to express my appreciation for the faculty in the Creative/Critical concentration at UC Santa Cruz—Micah Perks, Ronaldo Wilson, Karen Tei Yamashita, Rob Wilson, Gary Young, and Melissa Sanders-Self.

The arguments of this book have been honed in ongoing conversations with Sarika Chandra about the theoretical relationship between race and capital. Special thanks to Tim Kreiner, whose rich understanding of New Left and post–New Left movement history has shaped my readings of contemporary US poetry written over the course of the postwar "long downturn."

I have had the privilege of being in conversation with some extraordinary graduate students at the University of California at Santa Cruz. Thank you Angie Sijun Lou, Jane Komori, Luling Osofsky, Shu Chang, Whitney De Vos, Gabriela Ramirez Chavez, Kenan Sharpe, Cathy Thomas, Eric Sneathen, Nicholas Whittington, Ryan Lee, and Jose Antonio Villarán, for intellectual inspiration and for modeling a deep commitment to transforming the conditions of teaching and learning in public universities beyond visions of inclusion within precarity.

Finally, a lifetime of gratitude to Susan Maxwell and Sidney for seeing, and helping me to see, beyond the petrified forms.

I would like to acknowledge permission to reprint works cited within this study:

"Das Kapital." By Amiri Baraka, from *SOS: Poems 1961–2013*, copyright © Grove Press, 2016. Reprinted by permission of Grove Press.

"photo-essay." By Theresa Hak Kyung Cha, from *Exilée and Temps Morts: Selected Works*, copyright © 2009 by the Regents of the University of California. Reprinted by permission of the University of California Press.

Excerpts from *Piece Logic* in *Jump the Clock: New & Selected Poems*. By Erica Hunt, copyright © 2020 by Erica Hunt. Reprinted by permission of Nightboat Books.

"Toward a Personal Semantics." By June Jordan, in *Directed by Desire: The Collected Poems of June Jordan*, copyright © Copper Canyon Press, 2007. Reprinted by permission of The June M. Jordan Literary Estate Trust.

Excerpts from *Dura*. By Myung Mi Kim, copyright © 2008 by Myung Mi Kim. Reprinted by permission of Nightboat Books.

"nascent fashion." By Larissa Lai, from *Automaton Biographies*, copyright © 2010 by Larissa Lai. Reprinted by permission of Arsenal Pulp Press.

"rachel." By Larissa Lai, from *Automaton Biographies*, copyright © 2010 by Larissa Lai. Reprinted by permission of Arsenal Pulp Press.

Excerpts from *S*PeRM**K*T*. By Harryette Mullen, from *Recyclopedia: Trimmings, S*PeRM**K*T, and Muse & Drudge*, copyright © 2006 by Harryette Mullen. Reprinted by permission of Graywolf Press.

Excerpts from *City Eclogue*. By Ed Roberson, copyright © 2006 by Ed Roberson. Reprinted by permission of Atelos Press and the author.

"Ing Grish." By John Yau, from *Ing Grish*, copyright © 2005 by John Yau. Reprinted by permission of Saturnalia Books.

Introduction: Capitalism and Racial Form

The Triple Revolution

On March 22, 1964, twenty-six scholars, activists, and public intellectuals—from James Boggs and H. Stuart Hughes to Tom Hayden and Michael Harrington—sent a document to President Lyndon Johnson titled *The Triple Revolution*. Published by the Center for the Study of Democratic Institutions, a liberal think tank partially funded by the Ford Foundation, the short statement warned that industrial automation, Cold War nuclear proliferation, and a broader international "human rights revolution" would remake postwar life in the United States, with far-reaching global consequences. For the signers of the document, automation and "cybernation," or the computerized control of the industrial manufacturing of commodities, posed a grave threat to the gains of the civil rights movement and the future of US workers. At the end of an unprecedented national postwar economic boom, technological innovation promised ever-greater productivity gains while at the same time threatening workers with mass unemployment.

Civil rights movement aims of integrating Black workers into a racially desegregated US economy, the document argued, would be undermined by the increasing superfluity of industrial labor. Excluded from white-collar employment, Black workers were only partially incorporated into northern manufacturing industries and vulnerable to high unemployment levels in a booming postwar economy. This shift offers an understudied material context for understanding how discourses of Black racial difference came to register the historical transition from enslaved labor to persistent and elevated intergenerational unemployment amid lavish postwar consumer abundance. "The demand of the civil rights movement cannot be fulfilled within the present context of society," the *Triple Revolution* document continues, sounding a warning about the racial consequences of "being exiled from the economy by cybernation":

> The Negro claims, as a matter of simple justice, his full share in America's economic and social life. He sees adequate employment opportunities as a chief means of attaining this goal: the March on Washington demanded freedom *and* jobs. The Negro's claim to a job is not being met. Negroes are the hardest-hit of the many groups being exiled from the economy by cybernation. Negro unemployment rates cannot be expected to drop substantially. Promises of jobs are a cruel and dangerous hoax on hundreds of thousands of Negroes and whites alike who are especially vulnerable to cybernation because of age or inadequate education.... The Negro is trying to enter a social community and a tradition of work-and-income which are in the process of vanishing even for the hitherto privileged white worker. Jobs are disappearing under the impact of highly efficient, progressively less costly machines.

The automation-driven disappearance of work, the document warns, will raise already catastrophically high levels of Black unemployment. Here the possibility of freedom *without* jobs, or a kind of "workless society" in the words of signer James Boggs, would represent a perverse outcome of increasing efficiency and productive capacity due to technological change. The artificial boost in demand for labor represented by Cold War military spending, the document contends, is a temporary, wasteful, and socially destructive use of material resources that would be better directed toward other socially pressing needs in an era of expected rising living standards and economic growth.[1] The prospect of the disappearance of work, whether produced by labor-saving technological innovations or intensified global competition, has remained a significant touchstone within a range of subsequent debates over globalization, deindustrialization, the sources of urban poverty, and the creation of a permanent Black "underclass" (Trotter and Katz; Wilson).[2]

[1] In hindsight, we can read the *Triple Revolution* document's concern for the racial consequences of automation not only in relation to later Black "underclass" debates but also to a post-1960s white backlash politics to civil rights movement demands, chronicled by historians like Jefferson Cowie, emerging from an economically devastated US "Rust Belt" (Cowie) hollowed out by the long arc of postwar processes of deindustrialization.

[2] In an effort to preemptively address the possibility of mass unemployment, both King and the authors of the "Triple Revolution" proposed a guaranteed basic income among a number of other policies to delink employment from access to material goods and resources. Informed by a belief that "Automation and cybernation will make it possible for working people to have undreamed-of amounts of leisure time" (King Jr., *Where Do We Go From Here: Chaos or Community?* 179), King and the Southern Christian Leadership Council subsequently organized an interracial "Poor People's Campaign" that demanded $30 billion in additional social spending, full employment, and more low-cost public housing. Similarly, the "Triple Revolution" report recommended increased state spending—on education, public works, housing, transit, and power—made possible by more progressive taxation, the redirection of military spending, and greater protections for organized labor.

Although *The Triple Revolution* might strike contemporary readers as a historical curiosity with limited impact, Martin Luther King Jr., who wrote and spoke extensively about the dangers of automation throughout the 1960s, directly cited the document in his final Sunday sermon, "Remaining Awake Through a Great Revolution."[3] In his final book, published in 1967, *Where Do We Go from Here: Chaos or Community?*, King warns of the dangers of Black workers being consigned to a growing low-wage service sector as a result of automation "imperceptibly but inexorably producing dislocations, skimming off unskilled labor from the industrial force" (King Jr., *Where Do We Go from Here: Chaos or Community?* 149). "The displaced are flowing into proliferating service occupations," King continues. "These enterprises are traditionally unorganized and provide low wage scales with longer hours. The Negroes pressed into these services need union protection" (King Jr., *Where Do We Go from Here: Chaos or Community?* 149). For King and the authors of *The Triple Revolution*, how the nation might address the problem of automation was, at the same time, a question of racial justice. The demand for equal rights would have to confront the problem of high unemployment, poverty, and what I call a political economy of Black disposability.

Dreams and nightmares of automated "full unemployment" have periodically appeared within US political history, with significant ongoing debates over the causes of increasing precarity and job loss in the postwar period. As contemporary economic historians have argued, flagging profitability and low growth rates rather than automation could better account for accelerating processes of deindustrialization and offshoring, as well as patterns of chronic unemployment and underemployment.[4] While in hindsight, the authors of the "Triple Revolution" may have underestimated the extent to which the low-wage service sector would in subsequent decades both expand and absorb workers in a rapidly deindustrializing economy, the simultaneously feared and desired "end of labor" due to technological advances produced uneven and racially differentiated social effects. A combination of increasing automation and global competition battered the US manufacturing sector, where Black workers were concentrated in the immediate postwar period.

Increasing productive capacity made possible by automation, of course, required the cultivation of mass consumer demand. With the US populace no

3 In this sermon, King compares the coming workless future to the broken promises of emancipation without the redistribution of land and resources. For further speeches and writings on the impact of automation on Black workers and organized labor, see King Jr., *All Labor Has Dignity*.

4 See Benanav; J. E. Smith, "Nowhere to Go: Automation, Then and Now."

longer preoccupied with satisfying basic material necessities, postwar mass consumption in the United States represented democratized access to luxury goods in the aftermath of the Great Depression and the state-controlled production and reduced consumption of the war years. The postwar boom rapidly transformed the United States into what historian Lizabeth Cohen calls a "Consumers' Republic" (Cohen) based on the mass production of consumer goods and images of national life that established social consumption norms organized around the unit of white, middle-class nuclear families.

Presenting a peculiar and peculiarly unsettling warning of how facially race-neutral economic processes could continue to materially reproduce racial hierarchies in the aftermath of the formal end of Jim Crow, the "Triple Revolution" document is a part of a larger body of writing exploring the relationship between race and capitalism, or what scholars have called the "race/class problematic" (San Juan, Jr.). For the paper authors, Cold War images of material abundance promised by mass-produced consumer goods perversely reflected the mass production of Black populations without steady access to waged work in an era in which technological advances produced a glut of disposable consumer products as well as increasing numbers of seemingly disposable people—or, in the language of *The Triple Revolution*, chronic "surplus [productive] capacity and unemployment" (Ad Hoc Committee On The Triple Revolution).[5] For the authors of *The Triple Revolution*, technological advancements in production raised the possibility of the democratization of abundance while revealing the increasing irrationality of regulating access to consumer goods through the prior availability of employment within deeply racialized labor markets.[6]

The poems at the center of my study are similarly concerned with how racial subject formation is entangled with the production of things, or how race appears in what I call the mirror of the commodity form in the US postwar period.

[5] By the 1960s Black workers in northern industrial manufacturing confronted the threat of unemployment from automation and "cybernation"—a development that contributed to the formation of radical Black organized labor groups, such as the League of Revolutionary Black Workers. As a witness to the impact of automation in the Detroit auto manufacturing industry, James Boggs issued a provocative warning that "America is headed toward full unemployment, not full employment" (Boggs 118).

[6] For cultural critics and social scientists assessing the impact of the rise of postwar mass consumer culture on politics and culture—from German Frankfurt School critical theorists, to William H. Whyte (*The Organization Man*) and sociologist David Riesman (*The Lonely Crowd*)—the rationalization of mass production required a corresponding technical organization of consumer subjects and consumer demand. The bureaucratically managed mass production of commodities, from suburban homes to fast food, mirrored the social production a new kind of homogeneous mass personality.

Commodities do not simply refer to physical objects in these works but also to how such objects are bearers of socially determined value, which renders both human activity and the products of that activity exchangeable within capitalist economies. My study relies upon contemporary Marxist theorizations of capitalism as a form of social organization defined precisely through how value itself is created through the consumption and competitive exploitation of human labor as a specific kind of commodity capable of producing additional or "surplus" value. The commodity form is thus a crucial component of an entire recursive process in which, as William Pietz argues, value is appropriated, accumulated, and fed back into a self-expanding system of accumulation:

> The substance of capital itself is "value," that conserved quantity of social labor-time which seems to move through the metamorphic phases of the capitalist economy from one form to another (from laboring people to the things they produce, from these products to the money that purchases them, from this money to the new labor and materials it buys, etc). Commodities and capital goods, wageworkers and capitalists, money and credit, are forms or parts of a whole temporal-material system.
>
> (Pietz 149)

For the poets I examine, the dynamics of racial group formation are not an epiphenomenal expression of class relations but are nevertheless embedded within a process of capitalist accumulation in historically specific ways. Differential valuation functions as a mechanism of enforced racial comparison, which shapes and launders a history of racist practices while systematically reproducing racial groups in relation to each other over time. As what Karl Marx calls the "economic cell-form" (Marx 90) of developed capitalist societies, the commodity form does not simply reflect preexisting social relations but reshapes them. In the works I examine, capitalist imperatives bind together seemingly disparate domains of social life and incommensurable but materially interconnected colonial histories of expropriation, enslavement, and imperial war.

Rather than reproducing an entrenched opposition within contemporary literary scholarship between culture and political economy, these poets explore how the process of capitalist value formation becomes a measure of racial comparison, a field of racial competition, and an index of racial pathology and progress.[7] Poems by Erica Hunt, Myung Mi Kim, Larissa Lai, and

7 For a brief overview of the trajectory of the culture/political economy binary in contemporary Cultural Studies, see Peck.

Ed Roberson deploy a range of experimental poetic formal strategies to map the imbrication of class and racial group formation. The works I examine all explore identity's mass production as a serial social form whose dehistoricized, formally equivalent attributes increasingly mirror the concrete particularity and abstract exchangeability of commodities. Self-ownership and self-possession become a kind of internalized property relation and a condition of intersubjective, state, and institutional recognition.

Governed by what poet and critic Erica Hunt calls "Piece Logic" (Hunt), such serial identities orbit the normative figure of an atomistically isolated citizen-consumer as an imagined endpoint of racial integration and immigrant assimilation. The resulting generalized condition of market separation is represented across these poems as a fundamental barrier to further antiracist social transformation in the post–Jim Crow and post–Hart Celler era. Challenging the premise that a racially desegregated postwar economy will ultimately create the conditions of a "colorblind" social order, these poets explore how ostensibly race-neutral market mechanisms do not progressively dissolve racist practices but are instead deeply implicated in their reproduction.[8]

This necessarily narrow selection of writing explores the impact of capitalist processes on what sociologists Michael Omi and Howard Winant call "racial formation" (Omi and Winant 103). In their 1986 book *Racial Formation in the United States*, Omi and Winant contend that the meaning and material context of racial distinctions are not historically unchanging but instead "a synthesis, a constantly reiterated outcome" of ongoing historically specific social conflicts. "Racial formation" is the term Omi and Winant use to describe the resulting "sociohistorical process by which racial identities are created, lived out, transformed, and destroyed" (Omi and Winant 109). Distinct from categories of nation, ethnicity, and class, race is not reducible to isolable individual or group identities for these theorists but invokes "both a social/historical structure and a set of accumulated signifiers that suffuse

[8] The belief that capitalist market mechanisms will automatically reduce racial discrimination over time has long been a staple of mainstream neoclassical economic theory. The Nobel Prize–winning economist Gary Becker has influentially argued, for example, that market relations reduce what he calls a "taste for discrimination" (Becker 15), or prejudicial behavior and personal preference. Becker's argument is grounded in a neoclassical economic understanding of rational, utility-maximizing market actors. Becker's analysis presupposes that the market choices of owners of capital as well as consumers supported by sufficient information would necessarily reduce the irrationality of job market discrimination as costly under competitive market conditions. While Becker first makes this argument in the 1958 *The Economics of Discrimination* (Becker), and defends it through the latter decades of the twentieth century, versions of this argument continue to appear in mainstream political thought. See for example O'Neill and O'Neill.

individual and collective identities, inform social practices, shape institutions and communities, demarcate social boundaries, and organize the distribution of resources" (Omi and Winant 125).

As Philosopher Paul C. Taylor has pointed out, establishing the semantic referent of race has been an object of political struggle. "White supremacist societies created the Races they thought they were discovering," Taylor notes:

> Antiracist activists turned them into political interest groups, cultural nationalists treated them as incubators for ethnic groups, shifts in immigration patterns problematized and expanded their boundaries, and economic changes redefined their relations to the productive forces of society.
>
> (P. Taylor 86)

For Taylor, the association of intrinsic capacities and relative worth with differences in appearance and ancestry represents core features of the concept of race over time despite the term's various associations with biology, ethnicity, group culture, geography, lived experience, epistemic standpoint, normative political perspectives, ontological position, "identity," or some hybrid formulation of all of these. To develop a more parsimonious definition, Taylor focuses on how racial distinctions historically emerge in the United States through "the white supremacist determination to link appearance and ancestry to social location and life chances" (P. Taylor 86). This definitional clarification thus describes a recursive "link" between systems of belief and a range of historical policies and practices—or what the anthropologist Patrick Wolfe has recently characterized as the difference between "race as doctrine" (Wolfe 10) and "race in action" (Wolfe 10).

While my readings draw on some basic concepts of racial formation theory advanced by Omi and Winant, the poems I study reveal how race is indeed not "an ancillary aspect of inequality, an epiphenomenon of class" (Omi and Winant 67). As categories of analysis, however, class and inequality only partially capture how racial boundaries are drawn and redrawn across interlinked core features of capitalist economies—the commodity form, quantified expropriation and competitive exploitation, unwaged socially reproductive labor, and circulation. While I agree that racial formation is fundamentally irreducible to narrow categories of class and economic inequality, the poems I examine reveal a more capacious understanding of the historicity of capitalism as what Nancy Fraser calls a state-managed "institutionalized social order" (Jaeggi and Fraser 52) that is at the same time a racial-colonial order developed over the course of the Spanish and English conquest of the Americas.

The poems I read challenge widely accepted claims within mainstream neoclassical economic theories that competitive accumulation tends to progressively eliminate a "taste for discrimination" (Becker 14) and thus racial inequality and interracial conflict over time. Instead, I read these works as literary contributions to theorizing what Cedric Robinson and others have broadly labeled "racial capitalism" (C. J. Robinson 2).[9]

Asiatic Racial Form

Shortly after the publication of the "Triple Revolution" document and passage of the landmark 1964 Civil Rights Act—mandating the desegregation of education, employment, and public space—Congress signed into the law the Immigration and Nationality Act of 1965. As it was less commonly known, the Hart-Celler Act eliminated an older, explicitly racially exclusionary national quota system consolidated by the notorious Johnson-Reed Act of 1924. Spearheaded by Democratic congressman Emanuel Celler, who played a key role in passing the 1964 Civil Rights Act, and envisioned by Lyndon Baines Johnson as a part of a raft of "Great Society" programs, the Hart-Celler Act passed with overwhelming majorities in both houses of Congress.[10]

With its preference for professionals and highly skilled workers, the 1965 Immigration and Nationality Act reflected the hegemony of liberal and economic nationalist perspectives on antiracist state policy. Like the 1964 Civil Rights Act, the Hart-Celler Act also insisted on formal equality in its lifting of national quotas without regard for historical patterns of exclusion. For the era's liberal reformers, desegregated access to what historian Roland Marchand has

[9] While my use of the term "racial capitalism" is indebted to the work of Cedric Robinson, the term also describes a field of inquiry into the relationship between race and capitalism rather than a specific set of arguments derived primarily from Robinson's *Black Marxism* (C. J. Robinson). For a further history of the term "racial capitalism" see Melamed, "Racial Capitalism"; Hudson. For a compact critique of Robinson's theorization of "racial capitalism," see Ralph and Singhal.

[10] Opponents of lifting national quotas typically mobilized arguments about possible communist infiltration, as well as the capacity of the US economy to absorb global surplus labor that would potentially compete for jobs domestically, strain welfare programs, and threaten the white ethnic cultural coherence of national life. Supporters, including Southern and Eastern European interest groups subject to numerical quotas, argued for the importance of immigration reform as a key strategic asset in Cold War influence over an upsurge of global "third world" anticolonial movements. As Mae Ngai has pointed out, the passage of the bill "resulted from a constellation of political factors: the rise of Euro-American ethnics as important voting constituents in the urban industrial north; robust domestic-social movements (labor and civil rights); and the international embarrassment of discriminatory immigration quotas during the Cold War" (M. Ngai xxv).

called a "Democracy of Goods" (Marchand 217) would become a significant measure of racial progress and pathology.

Despite the polarized internal class structure of Asian America, the post-1965 mass entry of often highly skilled Asian immigrants into the postwar US economy conditioned subsequent mainstream media depictions of Asian Americans as both a hyperassimilable and politically quiescent "model minority" and culturally unassimilable perpetual foreigners. The competitive threat posed by a seemingly machinic and infinitely adaptable foreign labor pool undergirds these seemingly antithetical stereotypes. As Iyko Day contends, the racialization of Asian North American immigrant labor comes to embody one feature of what Karl Marx famously identifies as the split character of commodity form itself. For Marx, commodity form does not refer simply to material objects, but to the recursive social process by which the concrete particularity of human labor and the products of that labor is subordinated to a single abstract measure of comparative economic value. With origins in the nineteenth century, popular representations of Chinese immigrants to the United States and Canada have for Day historically "personified the quantitative sphere of abstract labor" as a racial threat to "the concrete, qualitative sphere of white labor's social reproduction" (Day 16) and a potential image of its degraded future. As exemplars of a kind inhuman mechanical efficiency, what Colleen Lye calls "Asiatic racial form" (Lye, *America's Asia: Racial Form and American Literature, 1893-1945* 9) has durably signified a racial population made both more and less than human by a unique racial capacity for mimicry and malleability that allows them to embody capitalist imperatives.

In the late nineteenth and early twentieth centuries, a series of exclusionary policies limiting or barring entry to Asian immigrants in the United States and Canada, as well as the removal of racial restrictions on immigration in both countries (in 1965 and 1967, respectively), proceeded in a remarkably synchronized fashion. "Beginning in the 1870s, racialized understandings of Chinese as economic, social, and cultural threats circulated throughout the hemisphere" (E. Lee 238), Erika Lee writes. Such ideas signaled the emergence of a "hemispheric Orientalism" (E. Lee 549) with significant consequences for immigration policies not only in the United States and Canada but also in Mexico, Peru, Australia, and New Zealand. Opposition to Asian immigration to the Americas and other British settler colonies has historically defined the contours of Asiatic racial form in transnational terms. In both the United States and Canada, the abstract protean character of Asian racial form has been associated with a range of historical threats to the health of national economies, from Chinese real estate investment capital to the uncertain political allegiances of alien labor.

When read together, the poems in my study offer readers an opportunity to reimagine the shifting terrain of Afro-Asian relations, and contemporary Black and Asian North American experimental and avant-garde poetry, in terms of economically interconnected histories. First, these works remap the historically changing ways in which capitalist processes have systematically reproduced Black and Asian North American populations within a single transnational economic geography over time. Such processes, of course, do not exhaustively describe every aspect of racialization but nevertheless constitute a crucial and relatively neglected condition of racial group formation that has in recent years provoked a recent revival of scholarly interest in and debates over the theoretical relationship between race and capitalism. At the same time, these poems radically reimagine such comparative or relational racialization processes, and the origins of interracial conflict, beyond existing discourses of incommensurable group consciousness or group cultural difference. The experimental poetic formal strategies these poems deploy, I argue, represent race not in terms of the inherent properties of fixed or fluid *identities* but as an iterative or serial social form whose contested meaning is produced by the interplay between *constraint* and *possibility* across materially interconnected social contexts. This study argues that how these poets reimagine race as a social form requires that we retheorize poetic form as a basic category of literary interpretation and a self-sufficient basis for disinterested aesthetic judgment.[11]

Afro-Asian Relations after Bandung

This book's comparative readings of Asian North American and African American experimental poets thus build on an emerging body of scholarship on Afro-Asian cultural exchange explored in two recent field-defining anthologies: *Afro-Asian Encounters: Culture, History, Politics* (Steen and Raphael-Hernandez) and *Afro Asia: Revolutionary Political and Cultural Connections Between African Americans and Asian Americans* (Ho, Fred and Mullen).[12] This scholarship

[11] For recent scholarly accounts of the entanglement of economies of racial difference with the eighteenth-century origins of concept of aesthetic experience as a "regulative discourse of the human on which the modern conception of the political and racial order of modernity rests" (Lloyd 3), see Gikandi; Armstrong; Lloyd.

[12] See Ho, Fred and Mullen; Steen and Raphael-Hernandez; J. H. Lee.

focuses on the historical promise of an anticolonial coalitional politics typically traced back to the 1955 Bandung meeting of "nonaligned" African and Asian nations. For 1960s-era US ethnic nationalist movements in particular—from Black Power, Chicanismo, and Puerto Rican nationalism, to the Third World Liberation Front and groups such as San Francisco's Red Guard Party—the Bandung meeting served as an inspiration.[13] For many scholars, the Bandung moment and its afterlives have served as a framework for understanding Black and Asian comparative racialization in the present. Promoting the concept of the "third world" as "an alternative to past imperialism and the political economies and power of the US and the Soviet Union" (C. J. Lee 15), third world national liberation movements offered a shared political idiom for postwar antiracist movements in the United States. The mid-twentieth-century wave of decolonization campaigns in Africa and Asia provided an opportunity for self-identified nationalist movements in the United States to signal international solidarity and frame the plight of non-white US racial groups through a shared experience of "internal colonialism."[14]

The poems at the center of my study explore a post-Bandung world where imperial histories have been encoded within unequal terms of global trade, debt repayment, and structural adjustment programs. It is a world where human migration is violently regulated through an international nation-state system that grants increasing freedom of mobility to transnational capital and an elite transnational capitalist class. With the achievement of formal independence for many decolonizing nations in the mid-twentieth century, the framework of a Third World "colonial analogy" (Blauner 63) uniting a range of US antiracist movements under the banner national liberation has been subject to extensive subsequent critique.[15] Although critics differ on the proximate causes of the decline of "third world" nationalist movements inside the United States, much current scholarship on comparative racialization is marked by a deep critical suspicion of what Afropessimist theorist Frank Wilderson calls "the ruse of

[13] For an overview of the impact of global Maoism on postwar US Black and Asian American radical groups that ideologically "wed Marxism, black nationalism, and Third World internationalism" (Kelley and Esch 14), see Kelley and Esch; Elbaum.

[14] See Gutierrez for an overview of the historical genealogy of theories of internal colonialism as "An American Theory of Race" (Gutierrez 281); (Chávez); and (Blauner).

[15] See Bannerji for a broad critique of the trajectory of twentieth-century anticolonial nationalisms in a post-Bandung era defined by "anti-imperialist politics in disarray and national liberation movements substituted by various right wing nationalisms or capitalist state inspired multiculturalisms which speak in the name of culture, tradition and identity" (Bannerji 1).

analogy" (Wilderson 35), an assumption of shared racial oppression which has historically underwritten earlier "Third World" coalitional visions.

In a poem like Myung Mi Kim's *Dura*, for example, Black–Korean conflict during the 1992 Los Angeles riots illuminate the fracturing of these earlier 1960s-era anticolonial imaginaries in the aftermath of the acquittal of four LAPD officers for the beating of Black motorist Rodney King. The poem does not, however, attribute non-white interracial conflict to historically unchanging forms of racial animus. Instead, the poet situates this conflict within the long arc of US imperial history where racial groups form in antagonistic relation to each other through "the articulation of a commodity form of real property," in the words of Brenna Bhandar, "in conjunction with a globalized 'economy of difference' " (Bhandar 6).

These poems reimagine the terrain of contemporary theories of comparative and "relational" racialization, including but not limited to postwar Afro-Asian relations, without positing analogous forms of oppression or "parallel minoritization" (Koshy 1546).[16] I situate my readings within a postwar economic history where differential claims to economic citizenship continue to position Asian Americans as a competitive threat to the nation in times of crisis, and the political and economic "solution" to the "problem" of Black political insurgency and perceived cultural deficiency.

These poems help readers to contextualize Asian Americans' model minority status, or what Claire Jean Kim calls their "racial triangulation" (Kim 105) between whiteness and blackness, as exemplary neoliberal subjects. At the same time, these works explore a political economy of Black expendability within a deindustrializing postwar economy beyond the reach of demands for formal equality. The resulting unique poetic vantage on a broader postwar "field of racial positions" (Kim 105) moves beyond images of populations stacked within a historically unchanging racial status hierarchy. Instead, these poems reveal how the meaning of racial distinctions is altered by a variety of social forms interlinked through the recursive circuit of capitalist production and social reproduction—from "broken families" and mass serial market identities to segregated cities, competitive blocs, and global logistics networks.[17]

[16] For an example of recent scholarship on comparative racialization, see Ferguson and Hong. For a selection on recent scholarship on relational racialization, see HoSang and Molina.

[17] Claire Jean Kim's influential account of the "racial triangulation" of Asian Americans in relation to white and Black Americans chooses a category of analysis, "relative devalorization" (Kim 107), that frames racial distinctions as hierarchical status categories. In my account, the meaning of such categories is continually made and remade by capitalist processes that continually reconfigure intergroup and intragroup relations.

Compared to What: Racially Marked Experimental and Avant-Garde Poetics

I draw on a number of contemporary scholarly studies focused on contemporary Black and Asian American experimental and avant-garde writing. These works include recent critical monographs on nationalist and post-nationalist Black experimental poetry by Aldon Lynn Nielsen, Evie Shockley, Anthony Reed, Phillip Brian Harper, Margo Natalie Crawford, and GerShun Avilez. At the same time, my study also builds on recent studies of Asian American experimental or avant-garde poetry—including books by Timothy Yu, Dorothy Wang, Joseph Jeon, Josephine Park, and Steven G. Yao.

Persistent questions emerge across these studies about how to define poetic experimentation and about the applicability of theories of avant-garde political and aesthetic oppositionality derived from early-late-nineteenth- and early-twentieth-century European literary and art movements. "The term innovation is a relative one," poet and critic Nathaniel Mackey observes, "it's haunted by the question, Compared to what?" (Mackey 240).

Innovation is for Mackey modeled both by postwar avant-garde jazz musicians and by an expansive poetic "other tradition," which includes authors from Robert Duncan to Guyanese novelist and poet Wilson Harris. Yet as Mackey's reference to the title of Gene McDaniels's famous song suggests, what counts as experiment is historically specific, context-dependent, and irreducible to the technical question of formal means. For Mackey, the "pursuit of greater complexity and sophistication in technical and formal matters" (Mackey 240) must be understood in relation to differing conceptions of conventionality across specific racially marked literary and musical traditions.

As a central value-laden category of analysis for early-twentieth century New Critics, poetic form has remained a ubiquitous, if troubled, basis for critical assessments of aesthetic novelty and avant-garde techniques within Black, Latinx, and Asian American poetic traditions. "The criteria of what counts as avant-garde, even in the twenty-first century," Dorothy Wang notes, "is judged according to High Modernism's purely formalist repertoire: disruption of syntax, fragmentation of the line, and so on" (Wang 32).[18] For Wang, this definitional

[18] In *Race and the Avant-Garde*, Timothy Yu maintains that because "after 1970 the question of race became central to the constitution of any American avant-garde" (Yu 1), Asian American poets could be understood as an avant-garde literary movement akin to groups such as the Language Poets. For Yu, both groups attempt to break "from the conventions of mainstream American poetry

premise consistently produces bifurcated readings of Asian American poetry where race is understood either in terms of the reproduction of "recognizable 'ethnic' content" (Wang 45) or subsumed within formal strategies "universalized as part of an avant-garde movement" (Wang 32). In both cases, race remains an undertheorized context of poetic experimentation.

Reading Mackey and Wang alongside each other highlights how Black and Asian American experimental poetry complicate existing narratives of postwar US poetic history that pit a postmodern, experimental, or avant-garde tradition against a dominant mainstream poetics committed to realist aesthetic values, "transparent" language, linear narratives, and coherent speaking subjects. This taxonomic distinction between experimental poetry and a formulaic "official verse culture" (Bernstein, *A Poetics* 6) has been subsequently routed through several other oppositions between "*open* and *closed*" (Hejinian 42) texts, poetic accessibility and difficulty, and an "expressive" lyric poetics grounded in the first-person testimony versus what Gillian White describes as "a powerful and increasingly canonical avant-garde antilyricism" (White 4) committed to exposing the lyric "I" as an ideological fiction.[19]

The underlying formalist premises marking the boundaries between a mainstream poetic tradition and its experimental margins have endured despite a recent turn toward a hybridizing "compromise aesthetics" (R. G. Smith) aiming to reconcile seemingly antithetical impulses toward "experimentalism and convention; difficulty and readability; and the underground and the mass market" (R. G. Smith).[20] The name of the influential poetry journal *Fence*, the stylistic eclecticism of a new generation of "elliptical" poets (Burt 354), and the titles of anthologies like *Lyric Postmodernism* (Shepherd) and *American*

of the 1970s and 1980s, and both develop their own institutions of publication and distribution, from magazines to small presses to anthologies. But central to both is a surprisingly acute sense of how race can inflect aesthetics, and of the relations of power that racial difference creates among contemporaneous avant-gardes" (Yu 2).

19 Lyric itself has been subject to extensive scrutiny as a coherent taxonomic category. For an account of the historical production of lyric as an contradictory and internally inconsistent genre, see Jackson and Prins. For a defense of the lyric as a generic marker with historically durable characteristics, see Culler.

20 This discourse of formal innovation comes to be redefined in "an age dominated by a highly polarized field," Greenwald Smith observes, "consisting of the experimentalists of the 1970s—Language Poets and postmodernists—on the one hand and the counter-revolutionary commitment to mainstream accessibility epitomized by the influence of New Formalism and the perceived conservatizing influence of Creative Writing MFA programs of the 1980s on the other. The new generation of writers are described by the proponents of this narrative as frustrated by the limitations of these two positions, and as a result rejecting en masse the notion that formally inventive literature requires intentional opposition to the norms of mainstream writing and the expectations of mainstream audiences."

Hybrid (Swenson and St. John) all narrate US poetic history in terms of an autonomous aesthetic logic of innovation pushing the boundaries of an ever-expanding repertoire of free-floating stylistic techniques. It is a narrative that has progressively decoupled experimental formal strategies from the historically specific institutional and political targets of critique of prior twentieth-century avant-gardes from Surrealism to Language writing.[21]

The Politics of Form and Poetics of Identity

Debates over how specific experimental and avant-garde formal strategies either disrupt or affirm an "expressive" lyric "I" have powerfully configured racial *identity* as a subject and object of formal innovation. Across scholarly histories of postwar US poetry, a persistent tension emerges between what critics and poets characterize as an experimental "politics of poetic form" (Bernstein, *The Politics of Poetic Form: Poetry and Public Policy*) organized around a critique of poetic speaking subjects, and a racial "poetics of identity" (LoLordo) premised upon autobiographical testimony, narrative realism, and racially representative voices. On either side of this postwar poetic divide, the question of poetic speaking subjects dominates discussion of the meaning and political significance of formal strategies.

In a 1988 article published in the pages of the *Socialist Review*, "Poetry and the Politics of the Subject," Language poet and critic Ron Silliman captures this historically durable, if controversial, taxonomic distinction between avant-garde and experimental traditions aiming to "call into question, if not actually explode, such conventions as narrative, persona, and even reference" by "many

[21] Although animated by a shared impulse to challenge literary conventions and often deployed interchangeably, the categories of avant-garde and experimental poetry represent two sometimes divergent ways of conceiving of the relationship between literary novelty and political oppositionality.[1] As Joe Bray, Alison Gibbons, and Brian McHale note, "Avant-garde begins its career in the military context, but then migrates to the political sphere, where the avant-garde is the faction that takes the lead ahead of the rest of a political movement" (Bray et al. 1–2); "Consequently, aesthetic avant-gardism continues to be allied with political radicalism in a number of twentieth- and twenty-first-century artistic and literary movements. Experimentalism's connotations, by contrast, are scientific. Experiment promises to extend the boundaries of knowledge, or in this case, of artistic practice. Strongly associated with modernity, it implies rejection of hide-bound traditions, values and forms" (Bray et al. 1–2).In his influential *Theory of the Avant-Garde* (Burger), Peter Bürger argues that a history of European avant-garde resistance to institutionalized aesthetic conventions is inseparable from a desire to renew aesthetic experience by overcoming the separation between art and what the critic calls the political "praxis of life" (Burger 22). By contrast, the category of experimental writing suggests alternative epistemic grounds upon which art and literature can make knowledge claims distinct from the growing authority of scientific discourses from the nineteenth century onward.

white heterosexual males, for example" (Silliman 63). At the same time, Silliman contends that writing by poets from historically excluded and dominated groups who "have a manifest political need to have their stories told" (Silliman 63) rely on more formally conventional modes of representation. Silliman's taxonomic distinction has been questioned by later critics, including other Language poets, for failing to adequately account for the work of poets from marginalized populations who also rigorously called into question "narrative, persona and even reference." From a rich Black vernacular tradition emerging from spirituals, secular songs, and folktales to the strategic deployment of "weird English" (Ch'ien) by Asian American poets, what constitutes conventional English varies widely across poetic traditions where nonstandard and often multilingual sociolects predominate.

Recent scholarship on contemporary Black experimental poetry has theorized poetic innovation in terms of the augmentation rather than abandonment of ideals of expressive capacity, for example, even where expressivity itself becomes an object of critical reflection. In the pioneering study *Black Chant: Languages of African-American Postmodernism*, poet and critic Aldon Lyn Nielsen's elaborates a theory of contemporary Black experimental poetry as unsettling the conventions of a Black oral vernacular tradition which has historically privileged "speakerly" rather than "writerly" texts. For Nielsen, Black experiment doesn't function as a critique of that tradition so much as an expansion of its boundaries. Echoing Nielsen, Lauri Ramey insists that "Formally innovative poetry is a constant in the African American poetry canon," Lauri Ramey, "though the experimental motives may not be mainly or wholly intended as a rejection or affront to the mainstream. Yet critical perspectives have tended to create dichotomies or binary oppositions about the themes and techniques of African American poetry, which reflect being either inside or outside the values of the Western lyric tradition" (Ramey 71).

As a basic premise of an increasingly institutionalized paradigm of "racialized reading" applied to racially marked poetry, such a demand is not simply a neutral imperative for writers and artists aligned with emergent political movements but ideologically contested terrain irreducible to the strictures of narrative realism or any specific set of formal strategies. The contemporary Black and Asian North American poems I read reconfigure the meaning of poetic experimentation by challenging the interpretive protocols of what Anthony Reed has called a "hermeneutic of racialized reading" (Reed 106) that both "suppresses or minimizes potentially radical forms of black politics" (Reed 7) while reducing Black poetry to "expressions and experiences of a singular intending consciousness that is in turn metonymic for race" (Reed 98).[22] Irreducible to either sociological testimony or socially unlocatable abstraction, Black experimental writing is thus often excluded both "from genealogies of presumptively white avant-garde writing, on the grounds that its concerns seem insufficiently 'universal' " (Reed 7) and "from disciplinary genealogies of African American literature" (Reed 7).[23] The protocols of racialized reading Reed and others describe, I argue, extend to contemporary Asian American poetry and other racially marked poetic traditions where such imperatives are the subject of ongoing critical engagement.

The observation that Black, Asian American, and Latinx poets "have a manifest political need to have their stories told" (Silliman 63) describes a longstanding demand of New Left and post–New Left feminist, antiracist, and gay liberation political organizations to highlight the role of autobiographical narratives as an essential component of consciousness-raising, community mobilization, and political education.[24] Silliman's calls for the textual demolition of the subject arguably reinforces a declensionist narrative of the balkanizing effects of the New Left turn to Black Power and "identity politics." Informed by an "anxiety over left fragmentation, with identity-based political groups seen as radically separatist" (Yu 48), Timothy Yu argues, Silliman's understanding of the critique of reference enacted in his own writing, and in the writing of Language poets more broadly, frames the group's formal experiments as a kind of "reintegrative force that brings together the shattered discourses of the new left" (Yu 50). A more comprehensive critique of linguistic reference that allows for the denaturalization of one's subject position thus "arrogates to itself the ability to provide a total view of society and culture, while limiting the work of 'oppressed peoples' to communication within the code of a circumscribed community" (Yu 50).

[22] Tyler Bradway characterizes institutional demands for legible racial subjects and subject matter in terms of "the cultural assimilation of so-called 'minority' writing to a logic of self-expression and a concomitant aesthetic of social realism—put simply, the expectation that these texts will primarily 'represent' the experience of social marginality and oppression" (Bradway 8). "In such a framework," Bradway continues, "literature is positioned as testimony, and nothing more" (Bradway 8).

[23] Poetic experimentation "does not refer only to the aesthetic category of innovation as typically conceived," as Anthony Reed argues, "but also to the use of literature to reconfigure blackness and of blackness to reconfigure literature" (Reed 8).

[24] See, for example, the edited transcripts of the 1982 Left Write Conference (Abbott) organized by Steve Abbott and Bruce Boone, where "over 300 persons of all ages, gender and ethnic backgrounds" gathered to debate that writers might play in facilitating coalitional alignments between organizationally distinct Native American, Black, Asian American, queer, and feminist political movements which shared "a unanimous sense of urgency about the need for Left unity" (Abbott 1) in the aftermath of the presidential election of Ronald Reagan.

Despite attempts to oppose or hybridize a "politics of form" and "poetics of identity," both taxonomic categories converge on the representational status of the subject or "identity" as a primary locus of aesthetic and political intervention. Recent controversies over the racial politics of contemporary avant-garde poetic movements like Conceptual Writing have continued to define avant-garde formal techniques in terms of a ludic transcendence of fixed identities and a celebration of the deterritorializing power of the internet to divorce texts from contexts.[25] Conceptual movement co-founder Kenneth Goldsmith's 2015 controversial poem "The Body of Michael Brown," and the author's subsequent defenses of the poem in the face of mounting criticism, offer a more recent example of the durability of this opposition between experimental form and identity.[26] Performing a version of the poem before an audience at Brown University, Goldsmith read excerpts from an autopsy report of Black teenager Michael Brown murdered by police—a document edited to conclude with a description of Brown's genitals. In defense of this project, Goldsmith averred that "If my identity is really up for grabs and changeable by the minute – as I believe it is, it's important that my writing reflect this state of ever-shifting identity and subjectivity" (Goldsmith):

> That can mean adopting voices that aren't "mine," subjectivities that aren't "mine," political positions that aren't "mine," opinions that aren't "mine," words that aren't "mine," because in the end, I don't think that I can possibly define what's "mine" and what isn't.
>
> (Goldsmith)

Goldsmith's defense echoes Silliman's earlier characterization of the uses of experimental form based upon a narrow understanding of race as a principle of social structuration that includes whiteness as an unmarked and socially "indeterminate" racial position. Literary strategies of citation and appropriation need not be understood in such terms, but in this case, such techniques mirror a universal, self-liquidating subject of avant-garde provocation capable of

[25] The politicization of appropriation as a literary technique capable of disclosing the grisly character of anti-Black violence arguably depends upon imagining political intervention in terms of a "zero degree of resistance," as Jasper Bernes has recently argued, "in which the artist can only imagine traumatizing or traumatized repetitions of the status quo" (Bernes 221). For two extended readings of both Goldsmith's poem and the critical responses it occasioned, see K. Young 411–30; Edmond 151–93.

[26] For an account of the performance and an extended discussion of Conceptual writing and the racial politics of literary appropriation techniques, see Leong.

imaginatively inhabiting all other identities within a social field. This particular framing of formal innovation and identity works to actively deconstruct the fiction of a stable, socially locatable speaking subject in ways that arguably reinforce rather than "explode" the literary conventions governing the representation and interpretation of whiteness as a normative, racially unmarked context of utterance, performance, and interpretation. The move to define aesthetic agency primarily in terms of social unlocatability reproduces the peculiar racial form of whiteness itself, which appears precisely as a deracialized and protean subjectlessness premised on the assignment of reified and particularistic "identities" to racially marked others.

But race as a context of signification is not reducible to contending affirmative or ascriptive processes of identification. Displacing an earlier political language of anticolonial national liberation and internal colonialism, the suturing of race to the concept of identity and cognate terms like "identity politics" is a recent postwar development emerging from a number of different sources: midcentury ego psychology, the language of advertising and mass consumer culture, political theories of possessive individualism, and political manifestos in the latter half of the 1970s.[27] While one of the earliest explicit uses of the term "identity politics" is contained in the Combahee River Collective's foundational 1977 "A Black Feminist Statement" ("The Combahee River Collective Statement"), the statement's drafters have lamented how in subsequent decades the "term has been used, abused, and reconfigured into something foreign to its creators" (K.-Y. Taylor 8).

Despite later scholarly attempts to offer more nuanced readings and defenses of the term, however, "identity politics" was not widely adopted by antiracist movements to frame their own political activity.[28] Entering widespread use in a post–New Left "culture war" context beginning in the 1980s, the term instead

[27] The use of a term like "identity politics" to describe not only the origins but ends of contemporary antiracist, feminist, and queer political movements is a fairly recent phenomenon arguably traceable back to the Combahee River Collective's 1977 "A Black Feminist Statement". Additionally, the concept of "identity" arguably does not assume a recognizable contemporary meaning until the mid-twentieth century, when it is consolidated across a number of distinct discourses—from Eriksonian ego psychology and commercial advertising to the political rhetoric of emergent Black feminist and nationalist political movements. See Marie Moran, *Identity and Capitalism*, and Philip Gleason, "Identifying Identity: A Semantic History." For a summary of the contradictory ways scholars have come to define the concept of identity, see Frederick Cooper and Rogers Brubaker, "Beyond Identity."

[28] See for example Alcoff.

transformed into a derogatory label applied by critics across the political spectrum to such movements in order to criticize their perceived failures and role in fracturing broader New Left and post–New Left coalitions. The designation has remained an amorphous placeholder for organizationally distinct postwar antiracist, feminist, and queer liberation movements with often divergent political objectives.

The works I read resist collapsing such specific political aims into discussions of the inherent properties of subjects by representing "identity" as an imposed social form whose political meaning is both continually contested and powerfully shaped by simultaneously atomizing and recombinatory capitalist market relations. The examined poems in this study challenge discourses of poetic experimentation that insist on the socially unlocatable character of formal innovation, but also paradigms of racialized reading that reduce race to a transhistorical and equally disembedded conception of identity abstracted from specifically capitalist histories of racial dispossession and exploitation.

Poets whose works have consistently challenged these conventions of racial representation have faced historical neglect—occasioning recent scholarly attempts to reconstruct underexamined traditions of Black, Asian American, and Asian Canadian experimental writing.[29] "'Formally innovative minority poets,' when visible at all," Harryette Mullen contends, "are not likely to be perceived either as typical of a racial/ethnic group or as representative of an aesthetic movement. Their unaccountable existence therefore strains the seams of the critical narratives necessary to make them (individually and collectively) comprehensible and thus teachable and marketable" (Mullen 10). For Mullen, how easily works might be consumed, commodified, and institutionally disseminated determine the often implicit aesthetic and political criteria governing what counts as legible racial "content" in the first place.[30]

Articulated in a brief essay entitled "Poetry and Identity," Mullen's remarks draw attention to the illegibility of racially marked experimental poetry within a literary and liberal multicultural imaginary emerging in the 1980s and 1990s

[29] For recent examples of anthologies of Black and Asian American experimental poetry in particular, see Tuma; Nielsen and Ramey, *Every Goodbye Ain't Gone: An Anthology of Innovative Poetry by African Americans*; Nielsen and Ramey, *What I Say: Innovative Poetry by Black Writers in America*; Lew.

[30] Nathaniel Mackey similarly contends that such judgments display a "Tendency to overlook variance and divergent approaches in the writing" from socially marginalized groups, and "especially to overlook writing that defies canons of accessibility" (Mackey 18). "It thus become easy and potentially self-fulfilling to characterize writing from socially marginalized groups in the most sweeping, totalizing terms," Mackey continues, "to posit a homogeneity of approach and inclination" (Mackey 18).

tied to "ideologemes of representativeness, authenticity, and 'gaining voice'" (Melamed, *Represent and Destroy: Rationalizing Violence in the New Racial Capitalism* 114).[31] Mullen's observations speak to the economic pressures shaping a broader post-1960s politics of representation oriented toward racial inclusion within liberal institutions.[32] I read Mullen's writing as an implicit commentary on two interrelated developments in post-1960s poetic history—the emergence of poststructuralist, feminist, and queer of color critiques of the normative heteropatriarchal subject of Black, Chicano, and Asian American cultural nationalist politics, and the subsequent rise of a multicultural literary imaginary premised upon the "idea of culture as property owned by people of color… within a consumer economy in which antiracism could be expressed by a desire for diversity, which consuming racialized cultural property presumptively fulfilled" (Melamed, *Represent and Destroy: Rationalizing Violence in the New Racial Capitalism* 36–7).

My study thus takes as its point of departure Mullen's playful and often scathingly satirical remixing of the language of advertising in poetry collections like the 1991 *Trimmings* and 1992 *S*PeRM**K*T*. In these books, the poet explores how race and gender are translated into the terms of an emergent postwar US consumer imaginary as attributes of typical, representative, and legible market identities. I read Mullen's poems as a sustained interrogation of the market logics that configure racial progress as multicultural integration into a postwar "democracy of goods." I do not read Mullen's poems as a moral condemnation of excessive or conspicuous consumption, but rather as attempts to diagram the modular, combinatory "grammar" of social relations mediated by the commodity form and the role of the latter in reshaping racial and gender distinctions.

This study diverges from prior readings of Black and Asian North American experimental poetry that have typically framed the political stakes of literary innovation in terms of a political evolution from the demands for uniformity encoded in 1960s-era cultural nationalist assertions of racial identity to the

31 What one might call "official" subjects of racial redress become legible, as Melamed and Roderick Ferguson argue, precisely through an acceptance of the fusion of "antiracist goals with property rights and market freedoms, limiting the horizon for racial equality to the extension of liberal freedoms and individual rights" (Melamed, *Represent and Destroy: Rationalizing Violence in the New Racial Capitalism* 221).

32 Despite increased attention paid to Black experimental poetry in the decades since the poet offered these observations, the rise of academic creative writing workshops, inaugurating what Mark McGurl has called a literary "Program Era", has continued to actively reshape the meaning of racial representation, visibility, and justice.

fluidity of poststructuralist models of racial difference. In field-defining works of contemporary Black and Asian American literary scholarship, postmodern critiques of literary mimesis have thus frequently been deployed against modes of racialized reading that collapse the highly mediated relationship between literary objects and lived experiences of racialization.

For Henry Louis Gates, for example, conflating racial difference with differences in "literary uses of language" (Gates Jr. 36) fails to take into account not only the "arbitrary relationship between sign and referent" (Gates Jr. 36), rendering "content… primary over form" (Gates Jr. 39) but also the intertextual lines of influence that cross racial boundaries. Such interpretive moves "demonstrates an alarming disrespect for the diversity of the black experience itself and for the subtleties of close textual criticism" (Gates Jr. 39).[33]

Within the context of Asian American literary studies, Lisa Lowe draws on the work of Louis Althusser and Korean American poet and performance artist Theresa Hak Kyung Cha to formulate a field-defining theory of racial interpellation based on an understanding of racialization as rooted in a demand for "identical equivalence as both a logic of domination and a legacy to be interrogated within the practices of resistance to domination" (Lowe 130). Lowe takes the experimental formalism of Cha's *Dictee* as a model for a politics of cultural difference reflective of the coalitional character and "Heterogeneity, Hybridity, Multiplicity" (Lowe 60) of a post-nationalist, pan-ethnic Asian American racial subject.

This discursive shift from identity to difference within existing scholarship, I argue, exposes a fundamental definitional instability at the heart of the concept of race itself. As what Stuart Hall calls a "sliding signifier" (Hall 18), race invokes both a fundamentally hierarchical concept, on the one hand, and, on the other, a sense of shared history, culture, and group solidarity in the face of racial domination and subordination. The poems at the center of my study radically reimagine race as a politically contested *social form* that pivots between oppressive and affirmative conceptions of racial group belonging. The turn to racial form as a framework for poetic interpretation circumvents ongoing debates

[33] For more recent reconsiderations of the legacy of the Black Arts Movement as what Larry Neal called the "aesthetic and spiritual sister of the Black Power concept" (Neal 29), see Crawford; Avilez. These works attempt to move beyond earlier critiques of the movement's reification of an "essentialized blackness" (Crawford 12) to offer more nuanced readings of the heterogeneity Black Arts Movement writing, art, and theater, including developing a more expansive sense of the era's queer "disruptive inhabiting" (Avilez 12) the movement's limits and possibilities. For Margo Crawford, such critiques ultimately relied "on a fetishism of individuality and the dead end of exceptionalism" (Crawford 16) that cannot convey the complexity of blackness as a signifier.

over the inherent and historically unchanging properties of either fixed or fluid *identities*, and instead reconceives race as a relational field of action, expression, and interpretation in which relations between subjects assume a range of formal "shapes" invested with sometimes contradictory racial meanings.[34] Across the poems I examine, these racial forms are objects of continuous political struggle that shapes and is, in turn, shaped by an aggregative relational "grammar" of racial group formation. In the aftermath of a series of epochal civil rights movement victories and the lifting of racial quotas in the 1965 Immigration and Nationality Act, I argue, that systematically reproduces racial belonging in an increasingly socially atomized or serial form.

Racial Form

In order to theorize race as a social form, or what Colleen Lye calls "racial form" (Lye, "Racial Form" 93), I place contemporary scholarship on literary form in conversation with contemporary theories of comparative racial group formation. Building on Raymond Williams's historical account of the concept of form as a descriptor of both literary genres and the organization of social life more broadly, Lye argues that the concept of race itself might be productively rethought in formal terms.[35] Employing a more expansive concept of form can help "mediate the usual divide between the aesthetic and the social, which is especially severe in discussions of ethnic literature" (Lye, "Racial Form" 97) where "the impasse between traditional formalism and sociological criticism" (Lye, "Racial Form" 97). The poems at the center of this study reimagine race as a field of constraint and possibility where subjects enter into shifting relational configurations with each other in ways that hinder or augment capacities for coordinated action under specifically capitalist conditions. This relational grammar of racial group formation constitutes a historically specific condition of possibility and limit

[34] This study builds on a recent relational turn in contemporary sociology and racial formation theory that has aimed to move beyond conceptualizations of race "as a 'thing' or a property," toward an understanding of racial distinctions as inscribed within relational fields (HoSang and Molina 6). "Race does not define the characteristics of a person," Daniel HoSang and Natalia Molina contend in the recent collection of essays on relational approaches to the study of race, "instead, it is better understood as the space and connections between people that structure and regulate their association" (HoSang and Molina 6–7). "Relational frameworks can provide purchase and insight even when different groups are not in frequent or direct contact," Molina and HoSang continue. "These groups share social fields and participate in and react to mutual social processes and practices even as they might inhabit distinct positions within shared structures" (HoSang and Molina 9).

[35] As Williams writes, within the history of literary criticism, form has "acquired two major senses: a visible or outward shape, and an inherent shaping impulse" (Williams 186).

of poetic experimentation in an era marked by seemingly intractable material barriers to further antiracist social transformation.

Drawing on a recent body of scholarship dubbed "New Formalism" (Levinson 558), I conceptualize racial form through the productive ambiguity of form itself as an "inquiry relative" (Kramnick and Nersessian 651) concept. A "noun in wait for its object" (Leighton 1), poetic scholarship has historically invested form with a range of sometimes divergent meanings—from shape, structure, container, and design, to prosody, syntax, ornament, and metaphysical ideal. Often taken to be synonymous with aesthetic experience as such, it is a concept which functions as a measure of novelty, estrangement, and conventionality in contemporary scholarship where poetic innovation is frequently assumed to be synonymous with formal innovation.

Suggesting both a shaping force and the patterned results of creative action, a capacity for abstraction as well as an apparition "greedy for substance" (Leighton 8), form can order, reorder, and dissolve the seeming chaotic irrationality of its antonym, matter. A traditional object of close reading, form vouchsafes the quiddity Calls for a "return to form" thus often accompany a "post-critical" (Polanyi 279) defense of aesthetic experience against more overtly politicized modes of poetic interpretation from symptomatic reading to ideology critique.[36]

Such arguments revive older philosophical elaborations of the non-instrumental character of significant aesthetic form. The entrenched conceptual opposition between form and identity bears traces of a tradition of Kantian and post-Kantian European aesthetic philosophy organized around the figure of a universal subject of aesthetic judgment counterposed to the "affectability" of non-European racial subjects especially susceptible "to a heteronomy of the laws of experience" (Kant 227) and to external determination by desire, prejudice, and "superstition." Despite scholarly efforts to free aesthetic judgment from explicit racial reference, the underlying conceptual opposition between aesthetic autonomy and "affectable" heteronomy persists, I argue, in contemporary debates over poetic form and identity.

Reading race as a social form which can be invested with a range of distinctive meanings departs from this specific formalist tradition and instead takes up the concept of "affordances" that New Formalist literary critics like Caroline Levine and others borrow from design theory. For Levine, forms describe

[36] On the "post-critical" turn in literary studies, see Felski. On as a highly influential articulation of what could be described as a "post-critical" method of literary close reading, see Marcus and Best. For a recent Adornian defense of the critical capacity of Kant's theorization of "purposive form," see Kaufman.

iterable or portable patterns that organize both literary texts and sociopolitical life. The language of affordances understands formal structures in terms of constraint and possibility. Specifying "the potential uses or actions latent in materials and designs" (Levine 6), the concept of affordance can illuminate how literary works reflexively thematize their own formal structuration and how social forms condition and enable human action. "Each shape or pattern, social or literary, lays claim to a limited range of potentialities," Levine writes. "Enclosures afford containment and security, inclusion as well as exclusion. Rhyme affords repetition, anticipation, and memorization. Networks afford connection and circulation, and narratives afford the connection of events over time" (Levine 6).[37]

Building on the premise that poetic forms possess no intrinsic political valence, however, I want to reconceive the concept of affordances as referring less to inherent properties of form than to an ongoing literary history of its

[37] Readers may find it peculiar that I take the recent work of Caroline Levine as a point of departure for studying poetic representations of capitalist processes. While appreciative of Levine's impulse to read forms socially and social life formally, some contemporary Marxist literary theorists have questioned how the critic conceptualizes the interaction and sheer variety of social forms. Echoing the work of Bruno Latour, Levine explicitly counterposes the ontological pluralism of social forms to Marxist interpretive frameworks, for example, that seem to exemplify totalizing forms of critique and causal explanation that posit an "ultimate causality" for manifold social phenomena. Explicitly working to displace an exclusive focus on dialectical thought, deep structures uncovered by ideology critique, and Manichaean binaries that define intractable political conflicts, Levine instead envisions a "democracy of forms" within an "overall view [that] moves away from the language of causality to that of 'collisions', crossings and the overlapping of social forms" (Lesjak). The resulting flat ontology eschews conceptual polarities while itself arguably reproducing a highly circumscribed and homogenizing image of liberal pluralist ideology.

The poems I examine in this study are not preoccupied with questions of "ultimate causes" or causal primacy that have provoked ongoing debates over the relationship between race and class as principles of social organization, conflict, and political identification. Capitalism is not represented in these works as a singular structural cause of all social phenomena that renders social life homogeneous but rather as a comparative measure of abstract value capable of comparing and connecting discrepant phenomena at a global scale. These poems explore how heterogeneous social structures, practices, and events are materially interlinked through what the theorist Moishe Postone calls capitalism's "historically unique form of social mediation" (Postone 5). In other words, my readings focus on how capitalism appears across these works precisely as a system of mediation that structurally reproduces social heterogeneity and homogeneity in integral relation to each other.

By considering literary and social forms together, Levine aims to move beyond an entrenched and thoroughly racialized opposition between formalist and historicist paradigms of literary interpretation, where ideals of aesthetic singularity and formal complexity are typically counterposed to crude reflectionist theories of literary representation. To argue that the relationship between literary and social forms can be productively thought together does not require endorsing Levine's broad adoption of Latourian flat ontology. Of course, there are alternative ways of reading form, and alternative theoretical definitions of the concept of literary form itself, that emphasize how form's antimimetic capacity construct a provisional space of aesthetic autonomy from the givenness of empirical "content." For example, on Frankfurt School theorist Theodor Adorno's reconceptualization of literary form's antimimetic capacity to refuse a capitalist commodity logic of representational equivalence, see J. Robinson.

potential uses.[38] At the same time, poems do not simply passively reflect given sociopolitical arrangements but actively construct and critically reflect on what counts as situation, context, and background for poetic signification, even and especially in works that announce their commitment to the aesthetic conventions of documentary realism. As Mutlu Blasing contends, the "essentialist, ahistorical alignment of given technical strategies with moral, metaphysical, or political values" is an enduring feature of both twentieth- and twenty-first-century formalist poetic analysis and "a historically specific confusion" (Blasing 2) largely derived from modernist aesthetic premises. New Critical aesthetic ideals have historically configured the formal structure of poems as the basis for claims that literature represents a specific kind of knowledge that presents a non-utilitarian challenge to the scientific quantification of social life and the pervasive means-ends rationality of industrial capitalism. The programmatic association of "open" and "closed" poetic forms with politically progressive or regressive values represents perhaps one of the most well-known recent examples of how accounts of postwar poetic movements have come to invest formal techniques with inherent political meaning and significance.

New Critical theories of the formal autonomy of the literary object promoted by John Crowe Ransom, Allen Tate, and Robert Penn Warren were deeply informed by a white Southern agrarian imaginary marked by the entanglement of race, literary form, and an entire regional form of life structured by a perceived conflict between the bureaucratic rationality of capitalist modernization and an economy of taste premised on Black chattel slavery. Echoing older Kantian theories of purposive form, Ransom, in particular, associates aesthetic experience with a capacity for non-utilitarian play that "does not reduce the [textual or commodity] object to a single, direct use, but acts as a restraint upon the rationalization and exploitation of the object" (Jancovich 37). In order to defend the cultivation of such non-instrumental aesthetic pleasures, as Mark Jancovich contends, Ransom "draws upon Southern paternalism, and its critique of capitalist relations" (Jancovich 37):

> The Southern paternalists argued that the capitalist was only interested in the labour-power of the labourer, and that, as a result, capitalist production failed to establish social or cultural restraints on the exploitation of the labouring classes. By contrast, the plantation was claimed to have established relations which were not purely economic, but more broadly social and cultural. Its organization

[38] As Madhu Dubey argues, "there is no straight line from form to politics and … aesthetic innovations do not inevitably produce politically subversive effects" (Dubey 10).

> was not designed with the sole aim of maximizing the productivity of the slave. Whatever the injustices of the plantation system, it was different from the capitalist system of production in which the only relationship between the capitalist and the labourer was that organized through the cash-nexus.
>
> (Jancovich 37)

New Critics could thus counter "purely economic interests with other interests" (Jancovich 37) through reference to the formal structure of textual objects as a balanced and stable harmonization of social contradictions. It is an image of the textual object as an organic whole modeled after images of Southern "unalienated pre-capitalist culture of the past" (Jancovich 18) whose coherence and continuity were secured through slave labor.[39]

Detaching form from this influential reading of the poem as a non-instrumental organic social whole requires critics to remain attentive to "both the political pressures that modify formal typologies and the formal negotiations of political imperatives" (Blasing 14). "Unless we differentiate how formal techniques may function in different ways," Blasing continues, "because the same forms may appeal to different rhetorical figures for their authority and because their rhetorical functions may change through time—we cannot make any substantive historical or political distinctions" (Blasing 14).

Instead, this study develops a more expansive concept of form to read poems that link literary techniques to sociopolitical arrangements understood in formal terms. Although there is a rich typology of aesthetic forms and rhetorical figures that might be brought to bear to describe the organization of texts, the concept of form ranges far beyond the boundaries of aesthetic discourse. "All of the historical uses of the term," Levine continues, "despite their richness and variety, do share a common definition: 'form' always indicates an arrangement of elements—an ordering, patterning, or shaping" (Levine 2–3).

Affording "repetition and portability across materials and contexts" (14), Levine's expansive sense of social forms includes patterns like bounded wholes, rhythms, hierarchies, and networks that can and do interfere with each other. This language of social forms, and formal modeling, already plays a significant role in contemporary scholarship on race—from what Paul Gilroy has called the

[39] How much of a break the emergence of New Critical interpretive methods represented from earlier formulations of a white Southern agrarian imaginary, implicitly or explicitly premised upon slavery and segregation and articulated in texts like *I'll Take My Stand: The South and the Agrarian Tradition* (Rubin, Jr.), remains a topic of ongoing scholarly debate. The key contributors of *I'll Take My Stand* would later become instrumental in defining New Critical interpretive methods. See also Maxwell.

"webbed network" (Gilroy 29) of the Black Atlantic world to Black feminist legal theorist Kimberlé Crenshaw's modeling of the interaction of racism and sexism in terms of intersections and basements. For Gilroy, the form of the network offers a potent challenge to "the coherence of all narrow nationalist perspectives" (Gilroy 29), while for Crenshaw, the metaphor of the intersection exposes how the prioritization of racial or gender oppression constructs nested hierarchies within legally protected populations in civil rights law.[40]

Reimagining the terrain of what E. San Juan Jr. calls the "race/class problematic" (San Juan, Jr.) through a politically engaged poetic formalism, the poems at the center of this study challenge the premises of a postwar liberal antiracism that has systematically separated anti-racist and anti-capitalist political imaginaries and narrowed antiracist political objectives to proportional inclusion within increasingly crisis-ridden capitalist economies. "Like race itself, antiracism 'floats' as a signifier," Daniel Martinez HoSang writes, "it has no inherent political valence or meaning" (HoSang 74):

> As the US military, Fortune 500 companies, and anti-union elites have learned, invocations of diversity, multiculturalism, and racial inclusion and equality can be fully commensurate with their agendas and interests. In many ways, the current regime of neoliberal multiculturalism represents the rise of a depoliticized antiracism—efforts presumed to stand against racial inequality and hierarchy that simply invite incorporation into existing systems of domination and power. (HoSang)

These poems can help readers of contemporary poetry envision racial justice beyond contemporary varieties of "depoliticized antiracism" designed to render capitalist institutionality impervious to collective political intervention.

These poems register the material demolition of the racial liberalism's promise of civic incorporation and offer vital historical soundings of the shapes that racial form might assume in the face of a resurgent twenty-first-century post-colorblind white nationalism and mounting interconnected global capitalist, ecological, and health crises.

These works can help readers of contemporary poetry to apprehend the Asiatic racial form of a "Chinese virus" and the diasporic reach of that "invisible enemy"(*Remarks by President Trump, Vice President Pence, and Members of the Coronavirus Task Force in Press Briefing*) infecting the nation from within. At the

[40] On Crenshaw's elaboration of the metaphor of a basement see Carastathis 69–102.

same time, this writing illuminates how Asian American claims on economic citizenship, for example, have fortified the economic logic undergirding calls for a civilizational war against China as a competitive threat, vector of disease, and emerging global hegemon. These works help clarify why the moral scandal of expropriated commodities both constitutes and fundamentally threatens racial order. In this order, the defense of property as a capitalist social form is routinely framed as the negation of Black insurgent political movements. Amid the largest political mobilization in US history in defense of Black lives, it is writing which speaks directly to why the national promise of a "democracy of goods" is routinely invoked to justify rather than challenge a political economy of Black disposability.

Chapter Summaries

In the first chapter, "Race in the Democracy of Goods," I read a selection of poems by Gwendolyn Brooks, Amiri Baraka, Theresa Hak Kyung Cha, and Harryette Mullen that offer differing critical perspectives on how the postwar production and consumption of commodities shape ideals of racial self-determination, immigrant assimilation, equal citizenship, family structure, and national cohesion. When read together, these poems trace a postwar economic history where postwar boom promises of material abundance give way to urban crisis conditions, deindustrialization, and austerity. These poems explore how such ideals are translated into racially differentiated claims on what historian Roland Marchand calls a "democracy of goods" (Marchand 217), where commodity displays compose a relational "grammar" that systematically connects market subjects precisely through their atomistic separation. Across these works, advertising images of post–civil rights movement racial inclusion for Black Americans, as well as post-1965 promises of economic citizenship for Asian immigrant subjects, are premised on identification with postwar US economic growth and the nation's excessive productive capacity.

In the second chapter, "In the Mirror of the Commodity Form: Race and 'Object Authority' in Erica Hunt's *Piece Logic*," I offer an extended reading of poet and critic Erica Hunt's poetry collection *Piece Logic* (2002) in relation to her 1989 essay, "Notes For An Oppositional Poetics." I argue that Hunt's compact volume of poetry reimagines a critique of what Karl Marx famously calls "the fetishism of the commodity" (Marx 163), or what the poet dubs "Object

Authority" (Hunt 10), from the point of view of the historically gendered, racially typed, and unwaged space of capitalist social reproduction within households. Across the poems in *Piece Logic*, the life cycle of disposable objects, such as malfunctioning kitchen appliances, mirrors the fate of racialized disposable or "surplus population[s]" (Marx 781) depicted as a kind of animate infrastructure for the production of full national subjects. Finally, I contend that the collection implicitly deconstructs the basic assumptions of a postwar discourse of Black matriarchal "broken families" and challenges the naturalization of capitalist value as a measure of racial progress and pathology.

The third chapter, "'Number, Form, Proportion, Situation': The Measure of Racial Comparison in Myung Mi Kim's *Dura*," offers an extended close reading of "Thirty and Five Books," a section from Korean American experimental poet Myung Mi Kim's *Dura*. *Dura* locates the historical origins of the US racial order within the process of the violent settler colonial creation of the United States as a national territory. At the same time the poet suppresses explicit racial reference in order to highlight the changing material forms of race structured through the insertion of expropriated indigenous land and enslaved labor into a recursive, ever-expanding transnational circuit of capitalist accumulation. A metrological imaginary emerges in Kim's book and across Kim's writings more broadly, I argue, which the author uses to renarrate colonial and capitalist history in terms of the evolution of systems of measurement. Such practices of counting and accounting have structured racialization processes in ways that, as the title of the book *Dura* suggests, have endured and that for the poet structure domestic non-white interracial conflict in the late twentieth century. For Kim, these metrological developments have historically defined a system of enforced racial comparison—from what Arjun Appadurai calls the "colonial numerology" developed to quantify the relative productivity of enslaved and colonized populations, to the parcelization and commodification of indigenous land required to construct the national territory of the United States. *Dura* employs an array of formal strategies that emphasize combinatory textuality. I argue that the poet does this to model how capitalist globalization brings formerly spatially separated populations into contact and often conflict. At the same time, the poem's combinatory textuality offers a potentially reparative vision of social coordination. In a section of *Dura* titled "Thirty and Five Books," Kim traces the long arc of an economic history of racial comparison, operationalized through entwined processes of quantification and hierarchical racial ordering. This racial comparison shapes the material terrain of Black–Asian conflict during the 1992 Los Angeles riots in the wake of four police officers' acquittal for the beating of Black motorist Rodney King.

The fourth chapter, "'In the Hollow Parts of Anything That Moves': Containing Asiatic Racial Form in Larissa Lai's "nascent fashion," focuses on a recent poem, "nascent fashion," from Asian Canadian poet and fiction writer Larissa Lai's 2010 poetry collection, *Automaton Biographies*. "nascent fashion" dramatizes how capitalist globalization renders spatially dispersed subjects both materially interdependent and subject to a logic of competitive devaluation facilitated by reconfigurable supply chains connecting distant sites of production and consumption. Centered on the cyborg-like figure of a self-assembling, abject, and ultimately replaceable "factory girl" (Lai 52), "nascent fashion" describes an emergent twenty-first-century global economic landscape whose logistical management transforms older imperial geographies into a spatially disaggregated "global factory." Facilitated by the military and later commercial development of the standardized shipping container, the hypermobility of commodities across this uneven landscape materially redefines global racial divisions in terms of the relative immobility of populations.

The fifth and final chapter, "Where From, Where To Are Faces of Here": Race as Seriality in Ed Roberson's "Sit In What City We're In," offers an extended close reading of Roberson's poem "Sit In What City We're In," from the author's 2006 book *City Eclogue*. Roberson's poem reimagines the rapid spread of 1960s civil rights movement lunch counter sit-ins across the South at sites of racially segregated consumption. He does this by reconfiguring the sit-ins in space and in time: spatially, by tracking how mirrors behind a lunch counter create an infinite regress of reflected images of protesters and counterprotesters alike, and temporally, by reconnecting the figure of a racially divided city to enduring cyclical geological processes. Registering an unresolved tension between ideals of abstract citizenship and divergent racially embodied perspectives on the scene, the poem critically reflects on a moment of political confrontation that promises reciprocity and the recognition of historical injustice but gives way to historical repetition and the persistence of spatial segregation. Trapping sit-in participants in a moment where they both confront and endure segregationist violence, the poem constructs a temporal loop that generates seemingly endless mirror images of serial subjects locked in struggle. At the same time, the poet presents a sweeping existential vision of desegregation that restlessly searches for a principle of relation capable of gathering together all of the disparate elements in the scene and imagining an alternative ground of collective life.[41]

In the Coda, I turn my attention to the poetry of John Yau and June Jordan. I argue that the interpretive framework that I develop to read for racial form in these works can be extended to poems that don't explicitly engage with the subject of postwar economic history. Yau and Jordan's poems both question language as a medium of "transparent" racial representation and insist on what I call, after Martinican poet and philosopher Édouard Glissant, the opacity of racial form.[42] These works imagine spaces of provisional abundance, grief, or repair through a refusal to render racial form legible as a subject of political recognition. Experiences of seemingly permanent racist misrecognition become in these poems a condition of possibility for the survival of the unsaid and unsayable, and for the imagining of alternative relational forms of collective life.

[41] In a recent study, Carter Mathes has argued that post–civil rights movement Black experimental literature, especially in its engagement with what Mathes calls "experimental sonority" (Mathes 11), is broadly characterized by a "potential to critically break from social realist literary form popularized in early to mid-twentieth-century political protest writing" (Mathes 11). Like the experimental literature Mathes explores, Roberson's poem challenges such strictures of aesthetic realism while at the same time dramatically reframing "late capitalist racial formation with a particular attention to the reconstitution of domination indicative of the post-Civil Rights era" (Mathes 11).

[42] My use of "transparency" refers in part to what contemporary Black feminist theorist Denise Ferreira Da Silva calls the "transparent 'I' " (da Silva xxiv) that regulates the terms of recognition of proper, sovereign, and self-determining subjects of emancipatory political claims. At the same time, "transparency" is here meant to invoke the historically changing formal and aesthetic conventions governing the racial legibility of subjects of poetic representation.

1

Race in the Democracy of Goods

At the center of mid-twentieth-century images of US material abundance broadcasted worldwide, the figure of the Cold War citizen-consumer powerfully redefined national belonging around both the productive capacity of the nation and the democratic freedom to consume. Studying advertising tableaux from the 1920s to the 1930s, historian Roland Marchand famously dubbed this national imaginary a "democracy of goods" (Marchand 217). In a nation where "the wonders of modern mass production and distribution enabled every person to enjoy the society's most significant pleasure, convenience, or benefit" (Marchand 217–18), Marchand writes, such images "offered Americans an inviting vision of their society as one of incontestable equality" (Marchand 218). Describing postwar consumer culture, economist John Kenneth Galbraith argues in 1958 that the merger of mass consumption and nationalism produces an "affluent society" (Galbraith) where the equalization of social status can finally be historically realized through the mass availability of standardized consumer items.

Representing social equality "in terms of equal access to consumer products" (Marchand 218), the promotion of the United States as a "democracy of goods" premises the power and legitimacy of the nation's global Cold War leadership in part on the egalitarian character of mass consumption. The assumed whiteness of the figure of the Cold War citizen-subject, whose consumption habits are a matter of patriotic duty, also functions as an emblem of the racially segregated social order that Robin D. G. Kelley and others have dubbed "Jim Crow capitalism" (Kelley and Camp). For most Black Americans, however, the technological advances in industrial production and the mechanization of Southern agricultural labor represented not the democratization of consumer abundance but economic expendability. In the immediate aftermath of the Second World War, as historian Jacqueline Jones notes, "For returning soldiers and all other Black people who had contributed directly or indirectly to the war effort between 1941 and 1945, the promise of full and equal American citizenship still seemed remote" (Jones 213):

> Increasingly, the country defined itself in terms of material well-being: Unlike Soviet citizens, the argument went, Americans could choose from a vast array of consumer items—from suburban tract houses so new and gleaming the paint was hardly dry, to fashionable cars and clothing… At the same time, transformations in regional economies called into question the notion that the United States was rapidly becoming an 'affluent society.' In the South, the mechanical cotton-picker continued to displace thousands of sharecroppers and tenant farmers, forcing them up north or out west, where they found contracting job markets borne of assembly-line automation, and rigidly segregated job markets borne of old prejudices and practices.
>
> (Jones 213–14)

Comprehensively structured by pervasive racial exclusion, violence, and terror, the distribution of the spoils of this postwar "affluent society" would powerfully shape the sites, stakes, and strategies of domestic antiracist political organizing. Indeed, the symbolic significance of what Lizabeth Cohen calls a midcentury "Consumers' Republic" would make racially segregated commercial sites of consumption and exchange, such as the five-and-dime Woolworth, focal points of civil rights movement sit-ins and consumer boycotts.

After a series of legislative victories, civil rights movement leaders turned their attention to the problem of material inequality, organizing a multiracial 1968 Poor People's Campaign centered on a social democratic "Freedom Budget For All Americans" (Le Blanc and Yates) designed to eradicate poverty in the United States within ten years.[1] At a moment of increasing access to what had once been considered luxury goods, made possible by the dramatically expanded productive capacity of US manufacturers, such "palaces of consumption" (Leach 339) crystallized an explosive contradiction between the rise of a postwar "affluent society" and Jim Crow.

Contemporary Black poets have offered prescient warnings of both the thwarted promise of equal citizenship as equal access to a "democracy of goods," and the absorptive power of an emergent culture industry working to commodify spectacular images of Black suffering and political unrest. From Gil

[1] For the authors of the "Freedom Budget," continued postwar economic growth would allow for the democratization of abundance without the need to raise taxes. For a history of the Poor People's Campaign see Laurent; Honey. For a book-length analysis of the "Freedom Budget For All Americans," see Yates and Le Blanc.

Scott-Heron's 1970 "The Revolution Will Not Be Televised" to Jayne Cortez's 2009 "Talking about New Orleans," images of a national "democracy of goods" in disarray suggest both surplus and the continued disposability of Black lives. These authors and musicians at the same time register a deep ambivalence about the ranks of what sociologist E. Franklin Frazier dubbed the "black bourgeoisie" (Frazier). In a controversial early-twentieth-century critique of this precarious class's social mores and political outlook, Frazier warned that the emulation of white consumption patterns would continue to constitute a failed strategy of racial integration. For Frazier, this strategy could only produce self-hatred and an obsession with status in a "world of make-believe" (Frazier 153)—highlighting the cost of accepting "unconditionally the values of the white bourgeois world: its morals and its canons of respectability, its standards of beauty and consumption" (Frazier 27).

Chronicling the lives of mostly poor Black residents of Chicago's Bronzeville neighborhood, the midcentury poems of 1950 Pulitzer Prize winner Gwendolyn Brooks explore moments of how this "world of make-believe" can become part of an alternative basis of community when repurposed and shared. For Brooks, commodities not only mark interracial and intraracial boundaries but allow her characters to imaginatively project themselves beyond daily rituals of rationed consumption and forms of spatial confinement tightly choreographed by poverty and the "plain old wrapper of no-expectation" (Brooks 36). In the 1953 novel *Maud Martha*, for example, the titular protagonist's sense of "what she felt life ought to be" (Brooks 192) is powerfully distilled by magazine stories of New York focused on the " 'good' objects there" (Brooks 190)—a "wood-paneled room, Chinese boxes, crystal, leather, rare plates, French figurines, expensive dresses" (Brooks 190), and "foolish food" (Brooks 191). Such objects don't simply mark the boundaries of racially segregated lives, however, but in their sharing or display cohere the Black communities Brooks represents as complexly interconnected and internally differentiated collective social forms.

For Brooks, the dreams that attach to "good objects" open up a margin of freedom from necessity—a space where communal sociality emerges in response to chronic material deprivation—from the "guiding awe / Of foodlessness" (Brooks 45) to the cramped and overcrowded rooms in kitchenette buildings her characters are forced to inhabit due to racially restrictive housing covenants. Brooks's characters, who populate the 1945 *A Street in Bronzeville* and the 1968 *In the Mecca*, are trapped in apartments that are themselves substandard commodities. Satin-Legs Smith's "wonder-suits" (Brooks 43) become emblems of a resourceful elegance that cannot completely cover over a betrayed promise of material equality "Below the tinkling trade of little coins" (Brooks 44). The playful economy of measured excess that comes to define the character becomes an implicit figure for Brooks's poetics. The poet restructures traditional European poetic forms such as the sonnet around non-traditional subjects evolving alternative measures of abundance under severe material constraint.

Brooks was not alone among poets in imagining postwar consumer goods as mirrors with the power to reflect ideal or stigmatized lives. Haunted by the history of the transatlantic slave trade, such objects in postwar contemporary Black literature frequently mirror what Saidiya Hartman calls the "afterlife of property" (Hartman, "Venus in Two Acts" 13) as an "ongoing state of emergency in which Black life remains in peril" (Hartman, "Venus in Two Acts"). As a small bit of supporting evidence in the 1954 *Brown vs. Board of Education* case, Kenneth and Mamie Clark's famous doll studies drew attention to how racially marked commodities could offer evidence of the psychic impact of racial segregation on childhood identity formation.[2] Similarly, what curator and sociologist David Pilgrim has called the widely circulated "racist objects" (Pilgrim 1) of Jim Crow America—from postcards and dolls to plates and parlor games—reveal the sometimes explicit racialization of postwar consumer objects in the form of racist Black memorabilia.[3] "Whereas the minstrel show animates the stereotype of the 'plantation darky,'" literary theorist Bill Brown argues, "these objects might be said to deanimate it, to arrest the stereotype, to render it in three-dimensional stasis, to fix a demeaning and/or romanticizing racism with the fortitude of solid form" (Brown 185).

Across Black and Asian American postwar poems, commodity displays mirror a relational "grammar" that systematically connects market subjects precisely through their separation as objectlike market identities. At the same time, these poems interrogate the racial meaning of social wealth and poverty in an era when the link between work and consumption has seemingly been severed. To take one prominent example of a poet consistently troubled by the "Affluent Society" as the product of historical theft and plunder, Amiri Baraka's short 1967 poem "Black People" (Bracey J.H. et al. 269) attempts to question the sources of consumer abundance in a world where human labor has seemingly

[2] For the definitive history of Brown v. Board of Education case, see Kluger. For a more detailed account of the institutional development of psychology as an academic discipline and the emergence of racial identification studies in the 1930s, see Jackson. As Jackson points out, however, the Clarks' doll tests, whose results were first published in 1947, were not central to the case for desegregation but instead one component of a broader body of social scientific evidence for the harm caused by continued segregation.

[3] For further discussion of racist Jim Crow memorabilia and advertising, see Turner; Goings; Brown.

vanished. For Baraka, consumer products bear the marks of a prior history of violent racial expropriation that marks a boundary between white property rights and Black enslavement. Such products also illuminate an intragroup split between the poem's speaker and "you"—an implied Black bystander who is prompted to repudiate a politically demobilizing possessive individualism.

The poem satirizes a hypocritical moral economy of money and debt, industriousness and idleness, possessive individualism, and productive labor to dispel the appearance of equal exchange premised on prior racial dispossession. In the poem, the speaker addresses poor Black residents of Newark, New Jersey—Baraka's birthplace—by drawing attention to their artificial separation from everyday symbols of postwar affluence sequestered in "palaces of consumption" (Leach 339)—"stoves, refrigerators, record players in Sears, Bambergers, Klein's, Hahnes', Chase" (Bracey J.H. et al. 269). The poem interrogates the apparent irrationality of socially engineered poverty amid plenty, building to an incendiary exhortation to loot items with "no money down, no money never" (Bracey J.H. et al. 269). This satirical reiteration of the language of easy access to credit evokes not only pervasive racially discriminatory lending practices and the spell of alienable property as a social form but also the appearance of money and goods as self-generating—conjured into existence as if by "magic."

Baraka's representation of these consumer goods not as the products of human labor but ultimately as the "fruits of the sun" (Bracey J.H. et al. 269) maintains that the link between work and consumption has already been broken—recalling the fears of the drafters of the "Triple Revolution" document. Repeating "magic words" (Bracey J.H. et al. 269) and performing "magic actions" (Bracey J.H. et al. 269) then might under these conditions redirect the force of a racial slur to break the spell of the commodity form in a post-labor world. "Magic" directly links the appearance of consumer goods seemingly created ex nihilo to the impossible condition of Black Americans expelled from steady waged work while remaining trapped inside a capitalist economy where material needs must be met through market exchange.[4]

In Newark, department stores such as Bambergers and Klein's, as historian Kevin Mumford points out, were long-standing targets of consumer activism and political boycotts organized by Black women—movements with origins

[4] For a discussion of the stakes of Baraka's transformation of "magic" as a racial slur into permission to, see Shaw 89–115. "We might say that 'magic,' in Baraka's analysis, is the shift in consciousness, the instantaneous charge, by which acts that seem to the prerevolutionary subject simply impossible suddenly become possible; magic explodes the common sense of liberalism, allowing the unthinkable to be thought" (Shaw 103–4).

in the Second World War "Double V" campaigns for victory against Axis forces abroad and against Jim Crow segregation at home. "By the 1960s, with the increase in credit cards and purchasing accounts for shoppers," Mumford continues, "African American women in cities across the nation protested discrimination in lending, inflated interest and terms, price gouging in the poor neighborhoods, and inferior merchandise" (Mumford 160).[5] Stripping apparel from white mannequins in local stores during the Newark riots, as Mumford writes, "many black female looters acted not only as nationalist dissenters but as agitated consumers" (Mumford 159). "As mothers, they routinely assumed responsibility for family shopping," Mumford notes, "and as shoppers absorbed the alluring advertisements, replete with photographs of white affluence and standards of beauty. Without enough income, for the average black woman the dream of consumption faded into frustration" (Mumford 159).[6]

Already controversial at the time of its publication, the poem was read out loud by Essex County Judge Leon Kapp at Baraka's 1967 trial, after his arrest and police beating during five days of civil unrest in the city, as evidence of the poet's criminal intentions. Written at a moment when 159 riots erupted across the United States, typically in response to police violence, "Black People!" doesn't simply expose how a defense of property rights could function as a technology of racial control but also echoes the demands of the "Triple Revolution" to democratize abundance in an economy that seemingly requires far fewer workers. "Money don't grow on trees no way, only whitey's got it," Baraka writes, "makes it with a machine, to control you you can't steal nothing from a white man, he's already stole it" (Bracey J.H. et al. 269). The poem's reference to the impossibility of stealing white wealth because it has already been stolen draws attention to the "origins of property rights in the United States [as] rooted in racial domination" (Harris 1716). In the poem, references to the power of "magic" refer in part to an occulted history of racial domination encoded in unequal property relations determining who and what is owned or owed. Simultaneously, the term draws

5 "In the mid-1960s, Black women led several demonstrations against the retailers on Springfield Avenue," Mumford continues about Newark-based Black consumer campaigns, "including a major action in which the police arrested nineteen protesters. The demonstrators eventually convinced the 'frightened merchants [to] clean up their stores.' Shards of information indicate pickets and other demonstrations against food stores in the South Ward before the riots… Despite several decades of concerted effort by angry consumers, white proprietors continued to gouge Black customers, and, when their accounts fell into delinquency, attempted to garnish their wages" (Mumford 160).

6 Attempting to explain the outbreak of looting to liberal audiences in the immediate aftermath of the Newark riots, Tom Hayden (qtd. In Mumford) drew similar conclusions. "They were tearing up the stores with trick contracts and installment plans," Hayden contended, "the second-hand television sets going for top-quality prices, the phone scales, the inferior meat and vegetables" (Hayden 30).

attention to how dreams of individual entry into the Consumers' republic separate Black subjects from each other.[7] Reappropriating and gathering together the dispersed panoply of products on display in "Sears, Bambergers, Klein's, Hahnes', Chase" (Bracey J.H. et al. 269) anticipates the aggregation of a Black collective insurgency out of serial experiences of material deprivation.

The liberation of these commodities, the poem suggests, will allow the poem's divided audience—the "you," distinguished from the looters—to rejoin and "Dance up and down the streets, turn all the music up, run through the streets with music" (Bracey J.H. et al. 269). The regeneration of an internally divided racial community here is made possible by "beautiful radios on Market Street, they are brought here especially for you" (Bracey J.H. et al. 269) dissolves the implied figure of a Cold War citizen-consumer, and a white nuclear family as a basic unit of privatized consumption, into images of communal use animated by a "critique of (private) property and of the proper" (Moten and Rowell 963). Commodities can be freed from private ownership, the poem maintains, into a utopian vision of communal abundance. It is not only money but a "democracy of goods" that also seems to be produced "with a machine." In an industrial economy restructured by "cybernation," the poem contends that the transformation of enslaved African labor into "living property" forms the basis for enduring corresponding claims of white ownership rights over expropriated land and labor.[8] Consumer goods in the poem reflect a doubled image of whiteness as property but also of fears that, in the words of Detroit activist and theorist James Boggs, "America is headed toward full unemployment, not full employment" (Boggs 118).

However, the poem does not demand full employment but freedom from industrial labor. The call to "make our own World" (Bracey J.H. et al. 269) and

[7] One might read in this act of resignification, a reversal of a language of moral obligation and indebtedness that since the nineteenth century have come to define what Saidiya Hartman has characterized as the "burdened individuality" of post-Emancipation Black subjects. Hartman has written extensively on the historical persistence of such a rhetoric of indebtedness and how it has systematically defined and been defined by the stepwise and revocable transformation of African slaves into rights-bearing liberal subjects and formally free wage laborers. "The mantle of individuality effectively conscripted the freed as indebted and dutiful worker," Hartman contends, "and incited forms of coercion, discipline, and regulation that profoundly complicated the meaning of freedom" (Hartman, *Scenes of Subjection: Terror, Slavery, and Self-Making in Nineteenth-Century America* 121–2) through a "liberty of contract that spawned debt-peonage, the bestowal of right that engendered indebtedness and obligation and licensed naked forms of domination and coercion" (Hartman, *Scenes of Subjection: Terror, Slavery, and Self-Making in Nineteenth-Century America* 120).

[8] Legal theorist Cheryl Harris has characterized this "property interest in whiteness" (Harris 1745) as "a line of protection and demarcation from the potential threat of commodification" (Harris 1721) through enslavement.

"gather the fruit of the sun" (Bracey J.H. et al. 269) after agricultural work had been rapidly mechanized in the first half of the twentieth century. Here Baraka offers a utopian vision of Black communal life, dreaming of the material basis for what abolitionist and Black nationalist Martin R. Delany called a "nation within a nation" in a post-labor world. By arguing that postwar consumer abundance originates in historical theft, the poem presents a world where "magic words" can break the spell of social atomization and the property form precisely because the latter's relationship to wage labor seems increasingly detached from social needs.

Asiatic Racial Form and the "Force of the Machinery"

In Korean American poet Theresa Hak Kyung Cha's "photo-essay," a short previously unpublished 1978 poem by Cha, such "palaces of consumption" (Leach 339) model a form of generic particularity as the endpoint of economic assimilation for newly arrived Asian immigrants. Along with the poetry of Kim, John Yau, and Mei-Mei Berssenbrugge, the writings, performances, and films of Theresa Hak Kyung Cha have powerfully shaped contemporary scholarly attempts to define the generic parameters of Asian American experimental writing. Cha's book-length experimental poem *Dictee*, in particular, has established durable protocols for reading Asian American experimental poetry as a challenge to what Lisa Lowe identifies as an earlier exclusionary, nationalist "logic of identity" (Lowe 131). *Dictee*'s formal strategies instead model an antiessentialist "politics of difference" (Lowe 153) that trouble "the notion of an essential Asian American, female, or postcolonial subject" (Lowe 153).

The initially indifferent or hostile reception to Theresa Hak Kyung Cha's *Dictee* among scholars of Asian American literature offers one of the most well-known examples of ongoing debates over the political ambiguity of the text's refusal to assert a legible and "representative" racial subject.[9] The book is composed of letters, photographs, translation exercises, film stills, stories, religious rituals, and highly fragmented descriptions of the difficulty of speaking and writing about the violence of Korean history and the challenges of Korean American

9 After a decade of relative critical neglect among scholars of Asian American literature, a collection of essays emerged—featuring contributions from Elaine Kim, Lowe, Laura Hyun Yi Kang, and Shelley Sunn Wong—positioning *Dictee* as a critique of the limits of a patriarchal and essentialist 1960s-era Asian American cultural nationalism. See Kim et al.

assimilation. A critical consensus has developed around *Dictee*'s fractured syntax and structural organization as a political critique of the violent imposition and ongoing regulation of normative racial, gender, and national identities.

The book's formal structure models an internally divided, yet integral, "subject" of Asian American politics at the intersection of identity and difference. Cha's writing has remained contested terrain for critics looking to reimagine the ground for configuring Asian America as an oppositional political formation in a post-nationalist era. Her work persistently poses the question of how to represent the populations that racial and ethnic categories describe after the "deconstruction of the very logic of 'identity' and its binary and exclusionary politics" (Radhakrishnan 199).

In my reading, "photo-essay" responds to this challenge that complicates existing interpretive frameworks generated to read *Dictee*. In "photo-essay," logics of identity and difference are not antithetical but share a market-mediated serial social form. The poem lingers over department store displays of consumer goods that reflect an image of national belonging in a "democracy of goods" and a narrow road to economic citizenship. The speaker puzzles over the "force of the machinery" (Cha, *Exilée and Temps Morts: Selected Works* 96) capable of producing collections of nearly identical mannequin faces, wigs, and mass-market paperbacks. The interplay between formal equivalence and variation among objects extends to the rest of the poem—from shelves of mannequin heads gradationally differentiated by skin tone to a display of nearly identical Harlequin Romance paperbacks, and from the geometrical regularity of church pews to scattered student desks in a Catholic high school classroom. The poem both compresses and updates a history of Asiatic racial form as machinic abstract labor in a post-Hart-Celler era. By assimilating into an order of commodities, the Asian immigrant speaker becomes multiplicitous and seemingly acquires the capacity of "self-regeneration" (Cha, *Exilée and Temps Morts: Selected Works* 96) from the object world.

Cha's poem pairs text and photographs across nineteen facing pages. The work lingers over commercial spaces where a new arrival to the United States searches for some reflection of her own life in what the speaker calls a "tyranny of objects" (Cha, *Exilée and Temps Morts: Selected Works* 96). Set against textual fragments of autobiographical memories, the poem's black-and-white photographs offer images of rows of consumer objects but no human figures. A photograph of an empty photo booth sits at the center of the poem. As a device capable of translating subjects into images and images into serial objects, it is a potent symbol for a kind of national image-making apparatus capable of generating the appearance of wealth and citizen-consumers who have seemingly vanished into the mirror of the commodity form.

Language acquisition in the poem is described in similar terms as a struggle to conform to a logic of serial equivalence. To discover their place among things and within a nation represented as a vast collection of commodities, the speaker must become fluent in a "vocabulary" (Cha, *Exilée and Temps Morts: Selected Works* 96) of objects. After two opening sections, describing early childhood memories and an overheard stranger's confession in a local café, "photo-essay" presents three photographs paired with three short pieces of text on facing pages. The first and longest text accompanies a photograph of rows of mannequin heads displaying women's wigs. The poem begins with a memory of entering the United States through San Francisco—called "Gold Mountain" by nineteenth-century Chinese immigrant laborers:

> ARRIVAL 31, AUGUST 1962 UNITED STATES OF AMERICA
>
> The most astonishing
> Of the first day
> Was the abundance, wealth, the excess.
> As a child, one imagined this "Gold Mountain"
> As having no two treasures alike, repetition became an inevitable
> Vocabulary member
> Inexhaustible duplication self-regeneration
> As necessity
> This absolute wealth tyranny of objects
> As force force of the machinery
>
> (Cha, *Exilée and Temps Morts: Selected Works* 96)

The speaker is disappointed that the nation's wealth does not display various "treasures" but instead the "Inexhaustible duplication" of things.

To assimilate to this "democracy of goods," the speaker must become an "inevitable / Vocabulary member"—an odd formulation can be read as a reference to how an individual word might take its place in a lexicon, as well as to the question of how a thing might become a "member" of a category of things. The jagged, paratactic breaks in the text suggest halting, effortful attempts at acquiring a new language through the recursive process of learning individual words. This language learning process entails mimicking the "force of the machinery" that efficiently produces the rows of objects pictured on the facing page. Attaining proficiency in this new language is implicitly framed as a method for securing recognition as an assimilated "member" of a nation where relations between objects model civic belonging.

The poem subsequently interrogates how the commodity form has seemingly captured the "machinery" of mass cultural representations of social life—creating combinatory, modular structures of repeated images and motifs. The following pages feature pictures of a photo booth and a display case of Harlequin Romance novels with nearly identical covers. Accompanying the image of the photo booth, the poet writes, "systematic. / Even with the image" (Cha, *Exilée and Temps Morts: Selected Works* 98). The missing subject of this textual fragment poses the question, Who or what is manipulating such images if not the "machinery" itself? In the poem, the "systematic" character of such manipulation hinges on a particular combination of sameness and difference, or standardized variation that does not simply reproduce an already existing reality but reshapes it—molding "even / desire" (Cha, *Exilée and Temps Morts: Selected Works* 100).

These mass-produced images of desire contrast with later photographs of what appear to be empty hallways and classrooms of a Catholic high school, accompanied by text that describes "the rigid obsessive order / skirts of measured lengths / interdiction of crossed knees" (Cha, *Exilée and Temps Morts: Selected Works* 106). Yet the poet is here also drawn to a "systematic" approach to representing and containing desire. In one photograph, several Freudian terms—*repression, reaction formation, introjection, defenses*, and so on—fill up a blackboard beneath a statue of Jesus. The accompanying text refers to "Reading D. H. Lawrence, Mary McCarthy, Henry Miller / in spite of" an atmosphere of tightly choreographed "synchronized gestures" (Cha, *Exilée and Temps Morts: Selected Works* 106), which seem to function as containers for unpredictable libidinal energies. The speaker subsequently confesses surprise at discovering a copy of Norman O. Brown's book *Love's Body*, underscoring how more frank discussions of erotic desire and sexuality have found their way into the otherwise ascetic institutional space. Such desire has become an object of study and conceptual ordering, producing another set of homologous objects as "containers" for otherwise unruly desires—from a set of scandalous texts to the mechanical psychic "apparatus" of the Freudian subject.

As a sign hung on its exterior reminds us, an empty photo booth placed at the center of the poem produces "wallet size" portable images one might exchange like currency.[10] The poem is itself structured around a series of formal shapes

[10] This "fusion between thingness and personhood" (Cheng 420), as Anne Cheng points out, has long marked media representations of the "yellow woman" as a figure for ornamental artifice.

generated through the aggregation and arrangement of basic visual motifs that, at an abstract formal level, illustrate the interplay between sameness and particularity. In my reading, this interplay recasts the pressures of assimilation in terms of a demand for homogeneity but instead as an ideal of market-mediated individuation premised upon social separation.

Market subjects are accorded representational visibility and coherence in ways that compel the speaker to interrogate the "apparatus" capable of producing citizen-consumers and naturalizing the boundaries between them. The poem lingering over the image of an empty photo booth anticipates the poet's later interest in cinematic apparatus theory. Initially promoted by two influential film journals, *Cahiers du Cinéma* and *Screen*, this approach to film criticism influenced by Althusserian Marxism and psychoanalysis reached the height of its popularity in the 1970s and 1980s. Apparatus theorists like Christian Metz, Jean-Louis Baudry, and Laura Mulvey maintained that any attempt to interpret the ideological content of films should focus on the historical evolution of cinematic technology itself, from the development of cameras and film stock to the emergence of sound. Having studied in France with Christian Metz in the 1970s, Cha ultimately edited a volume of essays, *Apparatus*, that featured the work of these theorists. Although the rigid formalism of apparatus theory has been subject to subsequent criticism, Cha shared with these scholars an understanding of cinema as a spatialized interpellative technology designed to produce passive viewers not primarily through the explicit ideological content of visual images, but through a logic of representation produced by the topography of camera, projector, screen, and spectator. The "concealment of the technical base" (Baudry 41) of cinema, as apparatus theorist Jean-Louis Baudry contends, produces ideological effects that can be dispelled by exposing this machinery of representation and insisting on an "actualization of the work process" (Baudry 41) that generates and naturalizes cinematic illusion.

Asiatic Racial Form and Abstract Labor

In offering readers an image of an image-making machine, Cha's poem attempts to expose the "apparatus" that has historically associated Asiatic racial form with the "force of the machinery" (Cha, *Exilée and Temps Morts: Selected Works* 96) itself. Fears of coolie laborers and low-wage workers in Asia, along with the wary fetishization of the productive capacity of model minorities, have historically framed the internal and external Asiatic threat in terms of an inhuman mechanical efficiency. By connecting images of anthropomorphic personified objects to the serial image-making apparatus of a photo booth, "photo-essay" evokes a history of Asian racialization in which immigrant workers have been persistently represented as machines whose consciousness and capacity for self-directed movement are an illusion.

Cha reimagines contemporary Asiatic racial form as the product of a failed translation of the speaker's concrete history and embodiment into a "Vocabulary" of things.[11] In the photographs, viewers are presented with images of the built environment and a world of things—from empty café tables and hallways to lecture notes on a chalkboard.[12] The discrepancies between text and image, where subjects and objects exist in different representational mediums, are examples of what W. J. T. Mitchell characterizes as a ruptural *image/text*—where each medium destabilizes the conventions of the other.[13] Textually invoked though visually unrepresented, the subject vanishes into things, becoming a kind of apparitional afterimage faintly visible in the patterning of objects within

[11] In calling attention to and exacerbating an iterative logic of subject formation as repetition and "inexhaustible duplication," "photo-essay" recalls perhaps one of the most famous passages contained in Cha's book-length experimental poem, *Dictee*. In that work, a speaker responds to the Catholic catechism by parodically overperforming the mimetic structure of religious ritual and embodiment: "God who has made me in His own likeness. In His Own Image in His Own Resemblance, in His Own Copy, In His Own Counterfeit Presentment, in His Duplicate, in His Own Reproduction, in His Cast, in His Carbon, His Image and His Mirror. Pleasure in the image pleasure in the copy pleasure in the projection of likeness pleasure in the repetition. Acquiesce, to the correspondence" (Cha, *Dictee* 17–18).

Critics have tended to read this passage as a key moment where the book's general challenge to aesthetic mimesis converges with the book's critique of the interpellative structure of a logic of generic and categorical identities. The problem of how categorization not only presupposes but produces uniformity, and actively suppresses the fact of what Linda McCall has called the "anticategorical complexity" (McCall 1773) of social subjects, has come to delimit the horizon of political agency in ongoing discussions of Cha's writings and artworks.

[12] Earlier in the poem, a photograph of empty chairs and tables in a café suggests how a range of objects seem to recontain the excessive grief of a stranger revealing intimate details of their romantic and familial life in an overheard conversation. It is a grief provoked by unmet desires and broken attachments that threatens to breach the boundaries of a blank, anonymous privacy seemingly enforced by things: "we pretend/that she does not/exist that/we did not hear/her saying/i am sick/i am hungry starving/i want Russ to take care of me/and my brother is dying/and i am not thinking of Phillip/that's an old affair/she has a toothpick in her/mouth he leaves her/she is crying by the/candle light in front of the lace/draped windows/legs crossed/camel coat/she looks my way" (Cha, *Exilée and Temps Morts: Selected Works* 94). Desiring to not only ignore the details of this overheard conversation but also to pretend that the person involved in it "does not/exist," the speaker instead confers recognition on a variety of objects: "candle light," "lace/draped windows," and a "camel coat." The interplay between text and image here produces a peculiar splitting of story and image where the painful, transient details of the sources of the woman's distress are displaced onto objects in the scene.

[13] For a reading of Cha's multimedia art objects in relation to Mitchell's theory of critical iconology and Apparatus theory, see Jeon (Jeon 110–13). Jeon argues that Cha's multimedia avant-garde art objects denaturalize and reconfigure the representational codes governing racial visibility. "The often befuddling objecthood of avant-garde objects—be they books, films, or sculptures," Jeon writes, "becomes a means of investigating the foreignness of radicalized bodies" (Jeon 3).

empty spaces. Asian immigrant assimilation is reimagined then as a process of dematerialization in which diasporic memory dissolves as immigrant subjects disappear into a "democracy of goods." The speaker is subsequently driven to search for their own "lost" corporeal reflection in a past that is not and cannot be spoken within a "Vocabulary" (Cha, *Exilée and Temps Morts: Selected Works* 96) of consumer goods.

The Nerveless Body of Abstract Labor

The poem's dramatization of the "inevitable" assimilation to an order of objects exposes a durable association between Asiatic racial form and machinelike labor. From the nineteenth century onward, the history of mass Asian migration to the United States has been powerfully conditioned by the need for labor in key industries—from the search for replacement "coolie" workers in the aftermath of the abolition of Black chattel slavery to the contemporary demand for highly skilled professionals under the H-1B visa program created in 1990.[14] The perception of Chinese immigrant labor, in particular as an economic threat to native-born workers, has long played a significant role in reshaping US and Canadian immigration policy. As Bill Ong Hing argues, "[Asians'] very presence fostered a fundamental rethinking and reordering of the role that immigration law might play in the construction of the United States as a national community" (Hing 19). As the first racial group to be banned by federal law from immigrating to the United States, Asian migrants subsequently faced racial bars to naturalization until the US government passed a series of congressional repeal acts in the mid-twentieth century. Asian immigration, in other words, occasioned a rethinking of US immigration policy as a mechanism that could alter the racial demographics of the country in response to economic crises and the perceived economically destabilizing effects of cheap and hyperefficient foreign workers.

The origins of Asiatic racial form lie in late-nineteenth-century images of "coolie" laborers who could subsist on inhumanly low wages and whose "nerveless" bodies were unaffected by pain. As Colleen Lye has argued, Chinese bodies capable of performing repetitive tasks condensed late-nineteenth- and early-twentieth-century fears that the increasing mechanization of industrial

[14] On Chinese "coolies" as a temporary replacement labor force in the aftermath of the formal abolition of slavery in the United States, see Jun.

labor processes in an era of monopoly finance capital might ultimately replace native-born white labor:

> The coolie… signifies the lowest labor price generated by the increasing transnationalization of labor markets. As the phantasmatically cheapening body capitalism strives to universalize, the coolie represents a biological impossibility and a numerical abstraction, whose social domination means that the robust American body will have disappeared.
>
> (Lye, *America's Asia: Racial Form and American Literature, 1893-1945* 57)

The efficiency that defined the threat of coolie labor formed the basis of a later public discourse of a US "model minority" that emerged in the 1960s and was later exported to Canada.[15] The framing of Asian Americans as a depoliticized "model" of successful assimilation for other racial groups has served a counterinsurgent domestic and international "pedagogical function" (Palumbo-Liu 409) that has consistently offered proof of "colorblind" capitalist dynamism and national exceptionalism. As many scholars have argued, the achievements of such "model" populations have been historically invoked to dismiss the political demands of the civil rights and Black Power movements domestically while calling for either protectionist measures against Asian competition or the emulation of Asian business practices. "While the domestic myth was deployed to contain and divert civil rights policymaking, to neutralize activism, and to promote a laissez-faire domestic urban policy," David Palumbo-Liu observes, "the international myth challenged the United States to modify its modes of economic operation" (Palumbo-Liu 172).

The body of the Chinese worker, in particular, has historically been understood in terms of both its stamina and minimal subsistence needs—a racial avatar of a degraded and dystopian capitalist future:

> Figured as enduring, impervious to physical pain, and mechanical or slavish in its relation to freedom, pleasure, and a volitional relation to history, this body spoke to Americans—or rather, was spoken, ventriloquistically, by them—most insistently of the possibility of a future that promised to rewrite the relationship between suffering and human being.
>
> (Hayot 139)

A model of endurance rather than strength, the body of the coolie is represented in nineteenth-century anti-Chinese tracts, such as Samuel Gompers and Herman

[15] See Pon.

Gutstadt's "Meat vs. Rice: American Manhood Against Asiatic Coolieism, Which Shall Survive?" (Gompers and Gutstadt), as uniquely suited to suffer light repetitive tasks, boredom, nutritional deprivation, and low levels of chronic pain. "The threatened triumph of the coolie," Hayot continues, "promised a victory of quantity over quality, of consistent small efforts over heroic large ones, of the faceless horse over the individual, and of mass production over unalienated, organic labor" (Hayot 142).

A persistent feature of anti-immigrant discourse into the present, the opposition between "alien" and "unalienated, organic labor" reflects not only national and transnational labor pools but also the divided character of the commodity form itself. As Iyko Day argues, the continued contemporary association of Asians in North America with either money or mechanization constructs a racial discourse of Asian immigrants as enduring representatives of what Karl Marx calls abstract instead of concrete labor. Defining concrete labor as work performed in a specific time and place that produces useful goods, Marx defines abstract labor in terms of a comparative and continually recalibrated unit measure of the "Socially necessary labour time" (Marx 129) required to produce a commodity "with the average degree of skill and intensity of labour prevalent" (Marx 129) in specific societies. This abstract measure renders the products of work exchangeable. In other words, the abstract exchangeability and concrete particularity of the commodity form reflect the similarly split character of the capitalist labor process. Although for Marx, abstract and concrete labor are mutually constitutive, Asiatic racial form, Day maintains, is constructed by separating the concrete and abstract dimensions of capitalist production and biologizing the latter.

The image of the Asian immigrant workers continues to be represented as rootless and bound to no nation, as opposed to the concrete labor of native-born white workers oriented toward practical use and the material reproduction of organic lifeworlds. Alternately mechanical automata and hyperassimilable model citizens, Asian workers represent a "monstrous personification of dehumanized equivalence" (Day 196) with an unsettling disregard for national belonging. The Asian worker is thus a "figure whose interchangeability as a value expression dramatizes the properties of money itself, Marx's 'universal equivalent,' " Day contends, "against which everything is commensurable and exchangeable" (Day 44).[16] As human emblems of the global mobility of capital

[16] For a study of contemporary literary representation of Asian Americans as "economic citizens" whose political visibility is significantly structured by their positioning within a capitalist process of accumulation see So.

intensifying competitive pressures to render labor more efficient and profitable, Asian labor continues to embody the possibility of a degraded capitalist future for US native-born workers.

In light of this history of contemporary Asian American claims on economic citizenship as proof of national belonging, we might return to a rhetorical question originally posed by Gary Okihiro in 1994, "Is yellow black or white?" (Okihiro 31). While Okihiro's question is meant to warn readers against conceptualizing Asian racialization as a derivative phenomenon, the very form of the question highlights how Asian Americans continue to be understood in terms of a unique racial capacity for mimicry—including a more and less than human ability to adapt to impersonal capitalist imperatives.[17]

One might read Asiatic racial form in a poem such as "photo-essay" as a specific experience of historical erasure conditioned by the Asian immigrant's reconstitution as abstract labor and mechanical apparatus. The poem invokes "excess" productive capacity as a metaphor for an affective "surplus" of historical meaning that the commodity form can neither adequately reflect nor contain. But it is precisely this excess that also appears as a kind of unreflected emptiness in the poem—a polarity that has historically defined Asiatic racial form as a personification of capitalist abstraction.

"Who Is the Maniac, and Why Everywhere at the Same Time": Baraka's "Das Kapital" and the Riddle of Value

Cha's brief meditation on the uncertain prospect of incorporation into the empty forms of "Gold Mountain" offers readers a series of snapshots of a national economy at the end of a thirty-year postwar boom. The poem's attunement to a peculiar hollowness at the heart of the commodity form depicts national identity as an inert and automated material apparatus bound to capitalist processes. At the same time, that hollowness also describes a psychic experience of privation that lends formal continuity to the non-narrative presentation of the poem's discrete scenes. As a psychic and material structure of atomized belonging, that

[17] What Colleen Lye calls the "analogical status of Asiatic racial form" (Lye, "Racial Form" 1735) opens onto a broader set of debates over cultural appropriation and exchange, as well as the impact of postwar Black cultural production on Asian American authors' attempts to articulate a distinctive antiracist cultural politics. Daniel Y. Kim has noted how Asian American cultural nationalist works by authors like Frank Chin have been inspired by the dream of an Asian American vernacular defined through both "an extravagantly parasitic relationship to a racist popular culture" (Kim 222) and an "idolatrous mimetic desire for whiteness" (Kim 35).

emptiness materializes relationally across various domains of social life—from the dissolution of intersubjective bonds within troubled romantic and familial relationships, to tightly choreographed spaces of pedagogical regulation and religious instruction.

The problem of how to both identify and denaturalize the elemental force of capitalist processes preoccupied Amiri Baraka during the decade of the publication of Cha's poem. It was a decade marked by several intertwined developments broadly characterized by politicians, planners, and scholars in terms of "urban crisis"—including accelerating deindustrialization, budget cuts, and municipal debt defaults, to white flight, decaying urban infrastructure, and deepening spatial segregation.[18]

After "Black People," Amiri Baraka's poetry registered the seismic impact of these economic developments rapidly reshaping US cities like Newark across the 1960s and 1970s. The poet trained his attention on both deepening class divisions among Black Americans and the economic imperatives establishing durable material constraints on municipal governance Increasingly critical of the conservatism of an emergent layer of Black politicians like Newark mayor Kenneth Gibson, whom Baraka had helped to elect in 1970, the poet broke with Black cultural nationalism and embraced an evolving version of Third World Marxism-Leninism-Maoism. "Although other intellectuals had offered Marxist critiques of nationalist politics," the historian Cedric Johnson notes of Baraka's political transformation, "the mid-seventies' adoption of Marxist-Leninist-Maoist ideology by Baraka and others sent shock waves through movement circles since many radical activists and intellectuals viewed such ideological converts as traitors" (Johnson 156).

While the controversial decision produced immediate organizational turmoil in his political milieu, Baraka persisted in his efforts to reconcile Marxism with revolutionary nationalist principles within an increasingly fractious New Communist Movement in the 1970s.[19] Inspired by a wave of midcentury global

[18] On the period of "urban crisis," see Pritchett. For an account of the role that racially segregated housing policies and credit programs, in particular, have played in the intergenerational reproduction of US racial inequality, see Rothstein.

[19] Jitu Weusi and Haki Madhubuti, two leaders in a Black Power organization led by Baraka, the Congress of African People, immediately resigned from the group after a speech Baraka gave on the need to incorporate "Marx's theories and the teachings of Lenin and Mao" into the doctrine of "revolutionary Kawaida" developed from the writings of cultural nationalist Ron Karenga. As Komozi Woodard notes of the organizational impact of Baraka's political shift, "The CAP transformed itself from a Black Power organization into a Marxist-Leninist group and changed its name to the Revolutionary Communist League in May 1976. A pivotal influence in Baraka's turn to the Marxist Left was the venerable Black Marxist, Harry Haywood. Haywood and his colleague Odis Hyde were veterans of the old Left who engaged 1960s and 1970s era" (Woodard x).

anticolonial movements, the resulting political synthesis advanced a vision of racism as functional to capitalist exploitation while translating antiracist and anti-imperialist political objectives into a language of national oppression, liberation, and self-determination:[20]

> People who cannot see that it is the economic system that supports, reinforces and continues racism are shortsighted, or simply want to get in on the oppressive system as a co-oppressor. Whereas, we must be mobilized and organized to eliminate this system entirely and replace it with a system that will see public control of land, mineral wealth, energy sources, supplies and factories, that is, all the means of producing wealth, under the absolute control of the working masses. For the benefit of the whole of society. This system, of course, is Socialism.

The problem of determining the precise theoretical relationship between capitalism and racial oppression remained an open question—with Baraka's poetry from the period often complicating the author's more sweeping programmatic pronouncements elsewhere.

Far from a settled issue, and despite Baraka's evolving attempts to formulate a "correct line" on these problems, poems from the 1972 collection *Hard Facts* sharply criticize the limits of his own earlier nationalist stances while exploring the theoretical relationship between race and capitalism beyond the author's more programmatic pronouncements elsewhere about racism as a byproduct of "monopoly capital" (Baraka, *Hard Facts* 8).[21] In particular, the poem "Das Kapital" resituates the urban sites of consumption, concentrated poverty, and insurrectionary rupture represented in poems like "Black People" within a broader postwar deindustrializing racial and economic geography. The poem ties the conditions of decaying cities to white flight into racially segregated suburbs and to the imperial reach of the "yanqui dollarrrr" (Baraka, *S O S: Poems 1961-2013* 162) abroad. Like "Black People," "Das Kapital" attempts to interrogate the racially unequal distribution of postwar property ownership as a kind of neutral market outcome. Unlike that earlier poem, however, the focus is less on commodities themselves than on an abstract system of domination

[20] As Baraka recalls in his autobiography, "moving away from the Black cultural nationalism movement, the criticism we received from the misguided that we had abandoned Black people for a White ideology was now matched by the Left, which not only criticized us for our cultural nationalism but staunchly tried to beat us up about our not having the correct Marxist line" (Baraka, *The Autobiography of Leroi Jones* xv–xvi). Despite the poet's break with Karengian cultural nationalism, race and nation, as well as racism and national oppression, remained largely synonymous categories of analysis for Baraka.

[21] See Baraka, "Nationalism, Self-Determination, and Socialist Revolution."

that organizes the production, ownership, and distribution of things and systematically mediates social relations between people in ways that are difficult to represent in their totality.

Translating this uneven spatial terrain and its devastating social consequences into the form of a mystery story, "Das Kapital" dramatizes a speaker's attempt to identify an elusive "maniac" (Baraka, *S O S: Poems 1961-2013* 161) that throughout the poem is responsible not only for a string of murders but also for the violence "hidden everywhere" (Baraka, *S O S: Poems 1961-2013* 161) in the decaying infrastructure of an unnamed city. The poem opens by describing an act of violence ignored by distracted "commuters looking for their new yorkers" (Baraka, *S O S: Poems 1961-2013* 161) while traveling back to the suburbs from work:

> Strangling women in the suburban bush
> they bodies laid around rotting while martinis are drunk
> the commuters looking for their new yorkers feel a draft
> & can get even drunker watching the teevee later on the Ford
> replay. There will be streams of them coming, getting off
> near where the girls got killed. Two of them strangled by
> the maniac.
>
> (Baraka, *S O S: Poems 1961-2013* 161)

Anticipating the poem's increasingly expansive understanding of what constitutes a murder scene, the very first word of the poem, a present participle attached to no clearly identified subject, raises the question of whether the speaker themselves or even the commuters may bear some direct or indirect responsibility for these deaths. These killings only seem to register in the poem as a momentary "draft" (Baraka, *S O S: Poems 1961-2013* 161), a slight disturbance in routinized suburban lives whose serial isolation is reinforced by what the poet will later call the "dead voice" (Baraka, *S O S: Poems 1961-2013* 162) of politicians on television.

Extending their search for the "maniac" beyond the suburbs to cities, the speaker implores readers to recognize that it is not only maniacs but also their victims who are "hidden everywhere" (Baraka, *S O S: Poems 1961-2013* 161) in the cities. As a frighteningly capacious signifier for violent disorder, the maniac is not simply a potential reference to a serial killer but also to racialized crime panics threatening to breach a segregated spatial order. The poem links commuters' fears of "dozens/and double dozens" (Baraka, *S O S: Poems 1961-2013* 161) of maniacs to an implied racial "minority" arriving "by the carload" (Baraka, *S O S: Poems 1961-2013* 161) perhaps from a decaying central city.

The speaker quickly notes that they and other city residents are also terrorized victims of violence typically represented as unexceptional when it is legible as violence a, but it is a form of violence at all:

> There are maniacs hidden everywhere cant you see? By the dozens
> and double dozens, maniacs by the carload (tho they are
> a minority). But they terrorize us uniformly, all over the place
> we look at the walls of our houses, the garbage cans parked full
> strewn around our defaulting cities, and we cd get scared.
>
> (Baraka, *S O S: Poems 1961-2013* 161–2)

The speaker's observation that "We cd get scared" (Baraka, *S O S: Poems 1961-2013* 161) draws attention to city residents perhaps resigned to the dilapidated condition of urban infrastructure which can "terrorize us uniformly, all over the place" (Baraka, *S O S: Poems 1961-2013* 161) and disenchanted by prospects of political transformation. At the same time, the passage addresses other city residents facing the challenge of determining who might be responsible for conditions that are clearly the work of more than one individual with murderous intentions.

The image of "garbage cans parked full/strewn around our defaulting cities" (Baraka, *S O S: Poems 1961-2013* 161) potentially refers to the 1968 sanitation workers strike in New York City or to the Memphis sanitation workers strike that drew the support of Martin Luther King Jr. shortly before his assassination. Such images conjure up some of the most famous municipal labor actions in an era of urban crisis, with the Memphis strike beginning two days after the conclusion of the New York City strike.

Such actions occurred in a period marked by a series of high-profile municipal defaults, where cuts to city services and layoffs signaled the advent of what geographer David Harvey has called a process of "neoliberalization" (Harvey 6) that for the theorist can be traced back to the near-bankruptcy of New York in 1973:[22]

> During the 1960s New York City had been losing jobs and companies had been moving out to the suburbs or out to the American South (not yet going to Mexico, Taiwan, or China, but they were moving out). As a result, industrial

[22] Economic historian Robert Brenner has called this period, beginning in the early 1970s, a "long downturn" (Brenner 2) defined by an "extraordinarily extended phase of reduced economic dynamism and declining economic performance, persisting through the end of the old millennium and into the new" (Brenner xix).

> employment was declining in New York City. Of course, this was going on in many American cities at the time. The result was that the centre of cities was occupied by disaffected, unemployed, marginalized and very often racially marked populations. These rose up in a variety of crises in the 1960s and it became known as the Urban Crisis of the 1960s.
>
> (Harvey 6)

Countering the drive to expand municipal public services and employment, particularly the "expansion of education, expansion of healthcare, expansion of garbage collection, and expansion of transit workers" (Harvey 6), Nixon ended federal aid to cities in 1973. The policy shift hastened the disintegration of a traditional system of federally backed commercial lending to cities that was created during the Great Depression to "provide short-term notes for budgetary shortfalls and buy small issues of long-term bonds as well" (Hackworth 30).[23] Financial institutions pushed NY into bankruptcy in order to impose strict conditions on municipal spending, breaking the back of unions and implementing "wage freezes and cutbacks in public employment and social provision (education, public health, transport services), and to impose user fees" (Harvey) on public institutions like universities—leading to the dramatic deterioration of physical infrastructure. The "urban crisis" of the 1960s–70s saw this general pattern of disinvestment in public goods and services remake the economic geography of northeastern and midwestern inner cities through urban redevelopment schemes and capital flight to racially segregated suburbs and "Sun Belt" cities before leaving the country altogether.[24]

By identifying a potentially vast conspiracy of "maniacs" responsible for decaying housing stock, crime, unemployment, and mounting personal and municipal debt, the speaker of "Das Kapital" is led to question whether the maniac is human at all. Here the poem reimagines the features of urban crisis as

[23] As Jason Hackworth has argued, "Banks were immediately less willing to cover budgetary shortfalls alone. Short- and long-term municipal finance through commercial banks became almost nonexistent. Rising interest rates compounded this obstacle to credit for cities, as bank money became more expensive" (Hackworth 30).

[24] As Jason Hackworh notes, "After World War II, capital made an even wider leap to the conurbations of the American South and West where land was cheap, labor tame and regulations lax. Midwestern and northeastern inner cities, once a symbol of might for the industrial mode of production, were forced to cede an increasing amount of power to both the suburbs within their own metropolitan areas and the 'sun belt' cities as well. The elite residential communities of the central city were the first to leave, followed by department stores in the 1950s and offices in the 1960s and 1970s. Many central cities went on a binge of slum clearance during the 1960s in order to spark a reversal of the dispersion of investment, but most were unsuccessful at returning meaningful investment" (Hackworth 152).

clues in an unfolding detective story marked by gothic elements and mounting ambient dread. Within the urban spaces of this mystery, a city in budgetary distress takes on the anthropomorphic characteristics of a dying murder victim, trapping residents within its collapsing structures. In what could be read as a compact political allegory of racial incorporation into existing institutional structures of municipal power, a rat "eases past" (Baraka, *S O S: Poems 1961-2013* 161) the speaker and crosses a boundary separating poverty from corrupt abundance. Parallel constructions featuring repeated rhyming words implicitly liken a murder victim's final "stumble" to how "old houses/crumble" and how the "unemployed stumble by us" (Baraka, *S O S: Poems 1961-2013* 161).

In the first half of the poem, the speaker quickly comes to suspect that the "maniac" may not be a person at all, but a kind of supernatural force possessing individuals and haunting the ruins of an era's "defaulting cities" (Baraka, *S O S: Poems 1961-2013* 161) hollowed out by capital and white flight. The poem translates the circumstances of a street shooting, for example, into a language of occult power. Detached from a specifiable human agent, "Blasts of fire" (Baraka, *S O S: Poems 1961-2013* 161) precede "some woman's son" (Baraka, *S O S: Poems 1961-2013* 161) dying "with a pool of blood around his head" (Baraka, *S O S: Poems 1961-2013* 161). The line's syntax echoes the agentless rhetorical framing of "officer-involved" police shootings but couched in an ominously prophetic future tense. The seemingly fated or preordained character of this killing that "will" happen, and the subsequent remark that the shooter and the victim "won't be the maniac" (Baraka, *S O S: Poems 1961-2013* 161), foreshadows the speaker's eventual identification of the "maniac" as a generic personification of social forces. One might read the acknowledgment that this "won't be the maniac" (Baraka, *S O S: Poems 1961-2013* 161) as a commentary on how such forces seem to continually reproduce the conditions of possibility for such murders only to vanish into a set of naturalized background conditions.

The stanza concludes with a sinister parade of figures who promise relief or distraction from urban crisis conditions but turn out to be potential suspects—from politicians whose hollow rhetoric "can not be stood, or understood" (Baraka, *S O S: Poems 1961-2013* 162) to religious saviors with melting faces and even a famous television character actor. "The baldhead man on the television set goes on in a wooden way/his unappetizing ignorance can not be stood, or understood," Baraka writes, "The people turn the channel/looking for Good Times and get a negro with a pulldown hat" (Baraka, *S O S: Poems 1961-2013* 161–2). The brief reference to actor Jimmie Walker's portrayal of the character J.J. on the 1970s CBS sitcom *Good Times* could be read as a brief commentary on a history of minstrel caricatures as a distinct but related process of racial personification.[25] As city inhabitants search for relief, they're instead presented with an early 1970s television show. The possibility of good times is replaced by *Good Times*. Evincing a deep skepticism about the politically atomizing effects of postwar mass media and echoing the poem's earlier description of commuters "watching the teevee later on the Ford/replay" (Baraka, *S O S: Poems 1961-2013* 161), the grim punning here also offers an implicit warning about the limits of an antiracist politics centrally organized around media and electoral representation.[26] Like the television character actor, the political figurehead who "can not be stood, or understood" (Baraka, *S O S: Poems 1961-2013* 162) are part of the same machinery of representation that can neither explain nor transform the landscape of urban crisis.

The speaker comes to understand the maniac as less as an aberrant individual than a relational structure connecting a growing sense of existential emptiness, or a "jumble of frustrations and unfilled capacities" (Baraka, *S O S: Poems 1961-2013* 162), with "dead girls, the rats noise, the flashing/somber lights" (Baraka, *S O S: Poems 1961-2013* 162), and suspicious preachers. The "death scene" (Baraka, *S O S: Poems 1961-2013* 162) expands to include thwarted dreams, daily work routines, and obligatory social roles that are not limited to sinister public figures but also condition the speaker's sense of themselves as a coherent self-determining social agent. Puzzling over a range of seemingly disconnected events, the speaker quickly reaches the explanatory limits of treating the conditions described in the rest of the poem as simply the aggregate results of individual action. Experiencing themselves as both a victim and an accomplice of whatever social forces the maniac might embody, the speaker shifts the investigation "from the image of the person," as Michael Clune points out in a recent reading of the poem, "to the analysis of the system" (Clune 43).[27]

[25] As Robin Means Coleman contends, while *Good Times* was a groundbreaking attempt to directly address the lives of working class Black Americans, the character of J.J. constituted a kind of "representational failure" (Coleman 98) and reversion to a "Jim Crow character" (Coleman 98). In my reading, the poem's critique of personification works to counter the capacity of such stereotypes to configure race as a *cause* of urban crisis.

[26] For an autobiographical account of Amiri Baraka's developing Marxist critique of the "verticality" of elite representation as an expression of deepening intragroup class divisions within the Black nation, see Baraka, *The Autobiography of Leroi Jones* xi–xxviii, 427–45.

[27] In *American Literature and the Free Market*, Michael Clune has offered an extended reading of Baraka's "Das Kapital" that ultimately reads the maniac not only as an example of fetishistic personification, but also as an example of how "The market system becomes an intentionality not locatable anywhere" (Clune 43). My reading diverges from Clune's insistence that "If the poem equates 'Das Kapital' with the maniac, it distinguishes the maniac from America's hegemonic social structures" (Clune 43), where "The maniac appears 'everywhere' against this social fabric not as its condensation, representative, symbol, but as its negation, its absolute other, its nemesis" (Clune 43).

The poem eventually turns toward the work alluded to in the title, invoking and reworking Karl Marx's critique of commodity fetishism and labor exploitation presented in the German philosopher's magnum opus, *Das Kapital*. For Marx, the specifically capitalist organization of commodity production and exchange produces the appearance of social activity directed by commodities that seemingly possess agency and value independent of that activity. Marx describes this appearance in terms of the "Personification of things and reification of persons" (Marx 209), or what the philosopher calls "commodity fetishism" (Marx 163). For Marx, the concept of "fetishism" functions as a broader category of analysis that describes how core features of developed capitalist economies are represented as natural, self-evident, and unchangeable.[28] Marx's complex critique of fetishism redirects Enlightenment philosophers' judgments of the ostensibly primitive religious beliefs of non-European groups back onto the societies of the critics themselves, where the "non-allegorical personification of material powers" (Pietz 138) such critics associate with religious fetishism appear in the form of historically unchanging capitalist imperatives seemingly impervious to human intervention.

Realizing that monstrous social conditions can't be reduced to the actions of aberrant individuals, the speaker of Baraka's poem presents capitalism as a social system that exhibits monstrous characteristics of a different order. Baraka's choice to depict urban crisis within the generic parameters of a supernatural mystery story here draws explicitly on the language of Marx's monumental "study of the monstrous forms of everyday-life in a capitalist world-system" (McNally 2) in the words of David McNally:

> As Marx searched for a means of depicting the actual horrors of capitalism—from child-labour, to the extermination of North America's indigenous peoples, from the factory-system to the slave-trade—he reworked the discourse of monstrosity that emerged with the rise of capitalism. Pillaging popular and literary imagination, from vampire-tales to Goethe's *Faust*, he cast capitalism as both a modern horror-story and a mystery tale, each inexplicable outside the language of monstrosity.
>
> (McNally 13)

In my reading, the figure of the maniac illuminates the unitary character of the nation's oppressive social structure by representing the capacity of abstract value to synthesize a specifically capitalist totality from "traces of dead used up/labor" (Baraka, *S O S: Poems 1961-2013* 162).

[28] For an extended discussion of Marx's critique of fetishism see Pietz.

Baraka's poem arrives at a peculiar conception of capitalism's monstrosity that ultimately emphasizes its relative invisibility and "the ways in which monstrosity becomes normalised and naturalised via its colonisation of the essential fabric of everyday-life" (McNally 2). "What is most striking about capitalist monstrosity, in other words, is its elusive everydayness," McNally continues, "its apparently seamless integration into the banal and mundane rhythms of quotidian existence" (McNally 2).

It is precisely the ordinary operations of this system in Baraka's poem that recursively translates human activity into the "skeletons of dollarbills" (Baraka, *S O S: Poems 1961-2013* 162)—an image that vividly represents money in anthropomorphic terms as the reanimated corpse of prior human activity and explicitly refers to Marxist accounts of the impersonal alchemy of capitalist production. In Marx's theoretical vocabulary, this consumption of living labor in the capitalist production process generates both abstract value and the "means of production" (Marx 985)—the "dead" machinery and materials made by past workers required to produce ever more commodities. For Marx, how the historical results of past human activity dominate the living is a particularly monstrous feature of the capitalist organization of social life, where "Capital is dead labour which, vampire-like, lives only by sucking living labour, and lives the more, the more labour it sucks" (Marx 342).

Both workers and the owners of capital inhabit purely functional roles in this process of production and exchange in which "Commodities, in short, appear as the purchasers of persons" (Marx 1003):

> This situation is the essential prelude and precondition of the actual process of production in which the commodity owner becomes a capitalist, capital personified, and the worker becomes the mere personification of labour for capital. The objective conditions essential to the realization of labour are alienated from the worker and become manifest as fetishes endowed with a will and a soul of their own. Commodities, in short, appear as the purchasers of persons. The buyer of labour-power is nothing but the personification of objectified labour which cedes a part of itself to the worker in the form of the means of subsistence in order to annex the living labour-power for the benefit of the remaining portion, so as to keep itself intact and even to grow beyond its original size by virtue of this annexation. It is not the worker who buys the means of production and subsistence, but the means of production that buy the worker to incorporate him into the means of production.
>
> (Marx 1003)

In this passage, what Marx characterizes as personification is not simply a cognitive error that can simply be dispelled through acts of ideological demystification. The appearance of things purchasing persons registers how the results of past labor captured by this system subordinate the activity of both capitalists and workers to a set of capitalist imperatives removed from the sphere of significant human influence.

Of course, Marx's theorization of the purpose of such processes is not primarily organized around commodity objects, narrowly speaking, but the "annexation" and accumulation of abstract value. In Baraka's poem, the image of "skeletons of dollarbills" (Baraka, *S O S: Poems 1961-2013* 162) invokes a more capacious "death scene" (Baraka, *S O S: Poems 1961-2013* 162) where capitalist abstraction not only feeds off of living labor but produces a medium of exchange that exists in the hollow spaces between the poem's vignettes. "Flashes of maniac shadows" (Baraka, *S O S: Poems 1961-2013* 162) in the empty spaces between anomalous incidents reveal that emptiness to be a form of abstraction that connects dispersed persons and events. Connecting seemingly discrete acts and modalities of violence, "Traces of dead used up/labor," like a trail of blood, "lead away from the death scene until we remember a quiet fit that everywhere/is the death scene" (Baraka, *S O S: Poems 1961-2013* 162). The dramatic reconstruction of this more capacious "death scene" (Baraka, *S O S: Poems 1961-2013* 162) offers a poetic vision of how the fractured and segregated landscape of urban crisis might fit together within a discontinuous but materially interconnected social whole.

But like the "maniac shadows" that seem to hover at the edges of the speaker's vision, the relational character of capitalist value similarly thwarts attempts at the direct representation of any isolable figure. As a measure and medium of social cohesion, such value relations are within the poem so naturalized and ubiquitous as to be virtually invisible. The poem's final stanzas offer a portrait of capitalism not as the primary cause of the violent scenes described in the rest of the poem but as a *medium of relation* that materially connects selves and others, interpersonal violence to infrastructural degradation, and wasted human development to a pervasive and naturalized system of economic compulsion.

Existing in the spaces "hidden everywhere" (Baraka, *S O S: Poems 1961-2013* 161) between things, the world value aggregates and quantifies both separates and connects the poem's characters while appearing as unremarkable as air—"a draft" (Baraka, *S O S: Poems 1961-2013* 161) in a commuter train compartment, a city street where "air is cold/winter heaps above us consolidating itself in degrees" (Baraka, *S O S: Poems 1961-2013* 161), or "leaves blown down the street to see the writing on them, the dates, the amounts we owe" (Baraka, *S O S: Poems 1961-2013* 162). Value relations quantify and measure human activity in ways that the poet likens to the elemental force of the non-human natural world. Winter is translated into the quantitative language of "degrees" (Baraka, *S O S: Poems 1961-2013* 161) and blowing leaves hint at the profound and profoundly underappreciated role that consumer and municipal debt has played, from racially exclusionary mortgage-backed securities to municipal defaults, in shaping the uneven postwar spatial geography described in the poem.[29]

It is not surprising then that the speaker likens their place within this system of value formation, "working for the yanquii dollarrrr" (Baraka, *S O S: Poems 1961-2013* 162), to the childhood memory of a "Radio City" song that "sighs through us like the wind" (Baraka, *S O S: Poems 1961-2013* 162). The speaker then recalls a childhood memory of mistaking this wind "scratching at the windows" (Baraka, *S O S: Poems 1961-2013* 162) for the maniac. Both the song and the image of the maniac promise some modicum of human control over systemic imperatives that seem to operate automatically in the interstices of social life, fragmenting and recombining subjects in ways that embed them deeper in what the poem suggests is a malevolent collective social body. A song that once seemed to command a "you" to labor for the possibility of individual success becomes a shared competitive burden—"we got to hit it" (Baraka, *S O S: Poems 1961-2013* 162). Visions of industry give way to repetitive work routines that conscript the speaker into the US imperial project of extending the global reach of the "yanquii dollarrrr" (Baraka, *S O S: Poems 1961-2013* 162).

Recalling the conclusion of Baraka's 1961 poem to his daughter Kellie Jones, "Preface to a Twenty Volume Suicide Note" (Baraka, *S O S: Poems 1961-2013* 3), "Das Kapital" similarly associates personification with childhood projections of fears and wishes. Unlike the former poem, however, dispelling childhood illusions does not expose a harmless natural phenomenon in "Das Kapital" but the lethal and thoroughly naturalized force of capitalist abstraction seemingly

[29] Because much of the existing social science literature on urban crisis has been framed primarily in terms of deindustrialization, neoliberalization, and white flight, Destin Jenkins has recently argued that it is easy to miss a deeper story about how "postwar inequality has been very much rooted in the political economy and sociality of municipal debt" (Jenkins 5), and in particular the "power asymmetries between elected and appointed experts, on the one hand, and the buyers, peddlers, raters, and holders of debt, on the other" (Jenkins 6). Baraka's poem offers an opportunity to consider how the quasi-objective character of debt and of how the "amounts we owe" (Baraka, *S O S: Poems 1961-2013* 162) conceal a deeper contradiction between democratic governance and the constraints of a low growth economy after the end of the postwar boom.

"everywhere at the same time" (Baraka, *The Autobiography of Leroi Jones* 163). "Who is the maniac," the speaker finally asks, "and why everywhere at the same time…" (Baraka, *S O S: Poems 1961-2013* 163)

Throughout the poem, the implied question of "Who is the maniac" (Baraka, *The Autobiography of Leroi Jones* 163) poses the problem of accepting a limited conception of what counts as social violence and its exceptional and episodic character. By the end of the poem, however, the line raises the question of how to represent capitalism as a system capable of conscripting living subjects to work on behalf of its perpetuation as a condition of their own survival. The image of the system cannot simply be analytically detached from the activity of subjects who are in a sense transformed into "maniacs" driven by uncontrollable structural imperatives. The introduction of explicitly Marxist categories of analysis here does not, in my reading, simply unmask the maniac as an epiphenomenal expression of underlying class relations better represented through the personae of capitalist and worker. Instead, the poem turns away from the image of the subject to value as a *medium of association* that materially connects selves and others, interpersonal violence to infrastructural degradation, and wasted human development to a pervasive and naturalized system of economic compulsion.

In the poem, it is a system that repeatedly produces the misleading appearance and material reality of social separation—a world in fragments where inequality and interpersonal violence can be explained entirely through reference to individual culpability. For the speaker, the wind is not simply the wind, but capital in motion meticulously recording "the dates, the amounts we owe" (Baraka, *S O S: Poems 1961-2013* 162) and driving the "straining, ashy fingered, harassed" (Baraka, *S O S: Poems 1961-2013* 161) unemployed out onto winter streets. The "substance of capital itself" (Pietz 148), abstract value, stalks the empty spaces of this monstrous world.

Harryette Mullen at the *S*PeRM**K*T*

Almost a quarter-century after the publication of "Das Kapital," two collections of poems by poet and critic Harryette Mullen, the 1991 *Trimmings* and 1992 *S*PeRM**K*T*, adopt a decidedly more comic approach to playfully exaggerate and distort the fetishistic language of mass advertising. Featuring a title made by deleting letters from the word "supermarket," *S*PeRM**K*T* in particular reimagines US racial history through a parodically warped compendium of "commercialized, debased" (Mullen, *The Cracks Between What We Are and*

What We Are Supposed to Be: Essays and Interviews 243) cliches. It is a language that the poet systematically attempts to disorder, reorder, and "recycle" (Mullen, *The Cracks Between What We Are and What We Are Supposed to Be: Essays and Interviews* 243). Like Cha's "photo-essay," *S*PeRM**K*T* discerns in commodity displays and advertising language a "grammar" of combinatory social relations and a normative model of national belonging.

Reading the first and last stanzas of *S*PeRM**K*T* side by side, for example, illuminates how racial distinctions are themselves represented and "recycled" both within advertising tableaux and the spatial arrangement of supermarkets:

> Lines assemble gutter and margin. Outside and in, they
> straightten a place. Organize a stand. Shelve space. Square
> footage. Align your list or listlessness. Pushing oddly eve-
> ning aisle catches the tale of an eye. Displays the cherished
> share. Individually wrapped singles, frozen divorced com-
> partments, six-pack widows all express themselves while
> women wait in family ways, all bulging baskets, squirming
> young. More on line incites the eyes. Bold names label fa-
> miliar type faces. Her hand scanning throwaway lines.
>
> (Mullen, *Recyclopedia: Trimmings, S*PeRM**K*T, and Muse & Drudge* 65)

> Flies in buttermilk. What a fellowship. That's why white
> milk makes yellow butter. Homo means the same. A woman
> is different. Cream always rises over split milk. Muscle men
> drink it all in. Awesome teeth and wholesale bones. Our
> cows are well adjusted. The lost family album keeps saying
> cheese. Speed readers skim the white space of this galaxy.
>
> (Mullen, *Recyclopedia: Trimmings, S*PeRM**K*T, and Muse & Drudge* 96)

The first stanza frames the space of the supermarket as an "environment of language" (Mullen, *The Cracks Between What We Are and What We Are Supposed to Be: Essays and Interviews* 243), in Mullen's words, where subjects are "hailed through your race, your class, your gender" and sometimes "divided up into compartments" (Mullen, *The Cracks Between What We Are and What We Are Supposed to Be: Essays and Interviews* 243). Such hailing invites readers to apprehend the interlinked "compartments" that enable and constrain relations between subjects. The "Lines [that] assemble gutter and margin" might refer to the gutters and margins of a page, but also the shelving and stands that display products. Such displays even implicitly model forms of social marginalization.

Indeed, the segmented, modular, and repetitive social form of "Individually wrapped singles, frozen divorced compartments, six-pack widows" pun on product packaging to describe the making and breaking of social ties, kinship structures, and marriage contracts. The family is centrally implicated in this form of social ordering, in which women are "straightened" into "family ways" and shunted into lines where they carry "bulging baskets" of "squirming young," who are themselves likened to consumer items. Beneath the "bold names," glossy packaging, and inflated advertising rhetoric, the poem suggests, lie "familiar type faces" and "throwaway lines." Images of postwar consumer abundance reflect the proliferation of standardized, modular social forms beneath apparent variation, and the systematic production and naturalization of human disposability.

The poem's final stanza foregrounds sites of consumption as places where fears of racial contamination and racial mixing are navigated—evoking fears of miscegenation in references to the deadly "fellowship" of "Flies in the buttermilk" and the existence of secret images in a "lost family album." Racial impurity must be rigorously disavowed, the stanza suggests, to preserve the coherence of the consumer tableau made up of a constellation of white or off-white objects: cream, milk, teeth, bones, cows, cheese, and a galaxy. As Mullen notes, such language is often drawn from memories of advertisements from her youth, in which Blackness, and Black womanhood, in particular, seemed to exist only as a flaw in an otherwise smooth white representational surface.

The reference in the final line to the "white space of this galaxy" redirects attention to how the collection comprises isolated stanzas surrounded by ample white space. The image helps us "read" race as an alternately marked and unmarked social form even and especially where the presence of race is disavowed. As a relation of figure and ground that organizes our reading experience before we parse the "content" of any specific utterance, the stanza primes readers to recognize whiteness as a normative, unmarked racial position that does not appear as a racial position at all.

The form of a "galaxy," perhaps mimicking a constellation-like arrangement of products, suggests that racial distinctions exist as much in the manifest promises of advertising rhetoric as in the invisible relations between compartmentalized objects. The figure of a galaxy might also suggest a principle of exchangeability, producing both the "same" and "different" as a conceptual binary—whether as sexual and gender polarities, or whiteness and Blackness as a visual mapping of racially segregated social networks. It is easy to "skim" these formal features of the poem and, as the pun on milk suggests, miss how whiteness constitutes a naturalized background condition against which nonwhiteness appears.

While Brooks, Baraka, Cha, and Mullen each offer critical perspectives on the postwar production and consumption of commodities as a model of racial order, my next chapter focuses on a poet who offers an extended reflection on how the structure of the postwar Black family became an imagined source of Cold War racial disorder within the "democracy of goods."

2

In the Mirror of the Commodity Form: Race and "Object Authority" in Erica Hunt's *Piece Logic*

After an agreement to host national exhibits in Moscow and New York, then-vice president Richard Nixon and Soviet premier Nikita Khrushchev engaged in a much-publicized postwar debate over the geopolitical significance of US postwar consumer culture. The July 1959 "kitchen debate" compared living standards in the United States and the Soviet Union as evidence of the capacity of capitalism or communism to deliver material prosperity for the average citizen. A widely broadcast portion of the exchange took place in the kitchen of an American model suburban ranch home in the US Trade and Cultural Fair in Moscow's Sokol' niki Park. With designers Ray and Charles Eames as chief consultants, the exhibit, meant to showcase the superiority of the "American Way of Life," involved a range of US artists, scientists, and major corporations, from architect Buckminster Fuller, filmmaker Billy Wilder, and photographer Edward Steichen, to Disney, General Mills, and RCA/Whirlpool. Within an exhibition hall featuring products from several hundred American companies, and against a backdrop of kitchen appliances meant to represent average US citizens' consumption habits, the model kitchen provoked a heated exchange between the politicians.

However, both figures took for granted the heterosexual nuclear family as a fundamental economic unit of production and consumption. The US model kitchen showcased suburban homeownership and normative family structures as the basis for a vision of democratized mass consumption. Of course, this Cold War vision of political stability secured through material abundance presupposed racially segregated suburbs and a "family wage" accorded primarily to white men as the single source of family income. "In Nixon's vision," Elaine

Tyler May argues, "the suburban ideal of homeownership would tame two potentially disruptive forces: women and workers" (May 156):

> In appliance-laden houses across the country, working-class as well as business-class breadwinners could fulfill the new American work-to-consume ethic. Homeownership would lessen class consciousness among workers, who would set their sights toward the middle-class ideal. The family home would be the place where a man could display his success through the accumulation of consumer goods. Women would reap rewards for domesticity by surrounding themselves with commodities; they would remain content as housewives because appliances would ease their burdens. For both men and women, homeownership would reinforce aspirations for upward mobility and diminish the potential for social unrest.
>
> (May 156–7)

This 1950s-era image of the suburban family inoculated consumers against any morally corrosive effects of affluence while providing "a means for assimilation into the American way of life: classless, homogeneous, and family-centered" (May 164).

Yet the Cold War kitchen was also notable for what it left unrepresented—the history of hidden, repetitive, and racially segregated labor replaced by new labor-saving devices:

> The exhibition presented a kind of science fiction of technological advancement. In the presence of automated appliances, labor became a kind of clutter to be expunged from the scene. The paradox of presence and absence is central to the Cold War kitchen: like the new technological innovations, women also are present there. But their work can be hidden behind labor-saving devices and, to a large extent, women and minorities were the "machines" removed from sight in the Moscow kitchen.
>
> (Baldwin 10)

Here one might read the array of mechanical appliances as making visible otherwise hidden and historically gendered forms of domestic and service labor—a hidden infrastructure of care work responsible for the intergenerational reproduction of wage laborers, children, and the elderly. The automated suburban home constructed in Sokol' niki Park not only represented the nuclear family as a basic unit of consumption within the United States but also what Neda Atanasoski and Kalindi Vora have recently called the "surrogate human effect" revealed by automatable forms of labor. Seemingly innocuous labor-saving appliances featured in these displays of the typical US kitchen materialize the "Unfree and invisible labor [that] have been the hidden source of support propping up the apparent autonomy of the liberal subject through its history, including indentured and enslaved labor as well as gendered domestic and service labor" (Atanasoski and Vora).

"Object Authority" and the Problem of Reference

Throughout her career, the poet and critic Erica Hunt has both modeled and theorized contemporary Black experimental poetry as a challenge to both "colorblind" experimental formalisms and dominant modes of racial representation. The poet has written two books and two chapbooks—*Local History* (1993), *Arcade* (1996) with visual artist Alison Saar, *Piece Logic* (2002), and *Time Slips Before Your Eyes* (2006). With Dawn Lundy Martin, Hunt co-edited a 2018 volume of experimental Black women's writing, *Letters to the Future: Black Women/Radical Writing*. Drawing inspiration from a range of cultural traditions, from bop improvisation to Oulipian procedural writing, Hunt's poetry remains a vital and relatively understudied example of a tradition of contemporary Black experimental poetry that, in the words of poet and critic Evie Shockley, has been historically "dismissed, marginalized, and misread: first, in relation to the African American poetic tradition, because its experiments were not 'recognizably black'; and second, in relations to constructions of the avant-garde tradition, because they were" (Shockley 1).[1]

In this chapter, I read Hunt's 2002 collection *Piece Logic* as a restaging of a critique of what Karl Marx famously calls "the fetishism of the commodity" (Marx, *Capital: A Critique of Political Economy. Vol.1* 163). The collection treats the enigma of the commodity form as a signifier whose semantic referent is unclear and whose origins, as Marx famously remarks, are shrouded in "metaphysical subtleties and theological niceties" (Marx, *Capital: A Critique of Political Economy. Vol.1* 163). Across these poems, commodities simultaneously "refer" to objects' physical characteristics, to other commodities through acts of exchange, and to a measure of abstract value governing the proportional

1 In a recent essay on Hunt's publication history, Kathy Lou Schulz has situated the poet's work in a broader "legacy gone missing… A legacy of avant-garde practice by African-American women poets including Julia Fields and Elouise Loftin. A legacy of work that has escaped the notice of most scholars, that has been allowed to go out of print, or was poorly published in the first place" (Schultz).

exchangeability of goods and services. The collection attempts to trace the referent of the commodity form not only to the "hidden abode of production" (Marx, *Capital: A Critique of Political Economy. Vol.1* 279) that for Marx determines the abstract value of commodities through the exploitation of wage labor, but also to a historically gendered, racially typed, and unwaged space of capitalist social reproduction within households.[2]

Like the poems examined in the previous chapter, *Piece Logic* reimagines the United States as a "democracy of goods" (Marchand 217) where the distribution of commodities in social space mirrors shifting relations between citizen-consumers. The first poem in the collection envisions an unnamed nation not as a country populated by citizen-subjects but as an "imagined community" (Anderson, *Imagined Communities: Reflections on the Origin and Spread of Nationalism*) of objects.

Possessing what the poet calls "Object Authority" (Hunt, *Piece Logic* 10), this immense national collection of commodities functions as "proof" of the justness and rationality of social hierarchies, including changing racial and gendered divisions of labor in homes and workplaces. Remapping the structure of what Cedric Robinson and others have called "racial capitalism" (Robinson 2), the collection interrogates how such "Authority" attributes intrinsic comparative value to both objects and subjects. The proliferation of self-multiplying consumer goods, and the technological automation of both industrial production and domestic labor, offer evidence not of material abundance but the systematic production of "broken things" (Hunt, *Piece Logic* 10) and disposable and thoroughly market-mediated lives.

To call "Object Authority" into question, the poet draws upon the legacy of a postwar poetic avant-garde, Language Writing, committed to a critique of normative syntax and "transparent" linguistic reference as core stylistic features of an increasingly commodified mainstream poetics.[3] For some of the movement's prominent theorists in the late 1970s—including Charles Bernstein, Steve McCaffery, and Ron Silliman—the referential "transparency" of language

[2] Restaging Marx's critique of commodity fetishism in the Cold War kitchen, Hunt's representation of "Piece Logic" is not reducible to a simple cognitive error but represents a form of thought, in Marx's words, that is "socially valid, and therefore objective, for the relations of production belonging to this historically determined mode of social production" (Marx, *Capital: A Critique of Political Economy. Vol.1* 169).

[3] My use of the term "racial capitalism" refers to a field of inquiry that includes but is not limited to the work of Cedric Robinson in *Black Marxism*. For a genealogy of this term whose origins lay in South African Marxist debates, see Melamed; Hudson. For a recent critique of Robinson's theorization of racial capitalism, see Ralph and Singhal.

could be understood as a species of commodity fetishism. The programmatic disruption of normative syntax for these authors could thus potentially decommodify poetic language.[4]

The crisis of reference that undermines "Object Authority" at the same time reshapes the meaning of racial and gender roles historically associated with types of unwaged socially reproductive labor. These poems map how postwar images of a normative "Fordist family" (M. Cooper 8), I argue, come to be defined against a discourse of Black matriarchal "broken families" (Moynihan 21). This discourse of cultural pathology features centrally in the 1965 "Moynihan Report," a government study of the sources of Black poverty, prepared by sociologist and then Assistant Secretary of Labor Daniel Patrick Moynihan, and the 1968 Kerner Commission Report on the causes of a wave of mid-1960s Black urban riots.

With its focus on the history of invisible labor reflected by kitchen appliances and increasingly automated production processes, these poems evoke a history of Black women's positioning as a kind of animate material infrastructure for the production and reproduction of full national subjects. Organized around a broader political economy of Black disposability in an era of rapid mechanization and deindustrialization, the construction of national identity across these poems traces a racial history of property as a capitalist social form. "Object Authority" is in other words continuous with "the racial form of slavery as the (not so) repressed or spectral frame for the imaginary of what surrogate technologies do, or who or what they are meant to replace" (Atanasoski and Vora 10).

Commodity Fetishism and "Object Authority"

Although this specific formulation of a shared poetics provoked some disagreement among other writers associated with the movement, Hunt both revives and reconfigures an anti-capitalist critique of what Language poet and critic Steve McCaffery calls "the referential fallacy of language" (McCaffrey 61).[5] "What Marx exposed as the fetishism of commodity," McCaffery argues in a

4 For a critical account of the overextension of language as a metaphor for social relations in general, see Altieri. For a brief interrogation of the relationship between the critique of reference and racial fetishism, see Marriott.

5 "There is a group of writers today united in the feeling that literature has entered a crisis of the sign," Steve McCaffrey writes, "that the explications of literatures have merged with the implications of language and that the foremost task at hand—a more linguistic and philosophic than 'poetic' task—is to demystify the referential fallacy of language" (McCaffrey 61).

special 1977 issue of the Canadian literary journal *Open Letter*, "is the same mode of mystification that is enacted in the fetishism of the referent, both being instruments for the displacement of human relations into an iconography of commodity" (McCaffrey 60). The third poem in the collection, for example, entitled "Administering the Atomic Kingdom," likens its formal strategies to a Fordist assembly line where occasional acts of rebellion, work stoppages, and slowdowns lead to "unauthorized / breaks on the line between one / thing and another" (Hunt, *Piece Logic* 13). Such "breaks on the line" in the poem interrupt the syntagmatic relations between words. Here Hunt reorients the critique of reference away from the mimetic capacity of language in general and instead toward the occulted origins of "Object Authority." The collection ultimately locates the ground or referent of this "authority" not in the physical properties of things but in capitalist value formation as a principle of social cohesion, family formation, and national belonging.

Hunt reimagines the avant-garde critique of commodified language as a historically specific crisis of meaning where a glut of commodities signifies both postwar abundance and racial disposability. The poet reformulates the problem of linguistic reference as a search for the sources of "Object Authority," where the commodity form offers seemingly incontrovertible evidence or "proof" of both plenitude and the cultural deficiency of devalued populations. For the poet, such abundance instead exposes the perversity of a measure of value that mandates the mass production of economically expendable populations. Investing both subjects and objects alike with a kind of complementary generic particularity, such value is revealed as the substance of a disarticulated and disavowed collective sociality.[6]

In a collection where the few examples of explicit racial reference seem to "function ambivalently in a poem concerned, in part, with the veils of ideology" (Williams 152), as Tyrone Williams argues, the problem of determining the material referent of race is inseparable from the search for the origins of "Object Authority." Under such conditions, "identity" appears as an objectlike social form embedded within a recursive chiasmic circuit where the personification of things requires the reification or "thingification" of persons, and vice versa—a process Marx famously identifies as a characteristic feature of commodity fetishism.[7]

[6] For an extended discussion of Marxist accounts of reification and mystification as socially objective forms of thought, and of why "Marx describes the consciousness corresponding to commodity-fetishism and both as 'inverted' and as one adequate to reality" (Rehmann 43), see Rehmann.

[7] For a discussion of the origins of concept of reification in Georg Lukacs' earlier writings on aesthetics, see Westerman.

Hungarian philosopher Georg Lukacs identifies this "thingification," or reification, as a fundamental ordering principle of developed capitalist societies that progressively subordinate subjects, human activity, and cognitive faculties to the demands of generalized commodity production.[8] Like the commodities they consume and resemble, capitalist subjects are threatened with removal from circulation, warehousing, and obsolescence due to repetitive use or failure to conform to market specifications. While the production of expendable groups seems to cut across racial divisions in Hunt's collection, images of a "democracy of goods" powerfully naturalize a rhetoric of Black cultural pathology, positioning Blackness as a kind of limit case of economic disposability. The increasing mechanization of production processes and socially reproductive tasks registered across these poems broadly illuminate postwar processes of deindustrialization, I contend, along with the racialization of what Marx calls "surplus population[s]" (Marx, *Capital: A Critique of Political Economy. Vol.1* 782) expelled from stable wage labor.[9]

Nation and Enumeration

The opening poem in the collection describes an unnamed nation as a vast collection of consumer goods, many damaged beyond repair. The poet compares this "House of Broken Things" (Hunt, *Piece Logic* 1) to a kitchen, department store, warehouse, and supermarket stocked with "miles of appliances, / lining the intestinal maze of its imposing architecture" (Hunt, *Piece Logic* 11). Appearing only as ghostly adjuncts to objects invested with seemingly irrefutable political and epistemic authority, national citizens exist in the spaces between things, and then only as part-objects themselves—laboring hands disconnected from bodies

8 In a reading of *Arcade*, a 1996 collection of poems and woodcuts co-created by Erica Hunt and visual artist Alison Saar, Linda Kinnahan contends that Hunt's poems consider the "public realm as spectacle that, within a commodity culture, absorbs, recirculates, and co-opts oppositional models of identity" (Kinnahan 165). For Kinnahan, the " 'body,' reorganized as a compendium of mechanized parts, itself becomes an expendable commodity" (Kinnahan 171). Kinnahan's description of *Arcade* captures how *Piece Logic* attempts to locate "the dynamics of racial construction along lines other than a naturalized identity politics" (Kinnahan 175).

9 As Roderick Ferguson has pointed out, the capitalist production of surplus populations has routinely constituted "the impetus for anxieties about the sanctity of 'community,' 'family,' and 'nation' " (Ferguson 17) within US history—often provoking state intervention to stabilize such categories "in terms of race, gender, sexuality, and class" (Ferguson 17). Grace Hong has similarly maintained that the systematic production of surplus populations, categories of "race, gender, and sexuality still indexes the importance of surplus labor, it is also the marker of purely surplus populations, populations who are existentially surplus" (Hong 92).

or fragments of advertising slogans and technical manuals. The collection's seven interlinked poems explore how capitalist imperatives regulate the pace of domestic labor, redefine racial progress, and demarcate the material boundaries of national belonging. "The codes and mediations that sustain the status quo abbreviate the human in order to fit us into structures of production" (Hunt, "Notes for an Oppositional Poetics" 200), Hunt argues elsewhere in terms that could also describe the nation imagined in these poems. "There is a place for everyone," the poet continues, "even the subordinate, if they know their place" (Hunt, "Notes for an Oppositional Poetics" 200).

Becoming hypervisible at the moment of its partial technological replacement by labor-saving devices, gendered and racially typed reproductive labor reproduces the nation as a kind of automated heteropatriarchal family unit in this work. Reimagining the home as a site where "Broken Things" are produced, I argue, counters converging liberal and Black cultural nationalist condemnations of Black matriarchal family structures as the source of what Daniel Patrick Moynihan dubbed the "tangle of pathology" (Moynihan 29) of Black poverty and civic marginalization.[10]

The Moynihan Report's analysis of the sources of Black unemployment, poverty, and social marginalization offers a strikingly different assessment of the challenges facing Black Americans than does the "Triple Revolution" letter and its warnings about the impact of automation and "cybernation" on the civil rights revolution.[11] Moynihan instead identifies "at the center of the tangle of pathology" (Moynihan 30) of Black poverty, youth delinquency, and crime, a "weakness of the family structure" (Moynihan 30). Although noting that bigotry plays a significant role in the continued civic and economic marginalization of Black Americans, the report nevertheless labels as pathological Black female-

[10] As Scott Brown writes, "Moynihan's contention that the quest for African American full citizenship was, in part, contingent on thwarting a 'subculture' of Black matriarchy found kinship with Black nationalist rhetoric, which… equated the rebuilding of the nation with the restoration of 'manhood' " (Brown 33).

[11] Leaked to the public in advance of its release, the report drew almost immediate criticism from liberal pundits and influential civil rights figures, such as Congress of Racial Equality (CORE) member William Ryan. The report found strong support from Urban League president Whitney Young and from some Black nationalist figures, such as Daniel H. Watts, editor of the *Liberator*, along with measured backing from Martin Luther King Jr. In a 1965 article, "The New Genteel Racism," published in the journal of the NAACP, *The Crisis*, Ryan questions the empirical data used to establish the report's conclusions—conclusions that seem to invert the causal relations between family structure and poverty. Ryan would later coin the phrase "blaming the victim" for his book-length response to the report, *Blaming the Victim* (Ryan, *Blaming the Victim*). In Ryan's words, the report's findings demonstrate that "unemployment and poverty cause 'family breakdown' rather than vice-versa" (Ryan, "The New Genteel Racism" 623). For an extended discussion of the mixed reception of the report, and the divergent ways in which its findings were interpreted, see Geary.

headed households marked by the "often reversed roles of husband and wife" (Moynihan 30).[12]

As a touchstone for my reading of Hunt's preoccupation with the quantifiability of household labor, the Moynihan Report configures these families as an object of social scientific study, quantification, and state management. Both the Moynihan and Kerner Commission reports assert that Black matriarchs are a fundamental threat to what Tiffany Lethabo King describes as "the coherence of the family as a property-generating institution and cornerstone of the nation" (King 74), and therefore require management through "a diffuse network of welfare case managers, monthly reporting and documentation of sexual behavior, children, income and daily activity" (King 75).

The opening poem in the collection measures such deviance against the responsibilities and potential rewards of belonging to a nation "that is not one but several" (Hunt, *Piece Logic* 1):

> In a country that is not one but several.
>
> In a country where it is common to assume that a new
> name gives you a new origin, leading to a different set of
> partners and possibly more exalted purpose. In a country
> that lives by its headlines, where explanations are clocked
> to correct enormity. In a country where a foreigner is
> welcome as long as s/he is generic. Or naturally naturalized
> and numbered.
>
> (Hunt, *Piece Logic* 1)

Pitched at a level of generality that makes historical specification conjectural, these flat, declarative statements invoke the principles of the American Creed. At the same time, the reference to "several nations" echoes the language of the 1968 Report of the National Advisory Commission on Civil Disorders, or Kerner Report, written by a Presidential Commission convened to identify the causes of a wave of urban riots in 1967. "Our Nation is moving toward two societies," the report famously concludes, "one black, one white—separate and unequal" (Disorders 1). The following stanza adds another layer of meaning to this statement, illuminating the paradox of how national cohesion can be premised upon multiplicity, or being "several." The conventions governing

[12] Moynihan's conclusions have continued to elicit polarized critical commentary in the decades following its publication. The report has continued to figure heavily in continuing debates over whether structural racism or group cultural norms or what anthropologist Oscar Lewis in 1959 called a "culture of poverty" adequately explains the persistence of racial group inequality.

the adoption of surnames, the naturalization of foreigners looking to become citizens, and the mass audiences conjured up by print media revolve around the "generic" particularity of a citizen-subject. Like the nation itself, the latter figure is both "not one" and "several"—a differential identity produced at the imagined intersection between ideals of formal equality and material inequality.

It is a figure ordered by what political scientist Benedict Anderson calls a "logic of the series… [and] a new grammar of representation" (Anderson, *The Spectre of Comparisons: Nationalism, Southeast Asia, and the World* 34) developed to describe nations as "imagined communities" (Anderson, *Imagined Communities: Reflections on the Origin and Spread of Nationalism* 13). Playing upon a Whitmanic use of catalog form, the anaphoric parallelism in these opening lines elaborates a "grammar" of combinatory sociality. The "generic" character of national citizen-subjects and assimilated foreigners is not opposed to but instead constitutive of social differentiation.[13]

The pun of "naturally naturalized" pathways to citizenship emphasizes how the massified, enumerable social form of national citizenship is not "natural" at all but the molecular unit of "serial, aggregable, counterposed majorities and minorities, which, starting as formal entities, were positioned in due course to assume political reality" (Anderson, *The Spectre of Comparisons: Nationalism, Southeast Asia, and the World* 38) within newly formed nations. The reference to enumeration in the context of US immigration policy gestures toward a racial lottery and national origin quota system, where per country numerical limits have historically determined the number of immigrants and refugees granted citizenship in any given year. For example, the national origin formula, established in 1921, strengthened by the 1924 Johnson-Reed Act and repealed by the 1965 Immigration and Nationality Act, was a central component of racially restrictive immigration policies that also established racial bars to naturalization and birthright citizenship.[14]

The poet presents the "generic" character of national citizens as evidence of an expansive liberal democratic right of free association seemingly unburdened

[13] On Whitman's distinctive use of catalog form, see Buell.

[14] On immigration policy as a mechanism of racialization, see Lopez; M. Ngai; FitzGerald. As Ian Haney Lopez reminds us, such racial prerequisites for full citizenship were a powerful legal mechanism for altering the demographic composition of the United States over time. "In 1790, only a few months after ratification of the Constitution," Lopez points out, "Congress limited naturalization to 'any alien, being a free white person who shall have resided within the limits and under the jurisdiction of the United States for a term of two years' " (Lopez 42). "Though there would be many subsequent changes in the requirements for federal naturalization," Lopez continues, "racial identity endured as a bedrock requirement for the next 162 years. In every naturalization act from 1790 until 1952, Congress included the 'white person' prerequisite" (Lopez 43).

by entrenched status hierarchies or stigmatized racial and ethnic origins. As scholars of the politics of names and naming observe about early-twentieth-century immigration waves from Southern and Eastern Europe, surnames could indicate professions and places of origin.[15] Adopting different surnames could allow immigrants to construct "a new origin, leading to a different set of / partners and possibly more exalted purpose." The Anglicization of both surnames and primary names—whether a voluntary decision made by immigrants during naturalization or a decision made by immigration officials at Ellis Island or Galveston, Texas—could conjure alternate familial histories and a corresponding range of possible futures.

The passage suggests that emergent mass media help to project an image of this nation as a space of associational freedom. The "headlines, where explanations are clocked / to correct enormity" (Hunt, *Piece Logic* 1) draw attention to how the visual design of newspapers, for example, synchronizes the experiences of disparate, spatially dispersed subjects in national space. Stitching together otherwise seemingly disconnected events—marriages, deaths, political appointments, and commodity prices—such "headlines" help to not only report but construct repetitive generic events for a mass readership of parallel national subjects.[16]

In a later poem, the rhythms of the production, circulation, and consumption of commodities serve a similar function of synchronizing labor globally. "The clocks / are locked to tick only the time / that objects keep," the poet writes, "whisked to the world / shelves, they can't keep stocked, the / goods sell so fast, manufactured by / invisible hands" (Hunt, *Piece Logic* 13). Suggesting "just-in-time" models of production developed in Japan in the 1970s, these lines gesture toward a revolutionary business innovation that minimized the time between production and sale to save on the cost of holding products or parts in storage facilities.

After listing basic principles of national belonging, the opening poem shifts its attention from citizen-subjects to the commodities circulating through national space. Blurring the boundaries between the abstract formal equality of citizens and the economic exchangeability of things, the "exalted purpose" of a

[15] See Clark-Oates et al.

[16] For Benedict Anderson, the formal strategies of the eighteenth-century novel also offer an example of how simultaneous, non-intersecting lives can be transformed into a kind of collective subject through the operations of a deceptively simple linguistic operator—"meanwhile." Both headlines and the novelistic space opened up by the "meanwhile" are a way of aggregating national subjects through the synchronization of events in national space.

national mission mentioned in the poem's opening lines is renarrated in terms of an "imagined community" of consumer goods:

> It is customary to give every object its count: To number
> the citizen and her possessions. Each object passing
> through enumeration is certified, and citizens are
> surrounded by certified belongings, a horde of things
> indemnifying identity.
>
> (Hunt, *Piece Logic* 2)

Describing the fusion of citizen and "her possessions" through "enumeration," testing, and certification echoes the language that government agencies, corporate inspectors, and consumer groups use to describe quality control procedures for evaluating the safety and standardization of consumer goods. That such testing typically involves verifying the industrial origins of products recalls the poem's earlier interest in the genealogical implications of names and naming. The poem likens citizens with revisable genealogies to consumer goods whose perceived quality and authenticity depend on traceable and potentially falsified origins.

To write that such products serve the function of "indemnifying identity" establishes identity and market citizenship as an object of calculation and species of property. As insurance against risk or payment for loss, indemnification presupposes a contractual obligation binding legal parties. In the poem, this legal relation materially compensates for the incompleteness, vulnerability, and finitude of "identity." The image of objects indemnifying identity invokes Lockean concepts of personhood as self-ownership, where "every man has a property in his own person" (Locke 19). Market identities become crucially dependent upon a "horde of things" to materially reproduce the former's sense of freedom and security—a surrogate relation that anticipates the poem's later investigation of the invisible domestic labor. Hunt's depiction of this object world and its regulative laws, I argue, ultimately remaps the material referent of race beneath the facially race-neutral language of the post–civil rights era.

The Time That Objects Keep

The poem presents family and nation as analogous social forms. Both are modeled on a "multiplying inventory" (Hunt, *Piece Logic* 10) of products that "Promises by the row what no / money can buy, belonging" (Hunt, *Piece Logic* 10).

The following poem in Hunt's collection, "Object Authority," represents such belonging in terms of a warehouse of kitchen appliances and other consumer products, including "Bread dough machines, rice cookers, vegetable / sculpting tools" (Hunt, *Piece Logic* 10). The poem's title might refer to someone with specialized knowledge or to a peculiar process of causal inversion where personified objects appear to possess independent agency and volition.

Reimagining the national motto, "E pluribus unum," the poem describes a nation of objects with "Millions of parts connecting characters and miles of appliances, / lining the intestinal maze" (Hunt, *Piece Logic* 11). Objects are the citizens of what appears to be a hollowed-out and mechanized interior of a human body. The poem likens this aggregation of items to a set of syntactical rules capable of "connecting characters" into words and words into even larger units of meaning. A closer investigation of this national warehouse reveals shelves of standardized, interchangeable parts. The seemingly self-assembling parts in this "intestinal maze"—with its "permutation of buttons and speeds, / convenience and silence" (Hunt, *Piece Logic* 11)—offer a vision of the comprehensive automation of manufacturing supplanting human labor.

The uncontrollable production of a glut of objects misleadingly appears as a rationalized "national standard of measurement" (Hunt, *Piece Logic* 10) applied to goods, labor time, value, language, and identity. Standardization constructs a "language" of objects to speed not only production but product repair and replacement. "Created to shelve / the volumes, miles of appearance and possibilities" (Hunt, *Piece Logic* 10), these self-assembling consumer products recall a history of twentieth-century movements advocating for the adoption of standardized subcomponents and interfaces across consumer products. "Advocating cooperation and interchange among industries," as historian Charles McGovern writes, "proponents of standardization sought higher productivity and efficiency through the adoption of common terms, units, and techniques" (McGovern 164). Such national standards create national cohesion at the level of the built-environment, aid in scientific research, and determine the most efficient methods of performing manufacturing and household labor.

Hunt's repeated reference to product testing, quality control, and the problem of "How the inventory gets out of/line" (Hunt, *Piece Logic* 13) gestures toward a history of "material nationalism" (McGovern 104) confronted with a range of technical problems posed by *nonstandard* consumer goods and production processes. Such issues led to the 1901 creation of the National Bureau of Standards, an agency in the United States Department of Commerce created to oversee the regularization of weights and measures. Over time the bureau's purview was expanded to include establishing quality assurance guidelines for commercial products, researching military weapons, and even creating consumer protection initiatives. "The bureau had been established in 1901 as the government authority over weights, measures, and physical constants," McGovern notes, "but it had gradually expanded its activities to assist American industries in solving production problems, especially regarding testing materials and ingredients… Additionally, the bureau made modest efforts to involve retail consumers in the movement in a series of guides to standardization within the home. These pamphlets illustrated uniform measurement and scientific efficiency for technically untrained consumers" (McGovern 164). *Measurements for the Household* (1915) comprehensively surveyed the role of standardized units of measure throughout the home, from gas and electric meters to kitchen tools (McGovern 164–5). The movement to standardize national weights, measures, and materials in commercial industries informed later business attempts to apply the principles of scientific management to fluctuating consumer demand.[17]

In the final stanza of the poem, commodities are "proof" of a range of knowledge claims that go far beyond merely verifying "consumer and existential confidence" (Hunt, *Piece Logic* 7):

> The house of broken things certifies status, a reference
> collection to be cited in courtrooms, schools, torture halls,
> parliamentary situations. Lighting up the corners of the English
> speaking world.
>
> (Hunt, *Piece Logic* 11)

The civic status conferred by things, in this concluding stanza, becomes a kind of evidence that can render legal judgments, shape the transmission of knowledge, select the victims of torture, and determine the distribution of political power. The nature of this "reference collection" of the differential value of objects corresponds to civic status hierarchies among subjects. The poem's concluding lines suggest that this classification of things has remade the English language as well, transforming it into a global currency of "Object Authority" and transnational vector of US national influence. Instead of verifying the status of persons or things, however, "Object Authority" ultimately proves that "we live in a broken world" (Hunt, *Piece Logic* 16) and so urgently need to imagine, in

[17] For a history of US consumer activist movements see Glickman.

the words of James Boggs, a "new standard of value" (Boggs, *Pages From A Black Radical's Notebook: A James Boggs Reader* 110).[18]

Value and the Kingdom

Hovering over this landscape of quantified subjects and objects, however, a kind of spirit of history emerges that the poem describes in overtly metaphysical or religious terms. This elemental shaping force creates, inhabits, and survives a succession of perishable objects:

> The objects arrive shrink wrapped, adamant, brilliant,
> resembling an illuminated text, ready to be admired.
> The tags claim the high ground of indestructibility,
> shamelessly wrapping themselves in the symbols of
> great empires, pyramid, halo, iron cross, to disguise
> their true membership in the atomic kingdom, with
> its currency of rust, dust, and ashes.
>
> (Hunt, *Piece Logic* 4)

Here product packaging can "shamelessly" obscure the origins of mass-produced objects by invoking the aura of traditional symbols of authority. New "shrink-wrapped" items can conceal their secular, modern, and ready-made character through an association with the painstaking and costly artisanal labor of earlier eras. However, likening commodities to illuminated manuscripts call into question the quasi-metaphysical character of capitalist value. At the same time, the poem offers a sophistic tongue-in-cheek description of how such value is encoded in the very atomic structure of matter.

In my reading, such objects "illuminate" not ancient Egyptian or Christian "great empires" but the unearthly "metaphysical subtleties and theological niceties" (Marx, *Capital: A Critique of Political Economy. Vol.1* 163) of the commodity form. By describing commodities as both new and "adamant" while being susceptible to damage and decay, the poem exposes not only the hollowness of promises of historical durability but the commodity object's "true

[18] "This technological revolution has brought mass unemployment to Negroes more than any other group of workers" (Boggs, *Racism and the Class Struggle* 23), James Boggs argues. "It has shown how the economic progress of the country and the social progress of other Americans," Boggs continues, "have been made possible only by keeping the Negroes as an underclass at the bottom of the ladder, an unskilled reserve labor force to be superexploited for the benefit of every other section of American society" (Boggs, *Racism and the Class Struggle* 23).

membership in the atomic kingdom, with its currency of rust, dust, and ashes." Items within this "atomic kingdom," which possesses a currency of its own, are not merely reducible to their "atomic" material form but are also defined through their location within a system of human production and exchange.

Mixing the language of economic value with references to an "atomic kingdom" of products not only points out the folly of attributing permanent value to evanescent phenomena but underscores the absurdity of describing the commodity form primarily in terms of the physical characteristics of objects. The poet similarly highlights how imagining the inevitable physical decay of things in economic terms, how items are exchangeable with the "currency of rust, dust, and ashes," invests historically specific human practices with an illusory permanence. This "currency" invokes two incommensurable ways of conceiving of the value of things: as a literal atomic property of objects or as a socially constructed measure of exchange that renders objects and activities commensurable.

The poem's telescoping or superimposition of these forms of value exposes the structure of what Marx calls commodity fetishism—the belief that commodities possess intrinsic value and therefore social relations between persons assume the "fantastic form of a relation between things" (Marx, *Capital: A Critique of Political Economy. Vol.1* 165). Governed by seemingly immutable natural laws, things pass through a life cycle ending in the brokenness of "object death" (Hunt, *Piece Logic* 5), mirroring the lives of the subjects who consume and possess them.

Hunt draws on the language of metaphysical or religious "incarnation" to dramatize how value survives the material forms it assumes:

> The objects are tested and assigned an incarnation, and
> Objects so tested are given a seal, an assignment of limited
> durability, by the House of Broken Things, a holy affiliated
> division of its original.
>
> (Hunt, *Piece Logic* 3)

Objects are born "broken," so to speak, precisely because they are perishable instances of an endlessly recreated social form.[19] A "holy affiliated / division of its original," the "House of Broken Things" may refer to a lab where product testing

19 "For all its ghostly objectivity," David McNally points out in relation to Marx's critique of commodity fetishism, "value flourishes only by attaching itself to entities whose objectivity is appreciably more palpable" (McNally 132).

occurs. The poem's punning mixture of the language of corporate subdivisions and wholly owned subsidiaries underscores how the "House of Broken Things" is itself, like the objects inside it, a degraded material copy of an "original" that is not an object at all but a seemingly eternal fount of creation.

Reworking earlier accounts of fetishism in the eighteenth-century scholarship of Charles de Brosses on religious development, Marx's critique of commodity fetishism targets not the physical properties of things but the "ghostly objectivity" of value. Here the poem echoes the language of Marx describing value's seemingly transcendental dominion over the earth, "ruling the whole world through the relation of supply and demand—a relation which… hovers over the earth like the fate of the ancients, and with invisible hand allots fortune and misfortune to men, sets up empires and wrecks empires, causes nations to rise and to disappear" (Marx, *The German Ideology* 54).

As William Pietz argues, "Marx understood 'capital' to be a species of fetish" (Pietz 129) not due to the commodities' "physical existence or concrete functions per se but in their reality as material forms ('part-objects') of a distinctive type of social system" (Pietz 129):

> "Capital" is the substantive name for the unity of a socially (if unconsciously) organized material system of growth and reproduction whose effective components and visible forms are things, people, and money. The substance of capital itself is "value," that conserved quantity of social labor-time which seems to move through the metamorphic phases of the capitalist economy from one form to another (from laboring people to the things they produce, from these products to the money that purchases them, from this money to the new labor and materials it buys, etc.). Commodities and capital goods, wageworkers and capitalists, money and credit, are forms or parts of a whole temporal-material system. They (we) are members of the body of Capital, whose value-essence transcends and yet incarnates itself in these material beings like the divine salvational power of Christ in the faithful members and sacramental objects of His church.
>
> (Pietz 149)

In Hunt's poem, the commodity form is simultaneously animated by an imperishable "spirit" of abstract value, but also by the perishable "truth of things, that they / self-destruct from the day they roll off the assembly line, / moving guilelessly toward object death" (Hunt, *Piece Logic* 5). By presenting capitalist products here as simultaneously perishable and imperishable, the poem echoes Marx's assertion that commodities possess both a sensible and a "supersensible" form. While material forms might degrade, abstract value is capable of surviving "object death."[20]

Later in the collection, what the poem describes as the "marketing of absolute / obedience to the thing as it mutates, as it was meant to be" (Hunt, *Piece Logic* 11) interprets the continual replacement of perishable things as incontestable "proof" of a kind of theodicy of capitalist value.[21] The unrepresentability of this substance of capitalist abstraction, whose material embodiment can only ever be fleeting and partial, presents a challenge for poetic representation. Hunt's collection initially approaches this problem by drawing on the parodic, quasi-religious rhetoric of advertising to describe the promise of commodities as "heaven's own brand" (Hunt, *Piece Logic* 11). However, as the collection proceeds, the poet traces the referent of value back to innumerable "invisible hands" (Hunt, *Piece Logic* 13) working in factories across the globe. The image of countless hands puns on economist Adam Smith's famous reference to an "invisible hand" (Smith 477) directing individual self-interested activity toward socially beneficial ends. Weaving together a "broken" world and synchronized to the time objects keep, such hands disappear into what they make.

The Cold War Kitchen and the Poetics of Social Reproduction

So far, I have been accounting for the upper portion of Hunt's poem. The lower half of "The House of Broken Things" describes a kitchen where domestic labor and consumption, and domestic labor as consumption, process the sensuous properties of objects. The proper classification, management, and enumeration of commodities in "public" national space alters the "private" form of the nuclear family, gender roles, and the rhythm of repetitive domestic tasks. Ever-increasing demands for efficiency within the home, the poem suggests, push commodities and their consumers to the breaking point.

The upper and lower halves of Hunt's poem not only maps a gendered split between public and private spheres but also how this split is processed through

[20] The abstract value that regulates the exchange of these products and that renders different forms of human labor commensurable is ultimately for Marx measured through the ever-shifting average time it takes to produce specific commodities—or what the theorist calls "socially necessary labor time" (Marx, *Capital: A Critique of Political Economy. Vol.1* 129).

[21] Here the poem echoes the rhetoric of incarnation that Marx repeatedly deploys to describe how money emerges from myriad acts of commodity exchange—in which a single commodity emerges to represent the value of temporal increments of human productive activity. Characterizing the money-form as the "universal incarnation of abstract human labour" (Hunt, *Piece Logic* 169), Marx draws attention to how this generally socially recognized "universal equivalent form of all other commodities" (Marx, *Capital: A Critique of Political Economy. Vol.1* 230) represents the fact of the abstract exchangeability of that labor.

the "chiasmic personification-reification structure of capitalist fetishism" (Pietz 147). Printed in smaller text and significantly more fragmented, the poem's lower portion offers impressionistic descriptions of the home as a sensorium patterned by discrete acts of consumption:

> Stewing in my own juice
>
> Minty, sour, strong, medicinal, narcotic, chalky, bitter,
> burnt, hint of frost, caramelized, envious, enchanted, dazzled,
> undressed, musky, briny, soapy, salty, oiled, interrupted,
> frozen, sticky, mucilaginous, squeaky, gritty, frothy, volcanic,
> round, wrinkled, shoe leather.
>
> (Hunt, *Piece Logic* 4)

The catalog of details here suggests the isolable attributes of products whose consumption segments sensory and emotional experiences, from taste and texture to envy and enchantment. "Stewing in my own juice," the speaker must helplessly suffer through a process of self-objectification that both supplants and fractures their experiences in ways that perversely mirror the commodity "Piece Logic" mapped in the upper half of the poem.

The space of the home—whose purportedly "private," nonmarket character has long constituted a locus of feminist theorization—becomes a figure for a nation in crisis as household labor is dramatically restructured by the postwar transformation of wage labor. The division between "public" and "private" space mirrored in the poem's spatial organization reproduces an older philosophical opposition between *polis* and *oikos* that distinguished Greek city-states from the private households taken to be the basic units of Greek civic life. In my reading, Hunt's collection offers a peculiar contemporary reinterpretation of *oikonomia*, or what Angela Mitropoulos describes as "the premise of the properly productive household" (Mitropoulos, *Contract & Contagion: From Biopolitics to Oikonomia* 28) at the heart of ancient Greek theories of the frugal and rational management of a family, slaves, wives, children, and property. "Literally translated, [oikonomia] means the 'law of the household,' or '*nomos* of the *oikos*.' It is also the etymological root of terms such as 'economics' and 'ecology'":

> In this sense, [oikonomia] describes both epistemological or scientific validity and the application of a valid measure: that which is presumably proper to household management (such as knowledge, conduct, measures, and techniques), the logical and normative procedures from which property right is derived and considered to be valid, including theories of ownership and equity

("fair exchange" or "just price"), and therefore also implying a theory of the role of money as a facilitator of exchange.

(Mitropoulos, "Oikonomia" 1026)

Reconstructed over time in historically changing forms, *Piece Logic* depicts the "law of the household" as a critical site where "the nexus of race, gender, class, sexuality, and nation" (Mitropoulos, *Contract & Contagion: From Biopolitics to Oikonomia* 28) is reproduced under capitalist conditions.[22]

Hunt's collection presents the properly productive household as the basis for erecting an entire moral economy of property relations, generational succession, and postwar racial order. The problem of measuring unwaged domestic labor as a component of household consumption registers the increasing commodification and mechanization of domestic tasks, or what feminist theorists have broadly characterized as socially reproductive labor. As opposed to spaces of public consumption, from restaurants to malls, the home as a site of private consumption depends on hidden forms of domestic work—from the work of preparing food to care for the very young and very old.[23] As Evelyn Nakano Glen observes, such work belongs to a broader category of socially reproductive labor that refers "to the array of activities and relationships involved in maintaining people both on a daily basis and intergenerationally" (Glenn, "From Servitude to Service Work: Historical Continuities in the Racial Division of Paid Reproductive Labor" 1). "Reproductive labor includes activities such as purchasing household goods," Glenn writes, "preparing and serving food, laundering and repairing clothing, maintaining furnishings and appliances, socializing children, providing care and emotional support for adults, and maintaining kin and community ties" (Glenn, "From Servitude to Service Work: Historical Continuities in the Racial Division of Paid Reproductive Labor" 1). Not simply reducible to biological reproduction, this labor's gendered and unwaged character has historically placed women in a position of structural dependence on wage-earning men.[24]

The changing racial and gender composition of US wage work in *Piece Logic* pressurizes the ideal postwar capitalist household modeled in places

[22] See Mitropoulos, *Contract & Contagion: From Biopolitics to Oikonomia.*

[23] "The shaping of the home as a private space of consumption," as Roberta Sassatelli observes, "is part of the larger historical architecture which gave rise to contemporary consumer culture" (Sassatelli 107). "More broadly, the domestic sphere is ideally constituted in opposition to that of production as a space of consumption and leisure," Sassatelli continues, "yet much of what passes for consumption is in fact mediated by the unpaid work of women and, increasingly, by their paid domestic services" (Sassatelli 170).

[24] For perhaps one of the most influential Marxist accounts of domestic labor that ties socially reproductive labor to women's oppression, see Vogel. See also Gimenez.

like Moscow's Sokol'niki Park. Under such conditions, the space of the oikos not only warps and fractures but increasingly resembles a workplace subject to competitive pressures and demands for greater efficiency. Thus, the collection represents household and wage labor in nearly identical terms, describing domestic labor as a kind of assembly line subject to speedup.[25] Arlie Hochschild famously characterizes socially reproductive labor as a "second shift" (Hochschild) for working women who are now left with less time to complete domestic tasks. The resulting "feminization of speedup" (Bernes 120) of the pace of domestic labor provides a framework for understanding why the speakers of Hunt's poems are frequently described as product testers who are themselves inevitably rendered inoperable by the performance of devalued and monotonously repetitive work. The physical and psychological limits of subjects frenetically performing domestic tasks are repeatedly compared to the point at which commodities "shatter" (Hunt, *Piece Logic* 7). Whether waged or unwaged, as Marxist feminists point out, such labor constitutes a crucial moment of the renewal of the economic relationship between capital and labor historically deemphasized in traditional Marxist accounts of workplace exploitation.

After the Second World War, women's mass entry into the workforce drove the dramatic growth of a low-wage service sector of formerly unwaged domestic labor—from the restaurant industry to childcare and eldercare. In the same period, technological advances fragment higher-paying jobs dominated by men, such as clerical work, into routine tasks performed by deskilled, feminized labor. The gender composition of a range of occupations shifts within a post-industrial economy characterized by a dramatically expanded service sector and the offshoring of industrial manufacturing.[26] Political theorists have typically narrated these broad transformations of the postwar US economy in terms of the historical transition from a Fordist to a post-Fordist society, where earlier assembly-line mass-production techniques give way to deindustrialization, service work, and white-collar administrative occupations.

[25] Jasper Bernes has argued that the writing of contemporary 1970s-era feminist poets like Bernadette Mayer dramatizes a "feminization of speedup" (Bernes 120), in which the character of paid and unpaid labor seems to blur in "a vertiginous mirroring of unpaid and paid activities" (Bernes 127) where "there is no escape from either waged labor or unwaged labor, as both reflect each other and intermix and merge into one long, endless workday" (Bernes 128).

[26] The term "Fordism" was first coined by Italian theorist Antonio Gramsci in an analysis of the impact of emergent US production methods on European economic development. See Gramsci 277–320. For a more recent overview of the various and contested meanings attached to "Fordism" and "Post-Fordism" as concepts, see Jessop. Fordism, of course, does not simply describe a particular organization of the capitalist labor process, but also a historically specific configuration of racial and gender relations structured by racially stratified labor markets, tiered welfare provisions, racially exclusionary immigration policy, and residential segregation.

Reimagining domestic space as a workplace, *Piece Logic* dramatizes new demands on working women to reduce the labor time allotted to complete household tasks. The resulting compression of the time of social reproduction erodes the distinction between paid and unpaid labor and traps the speaker of the opening poem in an endless and "windowless calendar workday" (Hunt, *Piece Logic* 8), in which "egg timers ration my phone calls" (Hunt, *Piece Logic* 8). The socially unrecognized and unwaged work the speaker performs requires an explanation of "How it's done. / First of all / Son. / 365 / Hot / Meals / On the table. / Every day. / No reheats. / No cold plates. / When you get there— / Hot. Second" (Hunt, *Piece Logic* 6). The speaker of this passage produces a series of meals and an experience of standardized units of time—a "Hot. Second" (Hunt, *Piece Logic* 6). Extensively regulated by a regime of "time management" (Hunt, *Piece Logic* 8), socially reproductive labor reflects workplace routines outside the home.

These representations of domestic work as a form of product testing that breaks the tester dramatizes the "transfer" between paid and unpaid socially reproductive labor. The commodification of such work simultaneously allows the wealthy to "outsource" such labor to a historically gendered workforce who are themselves left with less time to perform domestic tasks. In a process that sociologist Nona Glazer calls "work transfer" (Glazer 143), waged socially reproductive labor can suddenly be displaced back into the home due to private benefit cuts or state spending cuts in childcare subsidies. For Glazer, this transfer can also take "the form of shifting once paid work to consumers, making it part of consumption, and either eliminating or otherwise changing the work of paid workers" (Glazer 143). Citing the historical example of the labor of retail clerks supplanted by the unwaged "self-service" work of consumers who select their own goods, Glazer argues that working women are saddled with additional labor demands extending to "the myriad relations that people have in the marketplace and to state agencies as 'clients,' 'users of municipal services,' 'patients,' 'defendants and plaintiffs,' 'tax payers,' 'bill payers,' [and the] 'kin of dependents' " (Glazer 143).

The speaker of Hunt's poem goes on to describe the problem of measuring domestic productivity in terms of "Piece work as measured in throat sung pop anthems" (Hunt, *Piece Logic* 9). Unlike traditional wage labor, piecework usually occurs in the home and is remunerated according to units produced, tasks performed, time-rates, or some combination of these measures.[27]

[27] In recent years, labor scholars have argued that piecework is a kind of historical precursor to contemporary of algorithmically regulated, on-demand "gig work." See Alkhatib et al.

Hunt's linking of this type of labor to popular music brings to mind both the commodity character of mass culture and a form of labor often performed in the home like garment assembly or food preparation. The problem of measuring the contribution of unpaid domestic labor, including slave labor, to the process of reproducing workers within capitalist economies has remained a subject of ongoing feminist debates about the possibility and desirability of constructing an integral "unitary" theory of capitalist exploitation, racial oppression, and gender subordination.[28]

The Gender Factory[29]

Italian and US Marxist feminist activists and theorists of the 1970s—including Silvia Federici, Selma James, and Mariarosa Dalla Costa—formed the International Wages for Housework campaign to draw attention to the simultaneously unrecognized and indispensable character of these forms of domestic work. The campaign drew inspiration from 1970s Italian autonomist theory and politics, or "operaismo," while challenging the limits of traditional Marxist analysis in accounting for gendered divisions of labor and the restructuring of work within industrialized postwar societies such as Italy and the United States.

The campaign organizers both borrowed and reimagined the concept of the "social factory" (Tronti 20) elaborated by Italian autonomist theorist Mario Tronti to describe the increasing subordination of social relations to the needs of capitalist profit-making. The campaign organizers understood the home as a space where businesses could rely on "the free appropriation of immense areas of labor and resources that must appear as externalities to the market" (Federici 140), as movement co-founder Silvia Federici observes. Rather than a private space free from market compulsions, movement organizers viewed household socially reproductive labor as a terrain of political struggle:

> Equally important for the development of our perspective was the Operaist concept of the "social factory." This translated Mario Tronti's theory, in *Operai e*

[28] For an overview of Marxist and socialist feminist debates over whether capitalism and patriarchy constitute a unitary or "dual system," see Arruzza; Young. For some influential contemporary attempts to bridge Marxist critiques of capitalist exploitation with a theorization of the specificity of Black women's labor under capitalism, see C. Jones; E. V. Cooper; Cooke; A. Davis; "The Combahee River Collective Statement."

[29] The title of this section is drawn from Sarah Fenstermaker Berk's *The Gender Factory*, an empirical study of the distribution of household labor in the United States.

> *Capitale* (1966) according to which at a certain stage of capitalist development capitalist relations become so hegemonic that every social relation is subsumed under capital and the distinction between society and factory collapses, so that society becomes a factory and social relations directly become relations of production. Tronti referred here to the increasing reorganization of the "territory" as a social space structured in view of the needs of factory production and capital accumulation. But to us, it was immediately clear that the circuit of capitalist production, and the "social factory" it produced, began and was centered above all in the kitchen, the bedroom, the home—insofar as these were the centers for the production of labor-power—and from there it moved on to the factory, passing through the school, the office, the lab.
>
> (Federici 7–8)

The concept of the "social factory" that feminist theorists and activists such as Federici, James, and Dalla Costa extended to the home offers a suggestive framework for reading the complex figure of the "House of Broken Things" in *Piece Logic* as an amalgam of home, nation, workplace, laboratory, and warehouse.

The speaker of the poem repeatedly fails to escape from the "social factory" because both public and private workplaces are subject to the same "atomic measure" (Hunt, *Piece Logic* 9)—a phrase that simultaneously suggests a Cold War nuclear arms race and the "atomic kingdom" (Hunt, *Piece Logic* 4) constructed by commodity fetishism:

> Disconnect, to invent this life in phantom objectivity
> Step outside, as if the leash could reach that long, and
> Look back in, the heap uncoils a pile of props,
> Instruments for measuring speed useless for this atomic measure
>
> (Hunt, *Piece Logic* 9)

The backward glance into the house's interior reveals a heap of objects that, like theatrical props, expose the Lukacsian "phantom objectivity" (Lukacs 83) of domestic roles tethered to the commodity form.

The difficulty of getting "outside" the home described in this passage takes on a distinct political resonance in the context of Black women's occupational confinement in domestic service.[30] As Glenn points out, such work remained both gendered and racially typed as a range of unpaid socially reproductive tasks

[30] For a post–Civil War history of Black women's labor in the south, see Hunter. For an analysis of the contemporary social organization of care work within the United States, see Glenn, *Forced To Care: Coercion and Caregiving in America.*

were increasingly transformed into wage labor after the Second World War.[31] This division of labor had far-reaching implications for Black feminist critiques of the presumption that "typical" gender roles involved women being confined to unwaged family labor, a foundational premise of books like Betty Friedan's *Feminine Mystique*. "Of the black women who earned wages in the late nineteenth century," historian Jacqueline Jones observes, "fully 90 percent of them labored as domestic servants in private homes or commercial settings such as hotels and boardinghouses" (110).

In *History and Class Consciousness*, Lukacs famously describes how commodities assume an autonomous "phantom objectivity" (Lukacs 83), seemingly disconnected from human activity.[32] For Lukacs, commodity fetishism represents not only a central problematic of Marx's writings but also a "central, structural problem of capitalist society in all its aspects" (Lukacs 83). Lukacs deploys the concept of reification to describe how generalized commodity production reshapes different domains of social life in its own image, generating a range of distorting epistemic effects. A seemingly unbridgeable ontological chasm emerges between subject and object, thwarting the possibility of gaining a broader perspective on increasingly fragmented domains of social activity. Finally, this deepening process of reification encourages the development of a "contemplative" or spectatorial consciousness that treats this state of affairs as both natural and unalterable.

I want to connect the poem's imperative to "Disconnect, to invent this life in phantom objectivity" (Hunt, *Piece Logic* 9) to Lukacs's contention that deepening processes of reification fundamentally restructure the self-understanding of capitalist subjects:

> The transformation of the commodity relation into a thing of "ghostly objectivity" cannot therefore content itself with the reduction of all objects for the gratification of human needs to commodities. It stamps its imprint upon the

[31] As Glenn argues, the increasing commodification of social reproduction in the postwar period allowed white families to transfer caretaking duties to a labor pool composed predominantly of Black and immigrant women from the Global South. "Racial-ethnic women are employed to do the heavy, dirty, 'back-room' chores of cooking and serving food in restaurants and cafeterias," Glenn writes, "cleaning rooms in hotels and office buildings, and caring for the elderly and ill in hospitals and nursing homes, including cleaning rooms, making beds, changing bed pans, and preparing food. In these same settings white women are disproportionately employed as lower-level professionals (e.g., nurses and social workers), technicians, and administrative support workers to carry out the more skilled and supervisory tasks (Glenn, "From Servitude to Service Work: Historical Continuities in the Racial Division of Paid Reproductive Labor" 19–20).

[32] The essence of commodity-structure has often been pointed out," Lukacs argues, "Its basis is that a relation between people takes on the character of a thing and thus acquires a 'phantom objectivity,' an autonomy that seems so strictly rational and all-embracing as to conceal every trace of its fundamental nature: the relation between people (Lukacs 83).

> whole consciousness of man; his qualities and abilities are no longer an organic part of his personality, they are things which he can "own" or "dispose of" like the various objects of the external world.
>
> (Lukacs 100)

For Lukacs, the generalization of commodity form does not literally transform the capitalist subject into a thing but instead introduces a split within that subject between a passive observing consciousness and the subject's own "objectified and reified faculties" (Lukacs 100).

The subject of domestic labor in the bottom half of Hunt's poem understands their own "identity" as a list of partitioned qualities—a forensic catalog of permutable traits, feelings, and functions segmented by the "Piece Logic" of "Object Authority": "Part mammal. Part of it's 2/3rds's over. Part whack. Part loathing and part serene. Part failed can opener. Part mandatory loot counting to achieve status" (Hunt, *Piece Logic* 2). As the boundaries between domestic space, workplace, and marketplace erode, both the self and domestic space becomes an "object theater" (Hunt, *Piece Logic* 10) where seemingly non-monetizable conceptions of the value of kinship relations are subject to quantification. Reduced to a bit player in this "object theater," the speaker struggles to locate themselves among self-replicating objects that parody processes of biological reproduction:

> I didn't even understand lactation
>
> I inherited many small items and I go from house to house
> expecting to find a use for them. It is a long and tedious
> process but rather than belabor it, I believe in them. I discover
> money in quotes, and suddenly, these items amass tremendous,
> disproportionate value, amassing piles of appliances for some,
> and yards of lace. I wonder if the people of this place are at all
> in their right minds or if I stir admiration and desire to sell
> through the windows what cannot be obtained even in the dint
> of so much constant wage peonage, caged foliage, long work
> weeks, blank stock options, branded cars, the empty nights of
> the ice age.
>
> (Hunt, *Piece Logic* 5)

Family bonds and histories morph into rare objects of "admiration and desire" that accrue "disproportionate value" as heirlooms that cannot be put to any practical use but which nevertheless raise the question of their value. The passage highlights the absurdity of assigning family heirlooms a price or considering them a product of wage labor. Similarly, the subsumption of biological reproduction into circuits of capitalist social reproduction renders "lactation" alienable property—an incomprehensible object.

The poet's reference to both "yards of lace" and "money in quotes" seems to borrow liberally from the language of Marx's famous discussion of "20 yards of linen" (Marx, *Capital: A Critique of Political Economy. Vol.1* 161). In a thought experiment, Marx asks his readers to imagine linen as a hypothetical stand-in for money—a peculiar commodity that functions as an abstract "universal equivalent" (Marx, *Capital: A Critique of Political Economy. Vol.1* 161) facilitating exchange. Here "money in quotes" might refer to poverty but also to a problem of reference. What is the referent of a measure of exchange capable of translating objects into quantities of other objects—"amassing piles of appliances for some, and yards of lace" (Hunt, *Piece Logic* 5)?

As a "universal equivalent," money is compared in the poem to enclosing a word in quotation marks—a procedure that immediately raises the question of the force of social convention in determining the semantic referent of any linguistic signifier:

> So strong is the force of habit, a force measured in the
> power of " " (open quotes), in the house of broken things,
> there are objects that don't need to be fixed.
>
> (Hunt, *Piece Logic* 10)

The "power of ' ' (open quotes)" describes not only money's absence but how poverty is sanctioned by the "force" of social conventions renewed through innumerable acts of market exchange. The "objects that don't need to be fixed" doesn't just refer to replaceable consumer goods but also to the production of disposable populations.

The ontological equivalence between broken objects and expendable subjects suggested by these passages draws attention to unemployment as a permanent structural feature of the capitalist organization of production and consumption. Marx called the tendency of capitalist production to cast populations out of work a "law of population" (Marx, *Capital: A Critique of Political Economy. Vol.1* 783) specific to capitalist economies.[33] Contemporary theorists have resuscitated this

[33] It is "capitalist accumulation itself that constantly produces, and produces indeed in direct relation with its own energy and extent," Marx argues, "a relatively redundant working population, i.e. a population which is superfluous to capital's average requirements for its own valorization, and is therefore a surplus population" (Marx, *Capital: A Critique of Political Economy. Vol.1* 782).

category of "relative surplus populations" (Marx, *Capital: A Critique of Political Economy. Vol.1* 786) to analyze what James Boggs, writing in 1963, labeled millions of "outsiders" who because of automation and deindustrialization "have never been and never can be absorbed into this society at all" (Boggs, *Pages From A Black Radical's Notebook: A James Boggs Reader* 112).[34] In recent years, theorists have turned their attention to how "wageless life, not wage labour, is the starting point in understanding the free market" (Denning 81) and the systematic production masses of "surplus humanity" (M. Davis 201) on a global scale.

In a world where capitalist wealth and human disposability produce and presuppose each other, the dehistoricizing force of what the speaker calls "phantom objectivity" rigidifies into a creeping existential emptiness—a kind of blank "ice age." No longer a refuge from the marketplace or workplace, the home becomes a kind of tomb for the dead labor congealed in objects, or the "sublimated violence of the good life" (Hunt, *Piece Logic* 6), defined by "constant wage peonage, caged foliage, long work weeks, blank stock options, branded cars" (Hunt, *Piece Logic* 5). The striking off-rhymes that reverberate through "wage peonage" and "caged foliage" sonically embed a creeping "ice age" across the "social factory" of the workplace and home.

Here the stray reference to "wage peonage," or debt peonage, connects the vacuity of this "Consumers' Republic" to earlier forms of racialized unfree labor—in particular, a specific post–Civil War labor regime of sharecropping, tenant farming, and convict leasing after formal emancipation. By associating wage labor with an exploitative postbellum labor regime that preserved coercive features of enslavement through debt, the poem in part directs attention to the historical trajectory of the post-Emancipation Black subject circumscribed by what Saidiya Hartman calls the "indebtedness of liberty to property and to an alienable and exchangeable self" (Hartman 110). Cold War kitchens were sites of the reproduction not only patriarchal gender roles, but also of racially typed labor historically excluded from Social Security, pensions, or unemployment insurance.[35]

[34] For some contemporary critical reconstructions of Marx's concept of relative surplus populations, see Denning; Tadiar; McIntyre; Tyner.

[35] The 1935 Social Security Act exempted low-wage and irregularly employed agricultural and domestic laborers from eligibility though they constituted nearly one-third of the existing labor force of the country and despite lobbying efforts at the time by the NAACP and Urban League. For an analysis of the racial consequences of these exclusions within a broader history of the development of the US welfare state over the twentieth century, see Fox.

Race and the Fordist Family

The seemingly mystical origins of the "Object Authority" invoked throughout the collection embed changing beliefs about racial difference and family formation into a web of capitalist property relations. In 1974 Margaret Prescod and Wilmette Brown founded Black Women for Wages for Housework, "a network of Black/Third World women claiming reparations for all our unwaged work including slavery, imperialism and neo-colonialism" (*The International Wages For Housework Campaign*). More than a decade later, Prescod would confront then-senator Moynihan during the 1987–8 congressional proceedings about welfare policy, which established work requirements for Aid to Families with Dependent Children (AFDC). Despite its minimal budget, AFDC became, for conservative critics of the postwar welfare state, a powerful symbol of the Fordist family in crisis, racial dependency, and inflationary government spending. After being denied the opportunity to speak before a congressional committee deliberating these changes, Prescod took the stage with three other members of the Black Women for Wages for Housework campaign. "Black women have been paid for generations for doing housework in white people's houses," Prescod argued. "When we did that work for no pay, it was called slavery" (qtd. in Naples).

Analyzing how race and gender came to shape assumptions about the dependence and autonomy of Black women in ways that otherwise passed without comment during the congressional proceedings, Nancy A. Naples points out that Prescod was not only "committed to centering the value of women's work in the home" (Naples 934) but also to challenging an emergent consensus on welfare dependency in the wake of the 1965 Moynihan Report.[36] "In stressing Black women's contradictory position as paid domestic worker," Naples writes, "Prescod revealed the fallacy in separating women's domestic work from other forms of labor" (Naples 934) tied to less stigmatized forms of government assistance.

[36] As Naples argues, "Within new consensus discourse, poverty and so-called welfare dependence in America are constructed as direct consequences of individual behavioral factors such as out-of-wedlock births, reluctance on the part of women to enter the paid labor market, and unwillingness of biological fathers to support their children financially. African American poverty, when explained through these frames, is constructed as a consequence of Black men's personal inability to support their families economically and of Black women's transmitting dependency on public assistance to their children" (Naples 937).

Although the chapbook's rare references to race often appear as oblique euphemisms, likening a subject overwhelmed by domestic tasks to "broken" labor-saving appliances evokes that consistently displaces the "brokenness" of a crisis-ridden postwar economy, reliant on unrecognized household labor, onto specific racialized "broken" families and populations.[37] *Piece Logic* repeatedly juxtaposes this implicitly racialized diagnostic language against descriptions of appliances in a "typical" suburban household, much like the model home on display at the US Trade and Cultural Fair in Moscow's Sokol'niki Park. The image of a "House of Broken Things" invokes not only what Kate Baldwin calls the "Racial Imaginary of the Cold War Kitchen" (Baldwin) but also a social scientific discourse of "broken families" (Moynihan 21) that informed postwar calls from across the political spectrum for the provision of a Fordist family wage for Black men in particular, and the reconstruction of the Fordist nuclear family within Black communities, as a basis for racial progress.[38] "In effect, while it lasted, the Fordist family wage not only functioned as a mechanism for the normalization of gender and sexual relationships, but it also stood at the heart of the midcentury organization of labor, race, and class," as Melinda Cooper writes, "defining African American men by their exclusion from the male breadwinner wage and African American women by their relegation to agricultural and domestic labor in the service of white households" (M. Cooper 8).

If postwar images of a "democracy of goods" (Marchand 217) model both national abundance and an ideal "Fordist" family structure, Hunt's collection draws attention to how an entire racialized and gendered division of labor is exposed by the withdrawal of a stable "social wage" (M. Cooper 121) from a single, presumptively white and male, income earner.[39]

[37] Poet and critic Tyrone Williams reads Hunt's collection as an investigation of the "interdependency of consumerism, misogyny and state terrorism" in the aftermath of the attacks of September 11, 2001. "Recalling in part the logic of George Oppen's 1934 excavation of capitalist atomization, *Discrete Series*," Williams continues, "Hunt examines the 'pieces' of 'broken things' that both constitute and are contained within 'The House' " (151–52). For Williams, the few examples of explicit racial reference seem to "function ambivalently in a poem concerned, in part, with the veils of ideology" (Williams 152).

[38] Such demands for the extension of the Fordist family wage to Black men in particular faced increasing resistance to welfare provision in general after the 1970s.

[39] The preservation of this family form became a focus of converging postwar labor movement demands and elevated government social spending on public goods to create a virtuous cycle of increased consumer demand and in turn higher business profit rates. This combination of rising wages and rising government social spending has been called the Fordist-Keynesian "social compact" of the postwar boom, stretching from approximately 1945 to 1973, when the compact was eventually eroded and dramatically scaled back by what geographer David Harvey and others call the "neoliberal turn" (Harvey 9) of the mid-1970s and after.

Proof

The fifth poem in the collection, "Proof," shifts the implied referent of "broken things" from pathologized populations to the "Piece Logic" governing racial incorporation into the malfunctioning "social factory" of a deindustrializing US postwar economy:

> Proof that we live in a broken world and a broken world
> is unlivable.
>
> Proof that the carrot turns into the stick and vice-versa.
> Proof that that seems normal, self-sufficient.
>
> Proof that we sometimes destroy things that are broken and
> can't be fixed and sometimes fix things because to live with
> them broken is unthinkable.
>
> Proof that we switch roles, sometimes to destroy things
> that are broken and can't be fixed, sometimes to fix things
> because to live with them broken is unthinkable.
> Proof that we learn to live with the unthinkable.
>
> (Hunt, *Piece Logic* 16)

The allegory of damaged or destroyed commodities here confirms a "broken world" where the terms of economic incorporation require that subjects "switch roles" between attempts to repair social relations or living within a social order where such relations are treated as disposable things. The "social factory" that produces the "broken world" of the postwar US economy is maintained not only by consent secured through consumer abundance but also by state coercion—the "carrot" and the "stick." The latter emerges in the poem through a language of policing, provoking the "ruin and burn" (Hunt, *Piece Logic* 16) of implied civil unrest.

In the language of the Moynihan Report, the figure of the Black matriarch is understood not simply as unassimilable to the "democracy of goods," but as the source of the "scourge of urban rebellions that devastated the landscape of the American city" (King 80).[40] In a pointed reversal of the causal structure of Moynihan's analysis, *Piece Logic* identifies commodity form itself as "proof"

[40] "The Moynihan Report was as much a response to Black radicalism, urban rebellions and white fear," Tiffany Lethabo King writes, "as it was a liberal response to Black poverty" (King 80).

of the pathological character not of Black matriarchal families or "broken" populations, but of a social order subordinated to "Object Authority" at what the poet calls "the violent border of property and oblivion" (Hunt, *Piece Logic* 15).

Invisible Hands

In "Invisible Hands," the poet underscores how racial boundaries continue to be reproduced through contemporary property relations—connecting domestic racial politics to an expansive global capitalist "Object Authority":

> As in the phrase, "give me some skin," the slap of palms right
> hand to right hand empty, no weapon there, we come in
> peace we come out of the hypnotic circle that orbits and
> holds us in constant bind of stick em up and lap dancing,
> out of rigged destiny, across the violent border of property
> and oblivion, where hands can be detected in the bric a brac
> of the world.
>
> (Hunt, *Piece Logic* 15)

This passage connects what I have been calling a political economy of Black disposability not only to automation but to capitalist globalization and the offshoring of industrial manufacturing. As a pun on both Adam Smith's description of the efficiency of market allocated resources and the "surrogate effect" (Atanasoski and Vora 9) of invisible gendered labor, "invisible hands" (Hunt, *Piece Logic* 14) also represent an undifferentiated global labor pool capable of producing the "bric a brac of the world." Detached from bodies, hands are repeating and materially interconnected social forms that seem to possess their own mystified "Object Authority" across a range of social situations. Here the poem condenses an entire period of postwar racial and economic history into a synecdoche for labor—the human hand. At the edges of the world of objects, the poem presents two hands that cannot seem to "clap the other" (Hunt, *Piece Logic* 15). Despite the "piece logic" that connects them, a vast distance seems to separate the weaponless "empty" hand and the hands of low wage global workers that produce "key chains, sneakers, baseball gloves, flame proof nightwear, transmission, stereos, computer chips, Gap jeans, rugby polo shirts" (Hunt, *Piece Logic* 14).

"Invisible Hands" concludes by referring to forms of crime, policing, and sex work in terms of "rigged" destinies that aren't explained by reference to pathology but instead to property relations as an ongoing mechanism of racial ordering. Here a set of social roles is both enforced and naturalized as groups come to be partially defined through their relative risk of expulsion from the "hypnotic circle" of value accumulation, pushing populations beyond the "border" of wage labor into illegal or informal sectors of the economy. It is a border that suggests not only the boundaries of stable wage labor but also the boundaries of the nation within a global space of production. The poet represents the "hands" of workers beyond the United States as appendages of the same collective body of capital that measures and moves the "empty" hand with "no weapon"—a formulation that resembles the language used to justify police shootings of unarmed Black Americans.

The rise of the penal state as a particular management strategy of interrelated forms of "surplus" is, I would argue, the historical referent for the "stick" that accompanies the "carrot" in "Proof." As contemporary scholars of US penal history note, the construction of one of the largest carceral systems in the world in the 1970s constituted a vital component of a broad strategy to manage "surplus" labor and contain Black political insurgencies in the absence of a transformative restructuring of the US economy called for in documents like the "Triple Revolution" letter or the "Freedom Budget For All Americans."[41]

"Proof" questions how a seemingly "self-sufficient" (Hunt, *Piece Logic* 16) object world might be seen through—revealing the hands that ceaselessly make and remake it. This crisis of reference at the heart of "Object Authority" is destabilized by a moment of political upheaval, which disrupts an otherwise orderly taxonomy of things described in the rest of the chapbook and renders the meaning of things "far from self-evident" (Hunt, *Piece Logic* 13).

The concluding lines of the poem challenge readers to demystify "Object Authority" but also reports of a harmonious object world disrupted by the "tongue of ruin and burn" (Hunt, *Piece Logic* 16)—an image suggesting spreading social unrest and ecological devastation:

> Proof in the tongue of ruin and burn. Fluent in the language
> of minus.
> The forest comes apart and the trees have fallen.

[41] Sociologist Loic Wacquant has characterized the racially, economically, and spatially selective nature of policing and this emergent prison system as a form of "hyperincarceration" (Wacquant 23). Geographer Ruth Wilson Gilmore famously describes this carceral turn in terms of "the state-sanctioned… production and exploitation of group-differentiated vulnerability to premature death" (Gilmore 28). While Gilmore's redefinition of racism is often cited in the literature on the rise of the US carceral state, the description is premised on a less-discussed elaboration of the state capacity to control "various factors of production" (Gilmore 28), such as populations, capital, and land. State action enables these factors of production not only to be organized but also "to be disorganized or abandoned outright" (Gilmore 28). For Gilmore, the state is thus "not a thing but rather a capacity" to resolve a crisis of surplus labor, capital, or land—and a crisis of politically restive groups rendered superfluous from the point of view of production—in part through policing, imprisonment, and prison construction.

> Proof then by reading it on paper. Proof in unmarked bills.
> Line by line our eyes fill up with witness: Mornings as clear
> as glass.
>
> Can stones be far behind?
>
> (Hunt, *Piece Logic* 16–17)

The preceding passage initially seems to indicate the social and environmental cost of maintaining this material order of things, but the role and responsibility of human agents for sustaining this process is concealed. Even the oddly mismatched tenses in the description of the destruction of the forest feature a temporal caesura in which the implied observer can register the fallen trees only after the "forest comes apart." This stutter or gap in the line traces the outline of an absent subject, who can confirm that the event has occurred only by reading it "on paper." Language here is not simply a transparent or opaque medium of representation, but a salable product with specific material origins. The conversion of trees to paper, and from paper to "unmarked bills," traces the various stages of creating a commodity, paper, which subsequently functions as a symbolic representation of abstract value. As a result of these processes of conversion, paper can be reread as "proof" of the forest it once was part of, and "unmarked bills" as representing an abstract measure of value that renders the non-human natural world a fungible factor of production. At the same time, "unmarked bills" seems to invoke a demand for untraceable currency and the commission of a bank robbery in a "broken world" (Hunt, *Piece Logic* 16) undergoing a profound crisis of reference.

The poem reevaluates this crisis in its concluding stanzas, in which divergent concepts of "proof" are revealed as irreconcilable. On the one hand, "proof" that gathers in this poem "Line by line" evokes a world ordered by objects whose meaning and value are certified, secure, and "clear as glass" (Hunt, *Piece Logic* 17). On the other hand, such an order also offers "proof" of a "broken" world of disposable and "broken" populations. The accumulation of evidence "Line by line" produces radically divergent senses of bearing witness to either abundance or the multiplication of antagonistic social divisions. Here both senses of "proof" remain tethered to the commodity form and the measure of capitalist value. The more capitalist imperatives remake the world, the more self-evident and incontestable "Object Authority" appears. Readers are then presented with a scene of recognition in which the structure of this imagined community of objects becomes "transparent" and knowable as a form of social organization. What is witnessed at this moment is not the activity of persons or the "hands" of human labor "in plain sight and out of sight" (Hunt, *Piece Logic* 15), but an object, glass, that becomes a figure for epistemic certainty.

The presence of "invisible hands" throughout the collection, however, prepares readers for the question, "Can stones be far behind?" The line seems to dramatize the force of a historical rupture by introducing a temporal delay in which the stones that might shatter this dream of transparency are presented as an inevitable byproduct of the laws governing a "House of Broken Things" (Hunt, *Piece Logic* 1). This final interrogative returns us to a few preceding lines, which describe destruction as a "language of minus" (Hunt, *Piece Logic* 17). Without a locatable speaker—this language is also composed of part objects, stones, that seemingly move of their own accord back across the "violent border between property/and oblivion" (Hunt, *Piece Logic* 15).

The statements that make up this poem remain pitched at a level of generality that resists more detailed historical contextualization. But readers might nevertheless hear in the "language of minus" the poet's application of an avant-garde poetic critique of the "referential fallacy" onto the problem of how images of postwar consumer abundance "refer" to the continued systematic production of disposable populations. The contested interpretation of the meaning of this "language of minus" might be read, for example, as an echo of Martin Luther King Jr.'s widely cited observation that "riots are the language of the unheard" (King Jr.). This frequently quoted observation also describes a crisis of reference in which the causes of social unrest, King suggests, might be subject to radical misinterpretation, reversing cause and effect. After an upsurge of riots across Northern cities in the late 1960s, typically in response to police violence, King's argument implies that America has misconstrued the language as evidence of self-destructive irrationality and cultural pathology rather than worsening material conditions and pervasive racist practices.

For the poet, dereifying this world requires a practice of reinterpretation to expose both the shape of "things far from self-evident" (Hunt, *Piece Logic* 13) and integral relations between seemingly disconnected parts of a social whole:

> This is the world of objects we
> have made, and their silent rebel-
> lions are conducted under our very
> eyes. The inventory gets out of
> line, undermines truth by num-
> bers. There are unauthorized
> breaks on the line between one

thing and another.
[…]
The knee bone is connected to the
Thigh bone and the thigh bone to
The hip bone, eventually connects
To constantly moving persons.

(Hunt, *Piece Logic* 13)

Repeating the lyrics of "Dem Bones," a spiritual featuring lyrics that are rewritten passages from the book of Ezekiel and a melody composed in the 1920s by poet and novelist James Weldon Johnson, Hunt returns readers to the image of a collective social body that will one day be resurrected and made whole through divine power. As Allen Callahan observes, the prophetic vision of a valley of dry bones in Ezekiel "became a venerable topos in the African American vernacular" (Callahan 45), offering a "prophetic declaration of life after death, of a collective resurrection" (Callahan 45) for a dispersed and oppressed population. Hunt connects this Black vernacular transformation of the text of Ezekiel with a critique of capitalist atomization. Having clarified the "Piece Logic" binding both subjects and objects together in a web of capitalist social relations, the poet here dramatizes the survival of what theorist and poet Fred Moten calls Black "stolen life" (Fred Moten 179) in terms of property in rebellion as a necessary component of the resurrection of a collective "wounded social body" (Hunt, "Notes for an Oppositional Poetics" 201).

Reframing Oppositionality

The collection's diagramming of the social factory capable of producing a "democracy of goods" allows readers to radically reimagine the basis of an oppositional political and poetic imagination. In Hunt's 1990 essay "Notes for an Oppositional Poetics," the poet offers a broad framework for understanding the role that "Piece Logic" has played in helping to create "the illusion of a world at peace" (Hunt, "Notes for an Oppositional Poetics" 198) and obscuring the shifting terrain of a global "New War" (Hunt, "Notes for an Oppositional Poetics" 198) raging not so much between nations as within them against a range of persecuted, impoverished, and displaced internal populations. For Hunt, the resulting proliferation of unconventional "battlefields" across the globe—from the global arms trade and job loss to continued US support for authoritarian regimes and attempts to commodify and control Black women's reproductive capacity—appears as disparate, localizable phenomena rather than materially interconnected parts of a collective social body.

The "bonds of opposition" (Hunt, "Notes for an Oppositional Poetics" 200) that might potentially form across oppressed and exploited groups are consistently suppressed by a political "common sense" (Hunt, "Notes for an Oppositional Poetics" 199) that continually risks reproducing the terms of the dominant order. Promoted by the "bureaucratic rationalism" of the degraded language of state violence to the stock phrases of the nightly news, it is a "common sense" that reproduces a dominant culture's attempts to "transfer its own partiality onto the opposition it tries to suppress" (Hunt, "Notes for an Oppositional Poetics" 202). "Dominant modes of discourse," Hunt argues, "the language of ordinary life or of rationality, of moral management, of the science of the state, the hectoring threats of the press and media, use convention and label to bind and organize us" (Hunt, "Notes for an Oppositional Poetics" 199). The poet thus imagines both a poetics and a politics that does not simply reproduce those codes that discursively assemble an "us," but thinks through the conditions of possibility for coordinated action made possible by an expansive sense of collective belonging:

> The convenience of these labels serves social control. The languages used to preserve domination are complex and sometimes contradictory. Much of how they operate to anesthetize desire and resistance is invisible; they are wedded to our common sense; they are formulaic without being intrusive, entirely natural—"no marks on the body at all."
>
> These languages contain us, and we are simultaneously bearers of the codes of containment. Whatever damage or distortion the codes inflict on our subjectively elastic conception of ourselves, socially we act in an echo chamber of the features ascribed to us, Black woman, daughter, mother, writer, worker and so on. And the social roles and the appropriate actions are similarly inscribed, dwell with us as statistical likelihoods, cast us as queen or servant, heroic or silent, doer or done unto.
>
> (Hunt, "Notes for an Oppositional Poetics" 199–200)

The poet suggests that the imposition of inflexible, segmented social roles—a process that is not simply discursive but material—can frame inequality as the product of "natural" preexisting social differences. The comparison of the rhetorical structure of dominant discourses to the clinical vocabulary of forensic science or a public statement justifying state violence, "no marks on the body at all," underscores how responsibility for that violence is displaced onto targeted populations. Suggesting a crime victim or tortured prisoner, the figure calls attention to processes of racial marking and unmarking in particular that routinely invert the structural causes and consequences of violence, exploitation, and oppression.[42] The body without visible marks is also a figure that comes to represent how differential life chances are borne by specific populations as seemingly contingent "statistical likelihoods." Broad patterns of structural inequality are thus rendered "entirely natural" through a reversal of cause and effect in which domination and subordination are justified through reference to the inherent attributes of individuals and groups.

The metaphor of the "echo chamber" underscores how the political assertion of oppositional identities risks reinforcing the belief that racial distinctions describe normative or non-normative codes of behavior as inherent properties of populations. For the poet, such forms of political assertion risk trapping an oppositional poetics and politics within the imperative to perform rather than denaturalize recognizable social roles:

> The effect of this can be sensed in the feeling of captivity we have before there is a psychic or social advance, the state of alienation we reside in: somehow the codes fit and do not fit us, somehow we are the agents of the prescribed predicates and not the agents.
>
> (Hunt, "Notes for an Oppositional Poetics" 200)

The poet offers a complex analysis of the split character of race as a concept—alternately a mark of oppression and a signifier of oppositional subject formation, group culture, and shared history. The historically interconnected, but discontinuous, relationship between oppressive and affirmative senses of racial belonging exposes a complex historically unfolding dynamic of group formation in which members can "experience acute difference: autonomy without self-determination and group identity without group empowerment" (Hunt, "Notes for an Oppositional Poetics" 200). For the poet, the incommensurability of these two "moments" of racial group formation, alternately ascribed and asserted, also generates a peculiar rhetorical displacement of agency onto the "prescribed predicates" of subjects rather than to subjects themselves acting within historically and materially specific contexts.

In my reading of *Piece Logic,* Hunt's poems liken this process of causal inversion to a Marxist understanding of commodity fetishism and to the

[42] Later in the essay, Hunt draws on the writings of Elaine Scarry to present a stark example of the causal reversal established by these "codes of containment." For Scarry, victims of torture are often framed as responsible for their suffering when the scene of torture is understood as determined by the dynamics of a verbal interrogation rather than by power relations. See Scarry.

premises of documents like the Moynihan Report that, in the words of Barbara and Karen Fields, "transforms racism, something an aggressor does, into race, something the target is, in a sleight of hand that is easy to miss" (Fields and Fields 17). Echoing this critique of the concept of race offered by the Fieldses though not embracing the latter theorists' racial eliminativism, Hunt reimagines race as a social form whose meaning is itself an object of ongoing political struggle:

> In communities of color, oppositional frames of reference are the borders critical to survival. Long treatment as an undifferentiated mass of other by the dominant class fosters collective identity and forms of resistance. In a sense, then, oppositional groupings, be they based on class, race, gender or critical outlook, have traditionally been dependent, in part, on external definition by the dominant group—the perceived hostility of the dominant class shapes the bonds of opposition. And that quasidependent quality extends even further: we get stuck with the old codes even as we try to negate them. We experience acute difference: autonomy without self-determination and group identity without-group empowerment.
>
> (Hunt, *Piece Logic* 200)

Race describes for the poet a peculiar problem of defining individual and group identity, and the boundaries of the "bonds of opposition," primarily in terms set by "external definition." The poems that I have been examining over the course of this chapter dramatically reimagine oppositionality not primarily as a politics of the subject, but in terms of a "Piece Logic" that is the "connective tissue that joins" (Hunt, *Piece Logic* 207) the "conditions of sex, race, and class oppression" (Hunt, *Piece Logic* 207). Shaping both oppressive and affirmative conceptions of racial group belonging, such "Piece Logic" is inseparable from how capitalist imperatives simultaneously divide and recompose populations, producing material interlinkages between seemingly discrepant histories and disparate forms of oppression and exploitation. The poems dramatically reimagine how such interconnections might form the basis of an expansive, global conception of oppositionality capable of materially transforming the meaning of "old codes" beyond recognition.

3

"Number, Form, Proportion, Situation": The Measure of Racial Comparison in Myung Mi Kim's *Dura*

The poetry of Korean American author Myung Mi Kim represents an influential break with the activist polemics of Asian American poets of the 1970s, such as Janice Mirikitani and Francis Oka, and a departure from the Asian American lyric or confessional verse popularized in the 1980s by such acclaimed poets as Cathy Song, Marilyn Chin, David Mura, and Li-Young Lee. Born in 1957 in Seoul, South Korea, Kim is the author of seven volumes of poetry. Her writing sits at the intersection of two, sometimes overlapping, sometimes polarized, bodies of literature: Asian American literature and contemporary US avant-garde and experimental poetry. On the one hand, Kim's poetry represents a body of contemporary Korean American diasporic literature concerned with the pressures of cultural assimilation and the multigenerational impact of Japanese and US imperial violence.[1] On the other hand, Kim's highly fragmented, non-narrative formal strategies are situated within a genealogy of avant-garde, or experimental, writing that has rejected, as an ideological fiction, the stable speaking subjects and forms of autobiographical testimony that have come to define much contemporary Asian American poetry.[2] Although these audiences are by no means mutually exclusive, Kim's poetry nevertheless forces its readers to confront the shifting nature of poetic experiments among contemporary Asian American poets.[3]

1 See Grace M. Cho, *Haunting the Korean Diaspora: Shame, Secrecy, and the Forgotten War*.

2 For a reading of Asian American poetry as and against racially unmarked contemporary US poetic avant-gardes like Language Writing, see Yu. For further discussion of the theoretical problems raised by arguing for Kim as a specifically Korean American poet, see Liu.

3 For a detailed account of recent US poetic debates that have reinforced the conceptual opposition between formal innovation and a poetics of identity, see Wang 1–47.

By linking formal strategies associated with avant-garde literary movements to post-1960s Asian American diasporic poetics, Kim's poetry is, I argue, less interested in asserting a unitary ethnic or Asian American panethnic identity than in denaturalizing "Asiatic racial form" (Lye 70)—a set of underlying legal, political, and economic criteria that determine the legibility of Asian Americans as subjects and objects of representation.

For Kim, Asiatic racial form is *comparative*, meaning that it emerges and alters in relation to other racial distinctions in the United States. It is a racial position developed in relation to histories of Black chattel slavery, the expropriation of indigenous lands, and changes in intra-European ethnic hierarchies that formed whiteness as a marked and unmarked identity. Appearing as noncitizen alien labor, the demographic threat of a "yellow peril," contemporary images of model and/or "middleman minorities" (Bonacich 583), Asiatic racial form has long conjured up the image of a transnational population whose unique racial capacity to assimilate to capitalist imperatives continues to makes them both more and less than human.

Although scholars continue to situate Asian Americans within the US racial order, often questioning the very cultural and political coherence of a panethnic designation, which has its origins in the activism of the 1960s, Kim's poetry dramatically reframes such questions. This poet's writings trace the historical development of quantitative systems of measurement in relation to the historical emergence of the commodity form as a mechanism of imposed racial comparison structuring interracial contact, competition, and conflict.[4]

The increasingly compressed, oracular, and sometimes apocalyptic character of Kim's books—across seven volumes of poems, from *Under Flag* (M. M. Kim, *Under Flag*) to *Civil Bound* (M. M. Kim, *Civil Bound*)—makes critical interpretation provisional and highly speculative. Recognizably ethnic-speaking subjects fracture into seemingly disconnected textual fragments. What remains in the poetry increasingly resembles an archipelago of historical silences and traumatic ruptures, punctuated by oblique references to colonization, displacement, and war. At the same time, the accumulation of textual fragments begins to suggest innumerable possible networks of meaning. The seemingly disarticulated diasporic subjects of Kim's poems accrue the capacity to combine, aggregate, and bridge distant languages, cultures, and histories. In recent years

[4] See for example Claire Jean Kim's influential notion of "racial triangulation" (105) to describe the differential positioning of Asian Americans in US racial hierarchies primarily marked by what the author considers to be relative status differences and degrees of foreignness.

the poet has consistently posited an analogy between the "Fierce unsystematic recombinatory power of language" (M. M. Kim, "Convolutions: The Precision, The Wild" 251) and the "recombinant energy created between languages (geopolitical economies, cultural representations, concepts of community)" (M. M. Kim, *Commons* 110). The term *recombinatory* here suggests both the unsystematic possibilities of poetic language freed from normative syntax, and the multiplication of interconnected sites of cross-cultural contact, conflict, and coordination.

One of the most elliptical and hermetic texts in Kim's corpus, the 1999 collection *Dura* (M. M. Kim, *Dura*), dramatizes this linguistic tension between fragmentation and assemblage by taking the form of a historical primer for new immigrants to the United States. Kim's poems often mimic guides for new language learners, with the opening section, "Primer," of the poet's 1996 book *The Bounty* (M. M. Kim, *The Bounty*), dramatizing how the acquisition of English is both a negotiation with the pressures of cultural assimilation and a site for unruly translations of cultural norms. As a historical primer, *Dura* delivers a cryptic, compressed account of centuries of colonial history and traces a jagged itinerary through the archives of the Atlantic slave trade and settler colonial visions of the national territory of the United States.

As Kim and critics of her work point out, the poet's persistent interest in staging scenes of Asian immigrant assimilation as contradictory and self-undermining pedagogical exercises draws inspiration from the writings of Korean American author Theresa Hak Kyung Cha.[5] *Dura*'s focus on scenes of instruction, however, does not center its interlocking interpellative structures exclusively on Asian immigrant subjects or Orientalist tropes of perpetual foreigners, the "yellow peril," or model minorities. The text's examination of how units of measurement facilitate racialization processes and serve a kind of pedagogical function for diasporic subjects seeking political recognition complicates existing scholarly readings of Kim's poetry. Instead of resistance to identity-based models of racial

[5] The critic Anne Cheng has called these scenes of instruction in *Dictee* as part of a set of interlocking interpellative scenarios that form an overarching "dictaphonic structure" (Cheng 159) in which a kind of racially marked lyric voice "comes into being as injunction from without, but also that the injunction without is always already an echo of something within" (Cheng 158). Like *Dictee*, *Dura* blurs these inner and outer voices but in a manner that dramatizes colonial history and emergent capitalist social relations as a series of speech acts that seem to simultaneously describe and remake the world. In other words, what I call *Dura's* metrological imaginary blurs the distinction between constative and performative speech acts. The language of measure simultaneously describes and reorganizes land, labor, collective subjects, and historical change. The immigrant student or subject of instruction in Kim's earlier poems here almost completely vanishes into a matrix of legal codes, commodities, geometric spatial forms, and ancient and contemporary metrological systems, which the text uses to map European colonial expansion and capitalist globalization.

assimilation that critics of Kim's poetry highlight, *Dura's* pedagogical imperatives are not simply deployed to consolidate an affirmative conception of disobedient, unassimilated Asian immigrant subjects. Instead, the book's excavation of systems of enforced commensuration unsettles the reified, object-like character of racial categories considered as autonomous, transhistorical abstractions.

The more totalizing these systems seem in Kim's text, the more the possibility of a positive representation of identity seems to give way to how such an identity might appear in a slave trader's ledger, or from the point of view of the penal state, or as a palpable absence from a landscape scarred by war. *Dura*'s implied pedagogical subjects come to understand how they appear to colonial powers, states, and capital. Yet Kim's preoccupation with the inseparability of "Accounts and recounting" (M. M. Kim, *Commons* 4) does not simply point to the epistemic distortions of colonial history. It also indicates what I call a metrological imaginary, which blurs the difference between recording history and the seizure and salability of territories, populations, and goods—or, in the poet's words, the difference between "texts and trade" (M. M. Kim, *Commons* 4). Kim's pun on "recounting" here refers both to historical representation and to forms of bookkeeping that critic Katherine McKittrick has dubbed the "mathematics of the unliving" (McKittrick 17)—the "ordinary, proved, former, certified, nearly worn-out archives of ledgers, accounts, price tags, and descriptors of economic worth and financial probability" (McKittrick 17) both marking and masking the presence of blackness within colonial and Atlantic slave trade archives. For Kim, these archives suggest a grid of intelligibility in which space, time, bodies, and laboring activity are rendered measurable and exchangeable so that they can be incorporated into a contemporary world system that Cedric Robinson and others label "racial capitalism" (Robinson 316).[6]

My reading of *Dura* differs from other accounts of Kim's writings that have typically focused on the politics and poetics of Korean American subject formation but not on how the work highlights the dynamics of comparative racial group formation and nonwhite interracial antagonisms. Specific engagements with Korean history and diasporic identity are not absent from *Dura*. Still, my reading is primarily concerned with the entanglement of systems of measure and the colonial expansion of transnational capitalist networks that possess the

6 While my use of the term "racial capitalism" is indebted to the work of Cedric Robinson, the term also describes a field of inquiry into the relationship between race and capitalism rather than a specific set of arguments derived primarily from Robinson's *Black Marxism* (Robinson). For a further history of the term "racial capitalism" see Melamed (2015); Hudson. For a critique of Robinson's theorization of "racial capitalism," see Ralph and Singhal.

power, in the words of the poet, to both create "famine where abundance lies" (M. M. Kim, *Commons* 4) and establish the terms of later interracial conflict. In a book that rarely explicitly invokes specific racial categories, race is less a set of categorical identities than *a form of comparison* that produces and is produced by hierarchical metrics of value and evolving technologies of state control.

All this is to say that *Dura*'s pedagogical imperatives defamiliarize the referent of "race," so that its account of racialization is not centrally organized around cultural marginalization, but instead around a language of multiplicities, aggregates, and metrics—shifting forms of abstraction that both epistemically and materially organize social life, from colonial conquest to the contemporary commodification of immigrant labor. Unlike earlier texts, such as *Under Flag*, racial boundaries in *Dura* are defined not as much through symbols of cultural belonging as through the subdivision of colonial territories, the histories of imperial trade, and the bureaucratic enumeration of colonized or enslaved populations. The content of cultural representation here is denuded, reduced to what the text describes as "Number, form, proportion, situation" (M. M. Kim, *Dura* 73). A glance at its section headings—"Cosmography," "Measure," "Labors," "Chart," "Thirty and Five Books," and "Progress in Learning"—reveals the text's preoccupation with ways of measuring, ordering, and quantifying space, time, and bodies. Emergent systems of measurement facilitate the settler's colonial seizure and the spatial subdivision of an imagined map of the United States to impose the terms of political self-representation on populations both inside and outside the nation's expanding borders.

Even the book's title, *Dura*, implies a range of possible meanings that suggest the cognitive and spatial containers, borders, and boundaries that pattern and compartmentalize social life.[7] The title could be an abbreviation of *dura mater*, or the "dense, tough, outermost membranous envelope of the brain and spinal cord" ("Dura Mater, N.")—a border or protective boundary—or it could refer to what endures. What endures in Kim's text, I argue, is measure. If, as Kim explains in a 1997 interview, *Dura* is a "rereading of western civilization in a very coded way" (Morrison and Kim), the book is not simply full of indirect references to historical events. It is a book particularly preoccupied with the codification of knowledge and representing social relations as an aggregate of laws, regulations,

7 For an account of the mutually constitutive character of the rise of modern cartography and European colonial expansion see Mignolo; Schulten. See Mezzadra and Nielson for an account of how "the intertwining of geographical and cognitive borders" (28) has knitted together "the history of cartography and the history of capital" (28) over time.

principles, and numerical and linguistic sign systems. *Dura* explores how colonial accounting practices that undergird assessments of the properties of racial groups are systematically encoded into an emergent transnational circuitry of capitalist production and exchange, structuring everything from migrant labor flows to linguistic "contact zones" in late-twentieth-century Los Angeles.

Thus, Kim's formal strategies mimic the "recombinatory" segmentation and aggregation of standardized spatial, temporal, and monetary units of measure that trace the emergence of a kind of science of colonial management and the establishment of a shared metrological "language" for the nation. The poetry models the "recombinatory" power of language through repeated, permutable linguistic units—from words and phrases to typographical symbols and shapes. At times this reliance on combinatory textuality seems to play on the 1794 origin of the term *stereotype*. The term originally refers to the printing molds that facilitated the mass production of texts. "Borrowing the prefix from the Greek *stereos*—meaning solid, hard, or fixed—the term stereotype, by the 1820s, was beginning to evolve into a metaphor," Elizabeth and Stewart Ewen point out, "a common shorthand for 'the idea of unchangeability, of monotonous regularity and formalization' " (Ewen and Ewen 4). *Dura* exploits this double meaning of *stereotype* as a technical innovation in early printing and as a reference to mass produced racist imagery as a cognitive template subject to ongoing modification, rearrangement, and amalgamation:

> Propose: constant translation. Propose: the
> application of the compass to navigation. Propose: from
> a settlement, a capital grows. Propose: foray, expansion.
> Propose: as relates to an America. Propose: as relates
> to immigrant. Propose: knowledge becomes the parlance
> of the state. Propose: sound combinations. Propose:
> nameless days.
>
> (M. M. Kim, *Dura* 78)

Taken from the section "Thirty and Five Books" in *Dura*, this stanza offers a collection of seemingly modular sentences that could be rearranged without much difference in meaning. The call to "constant translation" (M. M. Kim, *Dura* 78) could refer to the difficulties of learning English for new immigrants, but also to the poem's heavy reliance upon puns and interest in the sonic echoes generated between languages. The phrase could describe the interpretive labor required to intuit connections between each proposition. Finally, when read in relation to the rest of the poem, this "constant translation" (M. M. Kim, *Dura* 78) suggests the "translation" of human activity into the economic idiom of labor and commerce.

"[A]s relates to immigrant" (M. M. Kim, *Dura* 78) the "constant translation" (M. M. Kim, *Dura* 78) required to learn the "sound combinations" (M. M. Kim, *Dura* 78) of a new language also exposes new language learners to cultural norms and national mythologies. For later immigrants the very knowability of "an America" is mediated not only through the English language but also through official histories and "the parlance of the state" (M. M. Kim, *Dura* 78). The long and short "o" sounds in "Propose" (M. M. Kim, *Dura* 78), "sound" (M. M. Kim, *Dura* 78), and "combinations" (M. M. Kim, *Dura* 78) begin to accrete an alternative order of sense-making tied to how sound might deflect the force of the passage's propositions. When read in relation to the rest of the poem, "nameless days" (M. M. Kim, *Dura* 78), here aligned sonically through the long "a" sounds in "nameless" and "days," potentially refers to the social anonymity of immigrants living in Los Angeles, the difficulties of acquiring the English language, and the uniformity imposed by standard units of time.

At first glance, these proposals, or propositions, don't seem to have much in common. But the fact that the statements are structured as imperatives emphasizes their formal equivalence. Similarly, the stanza's refusal to specify the languages, nations, settlements, capitals, communities, or states calls attention to the formal similarity of processes occurring at numerous sites and across historical epochs. The series of propositions could be read as a historical chronology that describes the spatial logic of settler colonialism. Together these historical propositions take on a cumulative, world-making force that brings the figure of "an America" (M. M. Kim, *Dura* 78) and "the state" (M. M. Kim, *Dura* 78) into being. This particularly dense passage models, in miniature, the historical panorama of the poem as a whole.

Yet if we do not assume that an immigrant subject is speaking in this passage, who is doing the proposing or being commanded to propose? "The subject is a proposition" (M. M. Kim, *Dura* 80), Kim writes later in the poem. In other words, the subject of the poem is the form of propositional logic itself—here a kind of colonial rationality that takes the form of a series of similar, "recombinatory" assertions. These statements seem to partition natural landscapes, urban spaces, and racially marked bodies into aggregates of enumerable units throughout the poem. The "foray" (M. M. Kim, *Dura* 78) and "expansion" (M. M. Kim, *Dura* 78) mentioned in the preceding stanza depend on the subordination of land and populations to the quantitative metrics of "Number, form, proportion, situation" (M. M. Kim, *Dura* 73). In the poem the enumeration of people, spaces, and things ultimately facilitates their commodification. In other words it enables the "constant translation" (M. M. Kim, *Dura* 73) of economic exchange.

The poet's interest in "geopolitical economies, cultural representations, [and] concepts of community" (M. M. Kim, *Commons* 110) reveals a structure of impersonal calculation and an extreme formalization of social relations that renders the particularity of lived experience largely unrepresentable. The exploration of these systems finds its most concentrated expression in the fifth section of *Dura*, "Thirty and Five Books." This portion of the text is particularly preoccupied with what Arjun Appadurai calls "colonial numerology" (Appadurai 121)—overlapping quantitative systems of measurement that have helped to produce and reproduce racial divisions over centuries. "Thirty and Five Books" establishes a deep structural relationship between textual segmentation and the spatial and economic quantification of human populations.

Scholarly accounts of Kim's writings often read the poetry's formal fragmentation as a record of traumatic historical violence and a reimagining of Asian diasporic subjects' existential dislocation as a kind of permanent unfitness for narrow nationalisms.[8] Although Kim's poetry makes space for what remains unassimilable or illegible about Asian immigrants' experiences in the United States, my reading of this work traces a different assimilationist trajectory that ends not with the preservation or repudiation of cultural otherness but instead with ideals of quantified economic citizenship. In *Dura*, *racial difference* is linked to the material production of an aggregative *racial sameness* within categories of identity shaped by divergent histories of enslavement, dispossession, and immigrant exclusion. Yet the very aggregative, serial form of these identities—described in the text as groups made up of substitutable bodies—also creates the iterative, exponential power of exchange, competition, and conflict across great distances and deep social divisions. Kim imagines what critic Lisa Lowe calls the "heterogeneity, hybridity, and multiplicity" (Lowe 509) of Asian American panethnic identity in the blank spaces of the colonial archive and a language of weights, measures, cartographic grids, and numismatics. In a body of poetry so often read in terms of the incommensurability of languages, cultures, and identities, the pervasive language of counting and accounting poses an interesting problem for critical interpretation. Departing from previous readings of Kim's writing, which emphasize the unrepresentability of cultural particularity or historical trauma, I argue that what exceeds representation in *Dura* is the inverted form of an abstract equivalence implied by systems of measurement—an aspect

[8] See for example Jean Uhm, Zhou Xiaojing, Laura Hyun Yi Kang, Joseph Jonghyun Jeon, and Jeannie Chiu.

of the poet's work that so far has generated little critical commentary. Kim's fluid diasporic subjects often appear in the poetry as bearing the marks of colonial accounting and the capitalist commodification of labor.

All this is to say that my reading of Kim's poetry tracks how the work complicates reading its formal strategies primarily as resistance to cultural assimilation rather than how the organization of social life through number and measure might transform our sense not only of racial subjects but also of the scale and impact of collective activity. Populations are racialized in *Dura* by being brought into spatial proximity through expropriation, enslavement, and economic competition and exchange. Instead of being directly racially identified in the poem, racialized populations are represented as bodies crowded in the holds of slave ships, massed at the borders of nations, dispersed through global networks of low-wage work, or forming mobile crowds in ruptural moments of urban unrest. The poem's formal fragmentation—the blank spaces, line breaks, and caesuras that punctuate the text—suggests both entrenched racial divisions and the utopian "recombinatory" possibilities of coordinated activity latent within an atomized yet nevertheless materially interdependent social order.[9]

It is unsurprising then that much of the poem describes the vanishing point of settler colonial frontiers. The language of legal contracts, currency, labor, and property circulates through this seemingly uninhabited space, marking the internal and external boundaries of race and nation. In the following stanzas, for example, justifications for colonial expansion are continuous with the logic of economic calculation:

> The dog will not eat the acorns assiduously placed in
> the dented bowl. Disguised as good will.
>
> Denomination. Promissory. Venture. Amass.
>
> In so locating a time of geography before the compass.
> Do not ask again where are we.
>
> Ones on the other side. Shaking sticks with strips of
> white rags tied at the top.
>
> Population gathered to population. More uninhabited
> space in America than elsewhere. Is that accurate.

[9] Lynn Keller has described Kim's modular arrangements of language as a "poetics of the aggregate" (Keller 156) in which repeated particles of language, from sounds to phrases, accumulate into larger formal structures that the poet often likens to geological strata.

> Riders wielding tall sticks with strips of white linen
> attached to them. Is that accurate.
>
> (M. M. Kim, *Dura* 163)

Like the previously quoted passage consisting of propositions, these stanzas display a sparseness and fragmentation of syntax, with the relationship between statements left ambiguous. Zhou Xiaojing (Zhou) offers an insightful reading of the possible historical references suggested by the lines—from stereotypes of colonized Korean or Chinese subjects as dogs to images of surrender evoking the July 27, 1953, armistice ending the Korean War. I focus instead on how what appears to be colonial "America" is in this passage defined primarily by a colonial frontier and by the racial and ethnic boundaries created through "Population gathered to population" (M. M. Kim, *Dura* 63). "America" here is characterized as seemingly "uninhabited space" (M. M. Kim, *Dura* 63) and by what the poem later calls the "Verities of seams and harbors" (M. M. Kim, *Dura* 77)—nodes within a network of global commodity exchange and an emergent global African slave trade.

In other words, the external borders and internal divisions of "America" in the poem are contested epistemological terrain, where inhabitants are made to submit to colonial measure or disappear. In these lines, America is represented as "uninhabited space," echoing the legal doctrine of *terra nullius* used to justify Native American genocide and national narratives of Manifest Destiny. What remains are not the proper names of racial or ethnic groups but instead a kind of colonial numerology. The poem's repeated references to "Number, form, proportion, situation" (M. M. Kim, *Dura* 79) invoke what Arjun Appadurai calls "the idea of number as an instrument of colonial control" (Appadurai 117):

> [C]olonial body counts create not only types and classes (the first move toward domesticating differences) but also homogeneous bodies (within categories) because number, by its nature, flattens idiosyncrasies and creates boundaries around these homogeneous bodies as it performatively limits their extent. In this regard, statistics are to bodies and social types what maps are to territories: they flatten and enclose. Therefore, the link between colonialism and orientalism is most strongly reinforced not at the loci of classification and typification (as has often been suggested) but at the loci of enumeration, where bodies are counted, homogenized, and bounded in their extent. Thus, the unruly body of the colonial subject (fasting, feasting, hook swinging, abluting, burning, and bleeding) is recuperated through the language of numbers that allows these very bodies to be brought back, now counted and accounted, for the humdrum projects of taxation, sanitation, education, warfare, and loyalty.
>
> (Appadurai 133)

In the poem, these "colonial body counts" echo later fragments of nightly news reports or police scanner broadcasts that seem to describe attempts by the police and military to contain the 1992 Los Angeles riots and commentators trying to explain the sources of the upheaval.

In describing "a time of geography before the compass" (M. M. Kim, *Dura* 63), the poem suggests, through the eye rhyme of "compass" and "amass," for example, a relationship between colonial wars and the Atlantic slave trade, a network that Paul Gilroy calls the "intercultural and transnational formation" (Gilroy ix) of the Black Atlantic, in which neither phenomenon is reducible to the other. The line "Denomination. Promissory. Venture. Amass" (M. M. Kim, *Dura* 63), itself couched in the form of a list, describes overlapping systems of measurement that organize colonial plunder and Black chattel slavery. The four-item list features repeated vowel and consonant sounds—the short "e" in "Denomination" and "Venture" paralleling the sibilance of "ss" in "Promissory" and "Amass." The named items and processes are interconnected both through a sonic patterning of items that might refer to religious groups, money, contracts, imperial trade, or the enclosure and parcelization of Native American lands.

In other words, it is difficult to tell if the lines are describing the movement of human bodies or the circulation of commodities—likely both. As Orlando Patterson reminds us, slaves were not only defined as "socially dead" persons but also were "the closest approximation to modern multifunctional money" (Patterson 167–8) in the ancient world. Thus the imperative "Do not ask again where are we" (M. M. Kim, *Dura* 63) functions as a refrain throughout the poem. The command closes the couplet "In so locating a time of geography before the compass. Do not ask again where are we" (M. M. Kim, *Dura* 63), and suggests a time before early navigational instruments such as the compass could radically expand and regularize global travel and trade by sea. This command to "not ask again where are we" (M. M. Kim, *Dura* 63) could also describe the transportation of human slaves unable to locate themselves in "a time of geography before the compass" (M. M. Kim, *Dura* 63) because they were chained in cargo holds, struggling to survive the Middle Passage between Africa, the Americas, and the Caribbean.

The previously quoted list moves from basic elements of human market activity, from the establishment of money as a universal equivalent or standard of value, to two terms, "Venture" and "Amass," which could also be read as colonial imperatives that transformed processes of enslavement, territorial expropriation, and colonial trade into the material basis of European industrial capitalist development. The poem's scattered allusions to slave labor, colonial frontiers, and the development of modern industrial capitalism maintain the mutually reinforcing spatial dynamics of these historical phenomena without positing a causal relationship between them. As Cedric Robinson explains, "From the fifteenth century on, that colonialism would encompass the lands of Asian, African, and New World peoples and engulf a substantial fraction of those peoples into the European traditions of slave labor and exploitation" (Robinson 98):

> First, African workers had been transmuted by the perverted canons of mercantile capitalism into property. Then, African labor power as slave labor was integrated into the organic composition of nineteenth-century manufacturing and industrial capitalism, thus sustaining the emergence of an extra-European world market within which the accumulation of capital was garnered for the further development of industrial production.
>
> (Robinson 112–13)

In the poem's representation of what appears to be the transition from European colonial expansion to industrial capitalism, colonial numerology is transformed into economic rationality. *Dura* thus comes to register how racial identity is rendered intelligible through what historian Walter Johnson calls an "emergent grid of settlement" (Johnson 39) that both made expropriated Native American lands "measurable, manageable, and salable" (Johnson 212) and "provided slaveholders (and their 'overseers') with a visual grid they could use to measure their slaves' labor" (Johnson 166).

Shifting from the colonial past to contemporary Los Angeles, interracial contact and conflict take on the aggregative form of "Population gathered to population" (M. M. Kim, *Dura* 63), except this time it is plotted within an urban spatial grid. The poem describes the 1992 Los Angeles riots in the aftermath of the acquittal of four Los Angeles Police Department officers for their videotaped beating of Black motorist Rodney King, in terms of the destruction and redrawing of spatial boundaries "Distended beyond assembly and parts" (M. M. Kim, *Dura* 55)—a possible reference to varieties of factory labor bringing communities together but also a system of global economic competition that "First assembled fire" (M. M. Kim, *Dura* 55). Proximity here is both a requirement of labor and a precondition of racial conflict. In the poem, the flames of the riots seem to fill the spaces between communities brought into contact through transnational labor migration. "What is nearest," Kim writes of the explosive results, "is destroyed" (M. M. Kim, *Dura* 67).

The speed at which the unrest spreads through urban space is likened to the speed of the circulation of money. Midway through the poem are percussive bursts of what sound like news reports of urban unrest, with allusions to coins that bear the residual marks of imperial authority:

> Litigious grounds. News a supreme pose.
>
> Riotous constitutes a fast designation.
>
> Fettered intention. Penalty teeming.
>
> Let a daughter be named perception: her name is economy.
>
> Coins imprinted with kings' and emperors' faces.
>
> (M. M. Kim, *Dura* 70)

The first part of this passage includes a series of mordant puns about what may be the "Litigious grounds" (M. M. Kim, *Dura* 70) of ensuing legal battles over restitution for property damaged during the riots; the "supreme pose," or ideologically distorted media framing of the unfolding events; and the "Fettered intention" (M. M. Kim, *Dura* 70) of looming mass arrests. The pun of teem/team in "Penalty teeming" (M. M. Kim, *Dura* 70) translates interracial antagonism through the idiom of competitive sports, suggesting both the unpredictable behavior of crowds and a framing of Black–Korean conflict as "Players in the field of manipulation" (M. M. Kim, *Dura* 69). The line "Riotous constitutes a fast designation" (M. M. Kim, *Dura* 70) puns on the parallel between a journalistic description of crowds and the speed at which the riots spread. The field of racial conflict and the dynamics of racial comparison are here structured by a manic competition and an economic rationality in which money as a form of measure deepens racial divisions and reproduces older varieties of despotic authority.

After six days, the riots resulted in 52 deaths, 2,500 injuries, 6,500 people arrested for riot-related crimes, and estimates of more than half a billion dollars in property damage.[10] As numerous accounts of the shifting demographics of South Central Los Angeles have noted, the core of the city was rapidly remade in the 1980s and 1990s by an influx of Latino and Asian American immigrants. As George J. Sanchez points out, "Latinos were the single largest ethnic group arrested during the period of the riots, not only for curfew violations and undocumented status, but also as looters of their local Korean merchants" (Sanchez 1018). "Riotous" (M. M. Kim, *Dura* 70), the subject of the previously

[10] Over half of those arrested for riot-related crimes were Latinos, a fact which Kim's poem seems to register in the line, "A third part of them are by no means/acknowledged" (M. M. Kim, *Dura* 66).

quoted sentence, is an attribute of persons, and a "fast designation" is used to pathologize Black responses to police violence and justify extreme forms of state and federal intervention. In the case of the 1992 riots, 4,000 National Guard soldiers were deployed to enforce an area curfew and to control crowds while federal agencies used the opportunity to deport individuals they said were undocumented immigrants.

The poem's snippets of reportage about the riots give way to language that seems to refer to a far earlier historical moment in which gender is subject to economic quantification: "Let a daughter be named perception: her name is economy. / Coins imprinted with kings' and emperors' faces" (M. M. Kim, *Dura* 70)—a ritual invocation that could be an updated version of the practice of calling upon muses in classical Greek poetry. The lines suggest that what is perceptible about this muse-like figure is the "economy," in which identities are rendered commensurable by male imperial authority. This line from Kim's poem also recalls the nine sections, each named after a Greek muse, of Theresa Cha's *Dictee*—a book and an author whom Kim acknowledges as an important influence on her work. In this couplet, the poem's concern with both epistemology and political economy suggests the poet's persistent interest in the "Feminization of poverty" (M. M. Kim, *Commons* 108), particularly in the global South, and in patriarchal social relations that render women equivalent, exchangeable, and analogous to currency.

The image of "Coins imprinted with kings' and emperors' faces" (M. M. Kim, *Dura* 70) is particularly striking for its numismatic linking of mimesis and equivalence, language and the money-form. Here, the coin as a container or signifier of value is backed by the authority of the face of the king or emperor, which functions as a kind of "referent," guaranteeing that value.[11] Additionally, these two lines acknowledge that the poem's formal permutations—in which units of text (often one- to three-word phrases) repeat, recombine, and migrate—mimic monetary circulation or the expansion of imperial trade networks. In the poem, linguistic sounds and the circulation of money seem governed by a similar recursive, self-expanding logic. So when the poem quotes a few lines from the nursery rhyme "Sing a Song of Sixpence," "The king is in / the counting house counting his money" (M. M. Kim, *Dura* 71), the repetition of "counting," echoing through the assonance of "house," mimics the strangely self-reflexive activity of the king, who is producing monetary value through accounting. In

[11] For more on the relationship between mimesis and numismatics see Jean-Joseph Goux.

other words the counting-house, in Kim's recontextualization of a line from an eighteenth-century nursery rhyme, is also a place where the king might be tallying images of his face:

> Antipathy. Gravity of action. Record that.
>
> Ranting rout. Evening bicycle rides display card players
> in windows who appear to be passing peanuts.
> Intercession of long avenues.
>
> Express the value of A over B. Dominant relation as
> that of owners of commodities.
>
> In plural. Numerous and countable. The king is in
> the counting house counting his money.
>
> Scale decimated. Columns engineered with kindling.
>
> (M. M. Kim, *Dura* 71)

The logic of the "numerous" and the "countable" animates the imperative to "Record that" (M. M. Kim, *Dura* 71), which might refer to George Holliday's widely circulated video of the Rodney King beating, a piece of evidence that helped bring to trial four officers from the Los Angeles Police Department. The poem's clipped references to state violence and social upheaval reverberate through racially and economically segregated urban space. Here the "intercession of long avenues" (M. M. Kim, *Dura* 71), "the value of A over B" (M. M. Kim, *Dura* 71), and "columns" (M. M. Kim, *Dura* 71) are all instances of what the passage characterizes as "plural" (M. M. Kim, *Dura* 71). The poem also begins to reveal how seemingly interchangeable, contiguous bodies resemble both "Moveable type" (M. M. Kim, *Dura* 56) and commodities: "Deployments to the assigned parallel" (M. M. Kim, *Dura* 54); "Ascension, declination, and distance of the measured body" (M. M. Kim, *Dura* 54); "first arrivals in rows and columns" (M. M. Kim, *Dura* 54); "Thirty sons who will domain. House by which houses will stand" (M. M. Kim, *Dura* 59); "Primitive tabulation of need" (M. M. Kim, *Dura* 60); "Distended beyond assembly and parts" (M. M. Kim, *Dura* 61); "Moving from twelve to counting on the ten fingers" (M. M. Kim, *Dura* 61); "Names of capitals. Names of cities" (M. M. Kim, *Dura* 62); "Population gathered to population" (M. M. Kim, *Dura* 63); "Assembly in tiers" (M. M. Kim, *Dura* 66); "Hordes" (M. M. Kim, *Dura* 67); "Players in the field of manipulation" (M. M. Kim, *Dura* 69); "To each note a number of officers, specially appointed, not only subscribe their names, but affix their seals" (M. M. Kim, *Dura* 72); "*pieces prices*" (M. M. Kim, *Dura* 73); "Vibrations per second" (M. M. Kim, *Dura* 75); "The fourth coordinate is any measure of time" (M. M. Kim, *Dura* 76); "Propose: sound combinations" (M. M. Kim, *Dura* 78); "Propose: nameless days" (M. M. Kim, *Dura* 78); "Time whose points are events" (M. M. Kim, *Dura* 79); "A million marching in the streets" (M. M. Kim, *Dura* 80); "Four roads meeting precisely as a grid" (M. M. Kim, *Dura* 80); "Effusion of ligatures" (M. M. Kim, *Dura* 82).

To return to the question of value in the poem, the lines that mention "the value of A over B. Dominant relation as / that of owners of commodities" (M. M. Kim, *Dura* 71) invoke the language of classical political economy. Echoing the language of "The Fetishism of the Commodity and Its Secret" (Marx 163), an early section of the first volume of Karl Marx's *Capital*, the lines provide a compressed description of hierarchical social relations nevertheless grounded in the apparent symmetricalness of a commodity exchange. For Marx, the commodity form conceals the fact that social relations between private individuals are mediated entirely through markets that render radically different objects and labor processes commensurable and calculable. According to Marx, the formal equality bestowed by the market upon individual subjects assumes their substantive inequality, flattening social difference while at the same time reconstituting social relations within hierarchies of economic value. Thus, sociality mediated through the commodity form becomes increasingly "thinglike," and commodities appear to relate to each other independent of human agency. "It is nothing but the definite social relation between men themselves which assumes here, for them, the fantastic form of a relation between things" (Marx 165–6), as Marx famously observes.

Although Kim's poem may deploy the language of political economy, the value of "A over B" (M. M. Kim, *Dura* 71) redefines exchange value to emphasize and "express" not simply the difference in value between two commodities but the "Dominant relation" of the market itself. The question of value here highlights how the terrain where racial conflict unfolds is mediated not only by the seeming reciprocity of commodity exchange—where what is "plural," "numerous," and "countable" refers to both bodies and money—but also by deep economic disparities.

After the previously quoted stanzas, which invoke the seeming interchangeability of "owners of commodities," the poem shifts backward in time to what appears to be the ancient Greek or Roman world: "Scale decimated. Columns engineered with kindling" (M. M. Kim, *Dura* 71). Again the poem returns to systems and instruments of measure, a scale in this case, and a serial architectural object, columns. "Columns engineered with kindling" might refer to classical Greek and Roman architecture, as well as to property destruction during the 1992 riots. "Scale" refers, of course, to a machine used for weighing items, as well as to an allegorical symbol of justice, and potentially to an implement the king uses in the poem when "in the counting house counting his money" (M. M. Kim, *Dura* 71) to ensure the authenticity of precious metals. "Scale" could also refer to proportion, degree, or even a series of sounds or tones that make up a musical octave. The poem is keenly aware of the latent etymological resonances between terms, such as "scale" and "decimated," in which the former suggests systems of measurement in general. At the same time, the latter's origins lie in a Latin root—*"decimā-re*: to take the tenth" ("Decimate, V.")—which could refer to either taxation or military execution by measured lots. Of course, "decimate" more commonly refers to the destruction or removal of 10 percent of a population. The ambiguous syntactical combination of these two terms, "Scale decimated," implies that the very social ground of comparability is both violently "engineered" and self-consuming.

Shifting suddenly backward in time, the poem's interest in the language of political economy also informs its reconstruction of early colonial American history and its interest in representing this period as a prehistory of contemporary racial conflict. In the following passage, the incommensurable, but nevertheless materially interconnected, histories of Black chattel slaves, European colonizers, indigenous populations deprived of the right of "possession" (M. M. Kim, *Dura* 67), and voluntary and involuntary migrants from Asia are inserted into a system of enforced competition that structures subsequent forms of Black–Asian interracial conflict:

> Make the surface plain.
>
> Hordes. Sides. One fish bowl and several shutting gates.
> None to receive action or to specify possession.
> Nations. Sty and pigpie.
> Natural motion of fire to move in a straight line.
> ____________ arrived in America. Bare to trouble and
> foresworn. Aliens aboard three ships off the coast.
> ____________ and ____________ clash. Police move in.
> What is nearest is destroyed.
>
> (M. M. Kim, *Dura* 67)

In this dense passage, the pun of making a "surface plain" signals how this version of national history has reproduced racial divisions as a set of antagonistic structural positions. Subsequently, these groups are organized into "hordes" or "sides" in contention—terms that also echo the media's racial framing of the Los Angeles riots. Of course, the word "hordes" has a long history as a stereotypical description of Asian immigrants as alternately a "yellow peril" and a "model minority."[12] The image of "One fish bowl and several shutting gates" (M. M. Kim, *Dura* 67) anticipates the penultimate stanza in this passage but also offers ways of conceiving of the spatial form of the nation as both a container and a fortress-like enclosure with a notorious history of anti-Asian immigration laws and legal barriers to citizenship. It is perhaps in reference to how these immigrant populations have often been figured in the public imagination as bestial, immoral, and carriers of disease that the poem offers the line, "Nations. Sty and pigpie" (M. M. Kim, *Dura* 67). Here the poem highlights how nation-building projects have been realized through repeated denials of the formal protections of full citizenship to a succession of seemingly interchangeable racialized populations who cannot "receive action or specify possession" (M. M. Kim, *Dura* 67)—a description of the poem's often cryptic concision, which frequently provides no grammatical object to "receive action" and no grammatical subject to "specify possession" (M. M. Kim, *Dura* 67).

The conclusion of this passage engages directly with the question of how "tables of distance and direction of the / principal portion of the inhabited world" (M. M. Kim, *Dura* 81) are at the same time maps of the core and periphery of a world-system defined by colonial conquest. The poem's repeated interest in the figures of sailing ships and oceanic navigation transporting anonymous human cargo situates these sections of the poem in the era of the Atlantic slave trade. In Kim's poem, ships appear to function as a figure for parataxis itself, joining otherwise discrete locations, histories, or peoples. Possibly referring to the Atlantic slave trade, Asian immigration across the Pacific Ocean or Portuguese colonialists described not as "discoverers" of America in 1492 but instead as "Aliens aboard three ships off the coast" (M. M. Kim, *Dura* 67), the underlined blank lines in the second-to-last stanza of the passage present a structural template. The first blank line could designate "Aliens aboard three ships off the coast," but are these "Aliens" slaves or immigrants, crew members or human cargo? Who is "Bare to trouble and foresworn" (M. M. Kim, *Dura* 67)—the nakedness of transported slaves or the immigrants who must foreswear allegiance to other nations before

[12] For more on the history of these stereotypes, particularly in relation to Janus-faced representations of Asian Americans as both model citizens and unassimilable aliens in media, film, journalism, and literature, see R. J. Lee.

becoming naturalized citizens? As a possible allusion to the bloody conflict between armed Korean American shopkeepers and Black and Latino looters during the Los Angeles riots, "____________ and ____________ clash. Police move in" (M. M. Kim, *Dura* 67) reads as a dispassionate account not of the cultural specificity of these groups but of the social forms and imperatives that position these groups in antagonistic relation to each other.

The passage also raises many urgent political questions about how such radically dissimilar communities and histories are increasingly rendered commensurable within a grid of intelligibility established by state and capital.[13] By "commensurable," I mean that the poem interrogates how populations are not simply made equivalent but have had political, economic, and spatial segmentation render them particularly exploitable, expendable, and vulnerable to state violence within a regime of racial capitalism. By representing commensurability in terms of colonial measure and as a medium of conflict, Kim's poem deviates from scholarly narratives of the riots, which have been increasingly criticized for rendering Black–Asian conflict as symmetrical and for assuming an antiracist coalitional politics that continues to reproduce anti-Black racism as its fundamental condition of possibility.[14] Critics such as Jared Sexton interrogate the implicit anti-Black racism of what Tamara Nopper calls the "abandonment narrative" advanced by Asian American activists, scholars, and literary authors who stress the lack of state or federal protection for Korean American communities during the riots.[15] According to Sexton, accounts of the riots offered by scholars of Asian American history tend to "gloss over discrepant histories, minimize inequalities born of divergent structural positions, and disavow the historical centrality and uniqueness of anti-blackness for the operations of 'global white supremacy' " (Sexton 90). This critique of particular accounts of the riots pinpoints these themes—questions of cultural (in)commensurability, racial and class hierarchies, and the regulation of social life through systems of measure—that we have been exploring in close readings of passages from Kim's poem.

A basic political ambiguity marks the poet's ventriloquism in speaking the language of state power. The poem does not focus on a narrative of state

[13] For two early influential theorizations of the precise relationship between Black chattel slavery and the dynamics of capitalist accumulation, see Williams; Du Bois. For more recent scholarship on the question of whether Black chattel slavery could be properly characterized as capitalist or non-capitalist, see Banaji; Rosenthal; Acemoglu and Wolitzky.

[14] See for example Wilderson, *Red, White & Black: Cinema and the Structure of U.S. Antagonisms*; Wilderson, "The Prison Slave as Hegemony's (Silent) Scandal".

[15] See Sexton; Nopper.

abandonment so much as explore the "measure" of racial comparison and how such "knowledge becomes the parlance / of the state" (M. M. Kim, *Dura* 78). In the poem, these racial metrics seem to recede into a naturalized background condition of possibility for the formation of racist attitudes, ideologies, or stereotypes. Here the proximity required by economic exchange, materially binding together populations across distance and difference, does not produce reciprocity but instead highly uneven economic geographies of disinvestment and competitive accumulation. Acknowledging the economic impact of Korean American businesses on inner-city communities, the poem describes "Not the return of money but its continued removal further / and further from its starting point" (M. M. Kim, *Dura* 72). The languages of economics, athletic competition, and political contests overlap and suggest how both socially sanctioned and unsanctioned forms of conflict mimic the "Traverse of operations" (M. M. Kim, *Dura* 69) of police and military actions. The poem provides a frequently bleak depiction of social life as thoroughly captured and conditioned by both economic competition and state power. Here racial comparison is decidedly not synonymous with coalitionist political ideals.

Yet the measure of race is also a condition of political possibility. Black, Korean, and Latino communities in conflict become "Players in the field of manipulation" (M. M. Kim, *Dura* 69), "Complete with motives" (M. M. Kim, *Dura* 66) of "Jobs. No Jobs" (M. M. Kim, *Dura* 66), whose "Bodies in propulsion" (M. M. Kim, *Dura* 66) in the following set of stanzas are packed together and tightly regimented by the physical choreography of low-wage service sector labor in South Central Los Angeles:

> Stamped by purse. Bone soldered. Labor open.
>
> Light and propagation. That stolen. Torment a sum
> of *pieces prices*.
>
> Bodies in propulsion. Guatemalan, Korean, African-American
> sixteen year olds working check-out lanes. Hard and noisy
> enunciation.
>
> A banter English gathers carriers.
> What is nearest is destroyed.
>
> (M. M. Kim, *Dura* 73)

The passage makes the bodies of "Guatemalan, Korean, African-American / sixteen year olds working check-out lanes" (M. M. Kim, *Dura* 73) difficult to distinguish from the commodities they handle and for which they "Torment a sum / of *pieces prices*" (M. M. Kim, *Dura* 73). Two pages later the poem describes "Repugnant items shelved and tagged" (M. M. Kim, *Dura* 75). These lines imply that, like commodities, entire communities have been "shelved and tagged," or geographically isolated and contained within an urban core subject to cycles of white flight and financial disinvestment.

But "Bodies in propulsion" could also describe the "Hard and noisy / enunciation" (M. M. Kim, *Dura* 73) of a pidgin English emerging from a chaotic, interracial linguistic contact zone created by low-wage service jobs and shifting patterns of global migration toward new centers of capital accumulation. The term "banter English" (M. M. Kim, *Dura* 73) doesn't describe a collective identity so much as the multiplicative power of coordinated activity emerging from the rhythms of commercial transactions and the racially restricted circulation of bodies across national borders. Here language is no longer simply a vehicle of individual expression, or a "carrier" of preexisting semantic content, but instead made and remade in the spaces between racialized populations "gathered" to the global North. By deforming the rhetoric of US racial panics around contagion, cultural pathology, and economic parasitism, Kim shifts the focus of *Dura* from a "poetics of identity" (LoLordo 11) to an exploration of what cultural meaning can be made out of the reticular networks of labor and exchange ceaselessly bringing populations together and splitting them apart.[16]

[16] While I agree with Margaret Ronda's observation that "Kim's central subject is the global multitude" (250) geographically dispersed and seemingly united only by "various forms of lack: illness, hunger, debt, pain, geographical displacement" (250), *Dura* repeatedly reminds its readers how histories of racialization fissure rather than unify this global collective subject *in potentia*. Recent attempts to theorize the lineaments of a global "multitude," by Michael Hardt and Antonio Negri (Hardt and Negri) in particular, remains, as Ronda points out, a "a deeply controversial and much-critiqued term" (250). The historical emergence of competitive accumulation and the capitalist value-form that I have been tracking over the course of Kim's poem both forms recombinatory networks of otherwise atomized individuals in antagonistic competition—a "grammar" of group formation that seems to structure a range of social phenomena that drive and reconfigure processes of racial and ethnic boundary formation in *Dura*—from riots to settler colonial expansion.

4

"In the Hollow Parts of Anything That Moves": Containing Asiatic Racial Form in Larissa Lai's "nascent fashion"

As contemporary scholars of migration and citizenship consistently argue, commodities and information move much more freely across transnational space than migrant populations. What scholars earlier called "runaway factories" (Safa 418), capable of relocating to different regions of the world in pursuit of lower labor costs, have been transformed over time into logistically managed global "supply chains" of spatially dispersed capitalist manufacturing.[1] Chinese Canadian poet Larissa Lai's 2009 poem "nascent fashion," part of a collection of poems entitled *Automaton Biographies*, maps this new geography of global production that both structures an evolving racial and gendered division of labor and depends upon transportation infrastructures historically developed to wage war. The title, "nascent fashion," suggests an emerging global sweatshop system of apparel manufacturing but also possibilities of materially interlinked capacities for coordinated action. The poem radically reimagines the terrain of a twenty-first-century anti-imperialist politics that might cut across complex histories of inter-imperialist rivalry, discrepant forms of racialization, and ideals of competitive national development.

In this chapter, I read "nascent fashion," alongside the poem "Rachel" from the same 2009 collection, as works that dramatize the increasing participation of women within this spatially distributed form of production through repeated images of androids, or of a half-human, half-machine "factory girl" (Lai 52). This new map of global labor shapes what Melissa Wright calls the "myth of the disposable third world woman worker" (Wright 2) inserted into low-wage, dangerous, and repetitive assembly-line work.[2] For Lai, this collective figure

1 On the phenomenon of "runaway" factories, see Safa.

2 Poets Rosa Alcalá and Daniel Borzutzky have similarly explored how this figure of the "disposable third world woman worker" (Wright 2) has been constructed as a simultaneously a singular and plural capitalist subject in mainstream US political discourse. See Alcalá's "Dear Maria" (Alcala 18–20) and Borzutzky.

does invoke not only the experiences of specific women navigating changing twenty-first-century labor regimes but combinatory networks of such workers who make up a transnational collective body continually made and remade by short-term labor contracts.

"nascent fashion" connects the creation of this networked figure to the invention of the standardized shipping container as a technology of both imperial warfare and international trade. The figure of the hypermobile shipping container facilitates the spatial containment of pools of "surplus" global labor whose intensity is governed by the rhythms of capitalist circulation across national boundaries "with migration flows frequently tracking (in reverse) the paths of earlier colonization" (Ferguson and McNally 5). At the same time, consumer products and the women who assemble them are represented in the poem as "containers" of labor power compelled to travel along the same pathways toward global centers of capital accumulation. In the poem, the intermodal container becomes a perverse metaphor for both the production of capitalist subjects and an aspirational symbol of free movement across a world where national borders are porous to commodities and impermeable to people.

Such technologies connect sites of consumption with distant export-oriented production zones—from maquiladoras in northern Mexico and factories in Vietnam to export-oriented "special economic zones" in China.[3] For Lai, such channels bear the historical imprint of earlier imperial supply chains, facilitating the spatial expansion of capitalism as "an integrated, if radically inconsistent, total system," in the words of Ruth Jennison and Julien Murphet, "stretched across and embedded within a vast, planetary matrix of institutions, states, supply chains, corporations, regulatory bodies, armies, police forces, and the brains and sinews of billions of laboring bodies" (Jennison and Murphet 18–19).

When read against the rest of the poem, the title suggests an emerging global system of apparel manufacturing but also materially interlinked capacities for coordinated action that exceed the "container" of the nation. The poet repeatedly links the emergence of labor pools to both military transportation infrastructure and the "mass racial graves" (Lai 58) left in the wake of twentieth- and twenty-first-century imperial wars. Contemporary "war and trade are both animated

[3] For an account of how the mass entry of *dagongmei*, or "working girls," into factories "correlates with global capital's rapidly rising demand for young, single female workers, evident in the special economic zones" (Schling 53), see Schling, P. Ngai.

by the supply chain," geographer Deborah Cowen writes. Further, "they are organized by it and take its form" (Cowen 1):

> At stake is not simply the privatization of warfare or the militarization of corporate supply chains. With logistics comes new kinds of crises, new paradigms of security, new uses of law, new logics of killing, and a new map of the world. For many, *logistics* may only register as a word on the side of the trucks that magically bring online orders only hours after purchase or that circulate incessantly to and from big-box stores at local power centers. The entire network of infrastructures, technologies, spaces, workers, and violence that makes the circulation of stuff possible remains tucked out of sight for those who engage with logistics only as consumers. Yet, alongside billions of commodities, the management of global supply chains imports elaborate transactions into the socius—transactions that are political, financial, legal, and often martial.
>
> (Cowen 1)

Lai's poem explores the "logistics space" (Cowen 219) of global commodity circulation that not only assembles and reassembles dispersed subjects of global labor but constitutes a mechanism of racial ordering that internally fractures Asian diasporic populations in particular.

The recurring references throughout the poems to bounded spaces and aggregative networks highlight a range of portable social forms or principles of social organization that help readers imagine racialization as part of a boundary formation process that doesn't only separate but connects populations.[4] Containers don't just enclose and immobilize in Lai's poem; they also enable and compel movement. Considered as social forms, the extendability of networks is often presented as a threat to rigid boundaries and borders, and to fantasies of nations as racially or ethnically homogeneous organic wholes. In the logistical space that the poem traverses, containerization is represented as a mostly invisible material infrastructure of racialization inseparable from capitalist exploitation.

The poem's turn toward containment, commodification, and capitalist circulation radically resituates existing theories of Asian racialization grounded in experiences of loss or unassimilable cultural particularity. Absorbed by an image of luxury goods in a magazine advertisement, the speaker of "nascent

4 While I reference boundary formation processes loosely here, my reading of Lai's poem is broadly indebted to contemporary sociological theories of racial and ethnic boundary formation. See Barth; Wimmer.

fashion" initially finds themselves caught in what Anne Cheng calls a "melancholic structure of identification" (Cheng 179) with an unattainable whiteness—a "white/girl in the white dress so pure" (Lai 52). Instead of introjecting whiteness as a lost object, however, the poem draws attention to how the products featured in this advertising tableau allow consumers, including the speaker themselves, to command the laboring activity of a collective "factory girl."

Reflected in the figure of a "dark" girl sutured together by renegotiable labor contracts, the speaker is forced into a troubled recognition of herself as a split diasporic racial subject of consumption and production. Tracing the objects featured in the advertisement back to the sites of their production, the poem begins to map a spatially dispersed group of women workers connected by the fact that they have all been injured in industrial accidents:

the factory girl who pinches
the girl who cries who pricks her finger
who strains her eyes
the girl with chemical burns
the girl who suffocated
the girl with the severed hand

the girl i want
not this dark

the white bed in the glossy
advertisement i saw and the white
girl in the white dress so pure
i wanted
not this ghost

a girl to do
what i say

not me

(Lai 52)

Here the speaker's dream of racial assimilation is premised upon a disavowal of the labor of a serial subject of global manufacturing vulnerable to increasingly calamitous workplace injuries. It is a subject that appears within the advertisement as a kind of "ghost" of abstract labor haunting an arrangement of luxury goods and hovering over the promise of an unattainable whiteness somehow available for purchase.

Proceeding beyond the frame of this structure of impossible racial identification, however, the poem maps a complex and evolving racial and gendered global division of labor made possible by global supply chains that carry and conduct "labour's liquid longing" (Lai 63). The remainder of the poem investigates processes of enclosure that both subdivide and integrate this new map of the world—from the commodity form as a container "whose arbitrary content/leaves labour power raw" (Lai 65), to nations as captive labor pools, to securitized transnational commodity flows. Even racial and gender distinctions are represented in the poem as conceptual containers that are continually remade by ongoing histories of imperial violence, international trade relations, and competitive national economic development.

For the speaker, this expansively recontextualized scene of consumption reveals an imperial history and diasporic trajectory in need of dereification rather than mourning. Echoing Cha's "photo-essay," "nascent fashion" reverses the arc of Asian immigrant assimilation from absorption into a national body to a shared desire to escape capitalist imperatives that reproduce hierarchical racial differentiation and abstract exchangeability as functions of each other.

Automaton Biographies

Author of three books of speculative fiction and three collections of poems, one co-authored with Asian Canadian poet Rita Wong, Lai has published several works that explore the boundaries between human, animal, and machine bodies. Whether imagining an ancient fox spirit possessing women's bodies across centuries or the dispassionate confessions of androids molded by the violence of human desires and fears, the protagonists of Lai's books are cyborgs, shape-shifting goddesses, and even a half-carp, half-human clone. Drawing inspiration from the writings of Donna Harraway on gendered cyborgs, Lai's depiction of multispecies or machine/animal assemblages troubles categorical distinctions that analytically separate humans from the nonhuman natural world and emergent technology. "The main trouble with cyborgs, of course," Harraway argues, "is that they are the illegitimate offspring of militarism and patriarchal capitalism, not to mention state socialism. But illegitimate offspring are often exceedingly unfaithful to their origins" (Harraway 151). Lai's writings routinely feature protagonists with decidedly "impure," hybrid origins in environmental catastrophes, corporate malfeasance, or military technology. They are characters who compel readers to rethink the interdependence of worlds that the taxonomic categories of human, animal, and machine work to separate. For Lai, the merger of human and nonhuman bodies dramatizes how the "determined eschewing of purities" (Villegas and Lai 124) might reveal new coalitional possibilities for action.

Automaton Biographies presents four long poems that investigate the interface between humans and technology, imperial warfare and global commodity chains, the Cold War and animal research subjects, and immigrant histories that remain unassimilable to narratives of national progress. Each poem in the collection is organized around figures who have historically been represented as automatons—machines or machinelike tools that appear to mimic persons and convey the illusion of self-directed movement. Aware of the automaton as a historically racialized figure, Lai's poems consider how these uncanny machines can evoke the emotionless, seemingly mechanical abstraction of Asian labor.

In recent years, critics have read the figure of the cyborg as a kind of late-twentieth and early-twenty-first-century version of nineteenth-century "coolie" laborer. As Rachel Lee and Sau-Ling Wong write, the cyborg "emerges as a convenient figure to project twenty-first-century anxieties regarding the porosity of national boundaries, the spread of global capital, and the transformation of a large domain of social relations into commodified exchanges" (R. Lee and Wong xiv). Like the coolie, the cyborg similarly comes to embody fears of human workers forced to compete with machines or machinelike foreign laborers, prefiguring a future of mass unemployment, impossible productivity demands, and generally unendurable working conditions. For scholars of contemporary Asian American cultural production, the figure of the cyborg also presents an opportunity for "interrogating, reimagining, and, perhaps, reinhabiting this figure of the Asian (American) cyborg," Lee and Wong continue, "the yellow body variously jacked into silicon chips and E-bay, to cybersociety and on-line forms of subjectivity" (xiv). The technologically augmented body of the Asian subject of capital also represents the possibility of manipulating deterritorialized forms of consciousness capable of surviving a dystopian future of full automation.[5]

"Rachel" and Racial Melancholia

In the opening poem of *Automaton Biographies*, Lai presents the imagined autobiographical testimony of the half-Asian android Rachel—a character

[5] For more on how contemporary literature, films, and media represent and respond to contemporary "techno-orientalism," see Roh et al.

represented in Philip K. Dick's 1968 novel *Do Androids Dream of Electric Sheep?* and Director Ridley Scott's 1982 film adaptation *Blade Runner*. When asked about the significance of the character for the entire collection, Lai has explained that Rachel "is such an immigrant figure—from the human side of the divide to the non-human one, from a misrecognition of self as European to a melancholic, then enraged, recognition of self as Asian" (Villegas and Lai 121). "Rachel" represents the boundary between humans and machines as a racial divide marked by eerily detached forms of self-consciousness and a welter of seemingly unmotivated affective intensities. Because their existence seems designed to produce categorical misrecognition, the figure of the automaton allows Lai to dramatize the uncanny combination of hyperassimilability and unassimilability that I contend broadly characterizes twenty-first-century Asiatic racial form.

Lai's reimagining of Rachel, both in the poem and in the author's earlier (2004) short story with the same title, represents a character who seems to move beyond mourning a lost humanity they never possessed into a kind of collective rage emerging out of networked and technologically mediated forms of distributed consciousness. Reframed as a racial allegory where Rachel is cursed with the capacity to mimic whiteness but never to fully embody it, the poem reimagines what Anne Cheng and David Eng characterize as a condition of racial melancholia—marked by experiences of absence, dissociation, or disembodiment—constitutive of Asian racialization.[6]

Building on Freud's account of ego formation in his essay "Mourning and Melancholia", Cheng contends that the force of racial assimilation lies in its power to compel Asian American subjects to identify with and internalize whiteness as a kind of unattainable ego-ideal. The Asian American subject is subsequently forced into what Freud would characterize as a melancholic position where the Freudian ego offers itself as a substitute for the lost object and is subsequently trapped within a suspended state of depletion and ongoing self-denigration. In contrast to what Freud describes as the temporary process of mourning, in which the subject's links to the lost object are steadily relinquished, melancholia describes a repetitive and seemingly interminable condition in which the subject's "self-reproaches are reproaches against a loved object which have been shifted away from it on to the patient's own ego" (Freud 248). The creation and internalization of this ideal produce psychic effects for both white

[6] See Eng and Han; Eng and Kazanjian.

and non-white subjects, situating them relationally within what Cheng calls a national racial imaginary "sustained by the exclusion-yet-retention of racialized others" (Cheng 10) that are "lost to the heart of the nation" (Cheng 10).

Lai's Rachel responds to this loss, triggered by her initial misrecognition of herself as "European," by moving from racial melancholia to rage at the circumstances of her construction. "[T]his melancholy pisses me off," the character confesses midway through the poem:

wars for us
the blunt rapes
the mass racial graves

i mourn purity
in guilt in fear
my perfect construction
the instrument of

(Lai 31)

The language Lai uses here is echoed in the following poem, "nascent fashion," which traces the historical transformation of imperial warfare's "mass racial graves" (Lai 58) into sites of global commodity production. This peculiar phrase, where "graves" and not populations are "racial," presents the reader with another image of a kind of container for anonymized human remains rather than an intrinsic property of individuals or groups. It is an image that highlights the historical construction of race as a social form whose meaning and boundaries do not precede but are instead produced by war, mass murder, and sexual violence.

Lai connects the circumstances of Rachel's fabrication to imperial violence projected outward toward subjects existing at the global periphery of an emerging capitalist world-system. Lai's Rachel is not only a spectral subject of racial melancholia constituted by loss but also a manufactured object whose production is governed by capitalist imperatives. In repudiating a melancholic "identification of the ego with the abandoned object" (Freud 249), Rachel instead comes to understand herself as a personified commodity animated by the racially "alien" sociality of abstract value. "I love her deficiency combined with her superefficiency," Lai has explained in interviews about why she is drawn to the character, "more human than human" (Villegas and Lai 121). Rachel thus appears in the mirror of commodity form as a kind of ghost in the machine of capitalist production, an updated version of the "nerveless," hyperefficient body of the coolie reimagined as abstract labor freed from the burden of human corporeality. Here, though, the character's self-awareness is grounded in a recognition that she is not one but many—a serial consumer product of both the profit-motive and patriarchal fantasies. "[W]e repeat / on department store shelves," the speaker observes in a passage that could just as easily belong in Hunt's *Piece Logic* or Theresa Hak Kyung Cha's "photo-essay" (Cha 91–111). As an ideal subject of transnational capital at home both everywhere and nowhere, the character dramatizes the uncanny enmeshment of the category of the human with the impersonal demands of global economic competition—demands that intensify patriarchal violence rather than ameliorate it.

The following poem in Lai's collection, "nascent fashion," arguably reimagines Rachel as a multiracial distributed subject continually assembled and disassembled by the rhythms and requirements of capitalist global production, competition, and development.

"nascent fashion": Racial Form in Global Logistics Space

As in Cha's "photo-essay," "nascent fashion" features a scene in which a speaker comes to understand the consumption of luxury goods as a mechanism of racial assimilation. The poem traces the historical emergence of two interconnected subjects: one a subject of consumption, trapped within an ambivalent identification with a "white/nation" (Lai 45), and the other a "dark" subject of production, or "factory girl" (Lai 52), distributed across the global South. Beginning with this subject of consumption, the speaker describes an advertisement of a woman in a white bed and struggles to articulate the anger and desire elicited by this image of luxury and ease. The image seems to reflect a racially fractured image of the speaker's own life, recalling moments of troubled self-recognition in "Rachel." Uncertain whether she covets the image of the woman on the bed or the bed itself, the speaker is faced with the question of who or what to identify with in the scene:

> i didn't know i wanted
> wanted the white bed
> was that so bad?
> white bed all crisp cotton and down
> high posts a girl
> i could yell at

> i'd make her pay make her
> anger i didn't see
> the mirror myself ghost
> white bed for ghost girl
>
> (Lai 51)

The speaker's desire for whiteness orients toward the "white bed" itself as a status marker tied less to a specific white body than to objects that signify wealth, leisure, and authority. The ambiguity of whether the speaker wishes to direct her "anger" at the girl in the white bed, or to occupy the position of the girl to make others "pay," displays an ambivalent melancholic relation to the internalized "lost object" of whiteness itself. Mirroring the seemingly immaterial abstract labor sedimented in consumer objects that make up the scene, the racial fantasy of a white "ghost girl" occasions a kind of crisis of racial recognition for the speaker. Unable to recognize herself in the mirror of the commodity form, the speaker imaginatively reverses the trajectory of immigrant assimilation, casting the poem's attention back through the networks and supply chains of globalized production to the "impure" materiality of laboring bodies forced to produce the objects in this advertisement.

The advertisement thus functions as a "mirror" in which the speaker can see how her desires and aversions are tied to the fate of workers whose lives are opaque to her. The speaker's "anger i didn't see" is displaced from object to object, alternately directed at the advertising image and what it promises, and then at the anonymous and abject laborers existing in the darkness beyond the frame of that image separating producers and products, and in this case, whiteness from nonwhiteness. In stark contrast to the brightness of the bedroom advertisement, the "dark" in which "my body their bodies all this rot / this shit this vomit this blood" (Lai 51) is, as the poem later suggests, a space of abject labor smuggled across national borders and asphyxiated within shipping containers.

The movement of these migrant figures mimic the movements of goods produced in what Diane Elson and Ruth Pearson have called export-oriented "world market factories" (Elson and Pearson 88). These production sites help to reproduce the image of women workers as naturally well suited to repetitive light manufacturing work with few labor rights and protections:

> Women are considered not only to have naturally nimble fingers, but also to be naturally more docile and willing to accept tough work discipline, and naturally less inclined to join trade unions, than men; and to be naturally more suited to tedious, repetitious, monotonous work. Their lower wages are attributed to their

> secondary status in the labour market which is seen as a natural consequence of their capacity to bear children. The fact that only young women work in world market factories is also rationalized as an effect of their capacity to bear children—this naturally means they will be either unwilling or unable to continue in employment much beyond their early twenties. Indeed the phenomenon of women leaving employment in the factory when they get married or pregnant is known as "natural wastage," and can be highly advantageous to firms which periodically need to vary the size of their labour force so as to adjust to fluctuating demand for their output in the world market.
>
> (Elson and Pearson 93)

For Elson and Pearson, these characterizations of women's labor in global factories are not a "natural" fact of gendered differences but the result of socialization into divisions of domestic labor and structures of economic opportunity. The subsumption of these workers into new regimes of export-oriented light manufacturing produces unpredictable social effects—alternately intensifying, decomposing, or recomposing new forms of gendered subordination.

The Imperial History of World Market Factories

Featuring sudden shifts between historical eras and events, Lai's poem consistently links the emergence of the "factory girl" to a broader twentieth- and twenty-first-century history of imperial warfare in Asia and the Middle East. From the August 6, 1945, US bombing of Hiroshima and Nagasaki to the 1955–75 Vietnam War, the poem suggests that these conflicts have prepared the ground for future "world market factories." In a possible reference to aerial bombing campaigns, the poem suggests that mass casualties create a kind of flattened historical surface where capitalist markets can take root and expand:

> the pilots who refused
> miraculous vision through heat
> memory stretches
> civilians crawl market still
> bodied stretches
> to where i wasn't
>
> (Lai 48)

The language of the passage is ambiguous enough to suggest a range of examples of bombing campaigns responsible for mass civilian casualties—from the aerial firebombing of Tokyo and Okinawa during the Second World War to the 1965–8 air campaign "Operation Rolling Thunder" of the Vietnam War. Despite mentioning the reluctance of some pilots to engage in these operations, the poem invokes a "miraculous vision through heat," in a possible reference to the nuclear weapons used on Hiroshima and Nagasaki, which nevertheless emphasizes the perverse sublimity of weapons of unprecedented destructive capacity. The moment vaporizes human bodies while leaving a "market / still bodied." The mordant pun on the crawling or still bodies of civilians suggests that the market can "stretch" into a zone of devastation where even memory cannot extend, remaking the meaning of war into a kind of theodicy of later national economic development.

The longer colonial, settler colonial, and imperial history of what the poem calls "the burning conquest the americas / trade slave the a-bomb reduction of place to death" (Lai 48) is reframed as a condition of possibility of late-twentieth- and early-twenty-first-century global capitalist development. The poem repeatedly likens the power of modern weaponry to disarticulate bodies to the assembly of consumer items out of modular components. Thus war prepares the ground for the peacetime "nascent fashion" of emergent sites of garment manufacturing and assembly located in such places as Vietnam and northern Mexico:

> only limbs and eyes
> and scattered sear the shard the shrapnel
> the peace we promise
> to keep materiel personal
> and flowing off assembly
> no right to unless it lines
>
> come unto these metal hands
>
> (Lai 49)

Here the factory girl is represented as a kind of cyborg whose prosthetic "metal hands" may be a consequence of war or workplace injuries within factories where feminized labor is a low-cost solution to the difficulty of automating aspects of manufacturing processes. This passage also tracks the historical transformation of "materiel"—or military technology, supplies, and personnel—into what could be read as the production of "personal" consumer goods. As an example of a formal strategy that the poem repeatedly employs to draw the reader's attention to relations of power and mediating figures hidden in the interstice of words and worlds, the additional phrase "no right to unless it," inserted between "assembly" and "lines," suggests that the workers who produce these goods cannot afford to purchase what they make. But this interrupted syntax also dilates the interval between products moving along an assembly line—where the "factory girl," and the extent of workplace "right," appears only in the form of a denied "right" of ownership of the manufactured goods. Productivity comes to define this subject "contained" in the interstices between products—a subject compelled to recursively manufacture her disposability and disappearance.

But this multiracial figure of the "factory girl" that Lai's poem represents as both a node and a network invites readers to reconsider different material possibilities of collective action that might cut across the reproduction of what Neferti Tadiar calls the "grid of intelligibility of race as social difference" (Tadiar 140):

> What, then, might it mean to reconsider "race" as a theoretical question and political intervention rather than a category of social exemption or exclusion or a descriptive category of "difference" (as a sign of marginalized social being)? It seems to me that it means attending to these subaltern pathways of social and self-formation that remain beneath the threshold of visibility of raced subjects (both dominant and subordinate), the proper borders of their own self-presencing. It means to ask how "race" operates within and results from practices of reproducing social life, generating lines of affiliation, stratification, and descent; determining and allocating proper distributions of value, right, power, and futurity; producing and maintaining relations of exploitation, expropriation, and violence at levels and through means beyond the ideological field within which "race" operates as a discriminatory, representational sign of social being.
>
> (Tadiar 156)

For Tadiar, contemporary global capitalism reproduces racial distinctions not as a series of discrete social identities but instead as a set of practices of social reproduction that produce material interdependencies subject to investment and disinvestment. Instead of simply naturalizing the inevitable transhistorical reproduction of older colonial-imperial racial categories, Tadiar draws attention to relational processes operating above and below the "threshold of visibility of raced subjects" as sites where racial domination might be contested.

For Tadiar, the racial socialities and solidarities of "Late imperial capitalism" (Tadiar 138) are better described by an analysis of processes of social reproduction operating "[b]eneath the level of given social identities" (Tadiar 155) and beyond "the macro process called 'identification' or even subjectification, as the other side of racialization" (Tadiar 149). In my reading of Lai's poem, the coordinated work of "dark" workers generates "accumulable or eliminable excess (value or waste)" (Tadiar 155), creating the material conditions of possibility for transnational solidarities that do not simply reproduce an existing imperial-colonial grid of racial positions. Lai's cyborg-like and serial "dark" workers ("she dark she poor" [Lai 58]) do not share a single racial identity but an experience of being reduced to the "arbitrary content" (Lai 65) of the commodity form's enclosure of "labour power raw" (Lai 65) in the darkness of enforced commensurability—from the commodity form of "my dark truck" (Lai 64) to the shipping containers (Lai 54) that "are dark inside" (Lai 54), to the borders of a country "in the dark" (Lai 65).

Like Cha's poem, "nascent fashion" directs our attention to the creation and spatial movement of what these poems frame as surplus or excess, which includes what Marx calls "surplus value" (Marx, *Capital: A Critique of Political Economy. Vol.1* 251)—or the unpaid labor time of workers appropriated as profit by the owners of capitalist enterprises. In other words, Lai's poem maps a recursive circuit of capitalist reproduction operating beyond and beneath existing categories of racial difference through the creation, appropriation, and expulsion of "surplus" capacities, resources, and populations.

Thus "nascent fashion" exposes how racial difference is assembled and reassembled not only by long imperial and colonial histories but also as the product of naturalized background conditions of capitalist production and social reproduction. The subjects engaged in such reproductive labor never become politically "recognizable" because their relative value is determined below the representational threshold of the "liberal democratic separation between the political and the economic" (Tadiar 158) that underwrites liberal antiracist "projects (and problems) of difference" (Tadiar 140).

Containing Asiatic Racial Form

As economist and historian Marc Levinson has argued, the late-twentieth-century globalization of production was facilitated by the development of both standardized shipping containers and an international infrastructure that allowed for the transfer of these containers across various modes of transportation—from cargo ships to trucks and trains. Although global commodity production and trade are not historically novel phenomena, new transportation technologies have made the cost of moving goods dramatically cheaper, faster, and more predictable. Although it "has all the romance of a tin can" (Levinson 1), the "box," as Levinson calls it, has enabled a process of deindustrialization that has devastated manufacturing regions in the global North:

> [H]igh transportation costs acted as a trade barrier, very similar in effect to high tariffs on imports, sheltering the jobs of production workers from foreign competition but imposing higher prices on consumers. As the container made international transportation cheaper and more dependable, it lowered that barrier, decimating manufacturing employment in North America, Western Europe, and Japan, by making it much easier for manufacturers to go overseas in search of low-cost inputs.
>
> (Levinson 268)

Older, slower, and more unpredictable forms of labor-intensive transport hindered more extensive forms of global business integration and the ability of states to project imperial power globally.

The contemporary standard shipping container was first developed in the late 1960s to deliver US military supplies to Vietnam. After the US buildup of troops began in 1965, the US military faced serious logistical problems and major delays in moving goods from ship to shore. After soliciting bids from private industry, the Department of Defense offered Malcom McLean, founder of Sea-Land Service, a 1967 contract to begin transporting materiel on container ships to South Vietnam. The fact that such containers could easily be transferred between different modes of transport largely solved the logistical problems exacerbated by the escalation of US military involvement in the country.

In "nascent fashion," the figure of the container reappears at several key moments in the text, not only as a technological innovation allowing for efficient transport of goods to the military but also as a way to represent the interconnections between dispersed workers. In the poem, containerization describes a process of race-making that includes the "trade slave" (Lai 48), a reversal of "slave trade" that, through one of the poem's repeated syntactical moves, transforms a noun into a verb and draws attention to a set of practices that produce the category of the slave. This subtle reversal highlights how what Christina Sharpe has called the "containerization of people" (Sharpe 29) has historically shaped the meaning of Blackness, but also how the terms of racial order are actively produced and reproduced.[7]

[7] Christina Sharpe has described not only Black chattel slavery but also the contemporary movement of Black migrants across the Mediterranean Sea in terms of the "containerization of people" (Sharpe 29).

Throughout "nascent fashion," the poet repeatedly calls attention to how the portability of things requires increasingly porous national borders and a predictable network of roads, "taxes," and "rapid transit" within countries. Tracing the emergence of twenty-first-century networks of production that build on and reconfigure earlier colonial and imperial supply lines, the poem also explores how national borders harden into "containers" of local labor power. The emergence of logistical space, the poem implies, redefines borders as a practice of managing supply chains and regulating differentiated types of mobility afforded to subjects and objects—from temporary and permanent workers to cheap consumer goods and intellectual property.

The shipping container becomes a potent symbol for these ramifying transformations of both labor and commodity flows within networks of global production that "unlimit consumption" (Lai 65) and erode remaining barriers to free trade and global markets for workers and goods:

> don't know which country
> matter the road
> which project labored
> which taxes
> which pride our rapid transit
> moves necessary packaging
> arbitrary content
> leaves labour power raw
>
> this rational economy begs transportation
> to unlimit consumption
> flows commodities in wastes out
> on pipe on wheel on rail by air
> my air i choke this moving dark
> standardize container
> to maximize swap of mode
> (Lai 65)
>
> all containers are dark inside
> whatever engine
> its oily ancient fuel
> whatever medium
> asphalt salt water fresh water track
>
> (Lai 55)

The description of the container as a "necessary packaging" enclosing "arbitrary content" is an implicit commentary on the commodity form itself, and the integral relationship between abstract exchangeability and concrete particularity. Or, better, the poem highlights how logistical management is less interested in the "arbitrary" particularity of transported goods or heterogeneous circumstances of specific workers and labor processes, and more concerned with the "necessary" imperative to accumulate capitalist value. The commodity form is here reimagined as an intermodal shipping container's ability to render what it encloses transferable across multiple sites and different modes of transportation.

The poem also imagines containers as a cyborg body, a metal shell around "raw" labor power—a body whose featureless, standardized "skin" allows for its rapid circulation across global spaces of production. In other words, it is a body that powerfully condenses a vision of a "frictionless" world. This vision of a smooth space of global circulation is double-edged, however. The shipping container is also presented as an imperative for workers to fit their labor, and sometimes literally their bodies, into supply chains that continually threaten them with obsolescence. The stowed away "i" aspires to literally and lethally mimic the movement of goods in order "to maximize swap of mode" and move illicitly across national borders in potentially lethal airless containers. Told from the perspective of a speaker choking and seemingly running out of air in "this moving dark," the poem reveals how a vision of global economic integration requires mechanisms that can differentiate between sanctioned and unsanctioned mobilities. The conceptual "containers" of older racial and ethnic categories historically constituted within nations are reconstituted in global logistics space.

Lai's poem lingers over images of workers repetitively assembling their positioning as racialized and gendered "containers" of labor power in a world where "body's repetitions mark modern woman" (Lai 69):

body's repetitions mark modern woman
my eye's eye
straining to acid scratch microchip
so fine my corridors
dexterous etching

[...]
i touch to know
my labour's incapacity
as hands spasm

already contained
contain me again

i doll my series
smaller and more enclosed with each collapse
towards stifled kernel
crooked fingers
coiled spring tight and full of rage

(Lai 69)

The references in these stanzas to the process of acid-etching microchips offer a figure for the production of the "factory girl" as a mass serial identity. Similarly, the speaker's explanation of how she must "doll my series" suggests the assembly of a series of distorted reflections of herself. As workers are pushed beyond their physical limits, the process seems to fuse bodies to "microchip" and machinery, creating an amalgam of a coolie laborer and gendered cyborg. Here the consciousness of the speaker seems to retreat into a series of nesting dolls "smaller and more enclosed with each collapse," pressurized by an increasingly mechanical rage at processes of social enclosure.

Imperial History and the Logistics Revolution

The standard shipping container required a new logistical infrastructure keyed to its specifications—a technological advance developed to facilitate the transportation of materiel during the Vietnam War. The continuous process of "assembly" described in "nascent fashion," in which goods are exported to more economically developed nations, seems to reverse the movement of supplies required by earlier imperial projections of military force. The poem's repeated allusions to the production and transportation of goods in wartime and peacetime don't simply describe the economic history of industrializing nations but also the evolution of the science of logistics—or the comprehensive management of the production and circulation of commodities across uneven global space.

The mid-twentieth century witnessed a logistics revolution that evolved increasingly sophisticated methods of tracking and coordinating the movement of goods from sites of production to sites of consumption. In the words of Deborah Cowen, this reordering of the world involves a "dramatic recasting of the relationship between *making and moving*, or production and distribution" (Cowen 103):

> At stake here is the rescaling and networking of production itself—the disarticulation of production into component parts that can be stretched out and rearranged in more complex configurations. In other words, the spatial arrangement of the reconfigured relationship between production and distribution is at the center of this question.
>
> The globalization of logistics marks not simply the global distribution of production but the invention of the supply chain and the reorganization of national economies into transnational systems that stretch the factory across national borders and even around the world... .The image of the factory as located in a single place is less relevant than ever before. Instead, the functions of the factory have been disaggregated and dispersed across space according to the logics of total cost. Commodities are increasingly manufactured across multiple states precisely to incorporate radically uneven modalities of labor into the production process. (103)

The spatial disaggregation of production requires more calculable, efficient, and standardized systems of circulation, involving multiple modes of transportation—from trains and container ships to trucks and mechanized ports. The logistical management of global space enables transnational firms the flexibility to exploit cheaper labor and resources while circumventing disruptions to the production process posed by organized labor, political instability, or natural disasters.

The new science of logistics is thus the backbone of "just in time" manufacturing processes that can more accurately tailor production to consumer demand while drastically reducing the cost of storing parts before they're made into goods, or of storing goods before they're sold to consumers. Logistical management aims to render more predictable the speed at which goods move from factory to consumer "flowing off assembly" (Lai 49). What Cowen calls the logistics revolution thus doesn't simply restore older supply lines for imperial armies but also updates and reconfigures imperial spheres of influence in ways that cut across national boundaries.

Alert to the human cost of this "new map of the world" (Cowen 1), with its "new kinds of crises, new paradigms of security, new uses of law, [and] new logics of killing" (Cowen 1), "the disruption of supply chains is understood as a matter of national security" (Cowen 116) and the costs of securitization are outsourced to states that depend on commodity exports. Lai's poem dramatizes how changes in the logistical management of global space create a self-regenerating collective body invested with a distributed form of consciousness:

> o parent
> corporation my body
> a cell to be bought
> i flash appear when you need me
> based in turkey
> shanghaied to Vietnam
> former yugoslavs slave as
> mexican labourers max hours
> push borders that pushed back
> illegal where once master
> carded now home without
>
> uniform my black hair
> flesh rip each time the contract
> relocated the girl
> the same girl different
>
> my dreams rust containers
> i slow boat from china
> to meet yesterday's demand
>
> (Lai 54–5)

In this passage, the poem arguably reimagines the cyborg body as a part-organic, part-machine network whose nodes are factory girls made, remade, and unmade through shifting labor contracts. The process of segmenting global production processes appears to clone a collective body of feminized labor by dismembering it, where the "flesh rip each time the contract / relocated the girl / the same girl different." Individual workers are imagined as the cellular building blocks of the larger body of a "parent / corporation"—a pun that merges the production of subjects of capital with a language of cloning and biological reproduction. Here Lai's poem likens these individual workers to the cells in a larger corporate body that can be disarticulated and aggregated through the relocation of work. In stanzas that seem to describe "runaway factories" relocating to different regions of the world in search of cheaper labor, the speaker is an anonymous avatar summoned into existence by the needs of capital. They might be an operator, for example, at an outsourced call center that "flash appear when you need me." Condensing at various sites of production and remote service work in Turkey,

Shanghai, Vietnam, the former Yugoslavia, and Mexico, the speaker is not any particular individual, but the personified "voice" of a supply chain that can be rapidly reconfigured in response to changing labor needs and local conditions.

The fact that these factory girls are both "the same" and "different" articulates a "grammar" of racial group formation embedded in the capitalist production of differential equivalence and what Erica Hunt calls "Piece Logic". The capitalist accumulation of abstract value does not tendentially produce social homogeneity but instead material differentiation, translating imperial and colonial racial distinctions into racialized and gendered labor markets within the "containers" of national borders.[8] Drawing on Marx's concept of "living labor" (Marx, "Grundrisse" 258), Sandro Mezzadra and Brett Neilson have noted how the "sexualized and racialized materiality" (Mezzadra and Nielson 110) of capitalist subjects is significantly defined through bounded labor markets. "Not only is labor power a commodity unlike any other... but the markets in which it is exchanged are peculiar," Mezzadra and Neilson observe. "This is... because the role of borders in shaping labor markets is particularly pronounced. The processes of filtering and differentiation that occur at the border increasingly unfold within these markets" (Mezzadra and Nielson 19).

The recombinatory capacity of supply chains enables the progressive erosion of working conditions and a devastating "race to the bottom" for workers forced to compete in a global marketplace. When Lai writes "mexican labourers max hours / push borders that pushed back," the poem draws attention to two types of borders: the boundaries of how much a laboring body can endure, and the racial borders of national citizenship created in part through the territorial annexation of large portions of Mexico by the United States.

The stanza suggests that the intensified demands on labor productivity simultaneously enable the accumulation of wealth in developed nations and help drive mass "illegal" human migration to these centers of accumulation. At the same time, this category of the "illegal" worker is inserted into a modified advertising slogan for a credit card: "illegal where once master / carded now home without." This reformulated advertising tagline evokes the dispossessive effects of postwar "structural adjustment" programs—leading to the privatization of state-owned enterprises and public services—imposed on Mexico beginning in the 1980s due to a dramatic rise in US interest rates on loans to the country.

8 For a useful feminist critique of factory production politics in Hong Kong and Shenzhen, for example, where owners exploit "the social organization of gender" (C. K. Lee 161) in order to lower the cost of the social reproduction of labor, see Ching Kwan Lee.

"In the Hollow Parts of Anything That Moves"

As racial categories internally fracture across a radically uneven global capitalist economic geography, "nascent fashion" locates possibilities of political transformation in what literal and metaphorical containers fail to enclose as they travel across nations and promise forms of collective coordination decoupled from capitalist imperatives. The poem dilates the lethally "hollow" (Lai 83) spaces created by imperial violence, the multiplication of securitized borders, and the rhythms of assembly-line labor.

Here the poem enlarges a moment of commodity circulation, where the relentless teleology of accumulation is interrupted and where persons and things are momentarily free from what Marx calls the "law of value" (Marx, *Capital: A Critique of Political Economy. Vol.1* 702). Moving along "late night highways" where "we signal our delight in time's hiccup / this momentary reign of pink petals" (Lai 82), the speaker wonders, "am i a girl dreaming i'm in a truck / or a truck dreaming i contain a girl?" (Lai 53):

> we ditch our furies to hiatus grim divisions
> our sores sprout music and soft lighting
> we boy our girls tender hands
> to dance these haunted roads
> time's momentary pocket of nothing
> in the middle of nowhere.
>
> (Lai 82)

Inhabiting a "momentary pocket of nothing / in the middle of nowhere" allows the speaker to experience a temporal gap, "time's hiccup," as collective possibility freed from the capitalist organization of human activity. In this hollowed-out space and time, the poem's "i" becomes "we," both singular and plural—a kind of intermodal subject who is both truck and "a girl" in blurred motion across borders and other "grim divisions" in a networked global economy.

We might read the "hollow" nighttime landscape that the speaker travels through not only as logistical space but also as the time of capitalist circulation between the production and sale of commodities. This interval in the circuit of accumulation allows the speaker to imagine alternative social possibilities and forms of wealth "in the middle of nowhere," unmapped by capital. The speaker's work injuries are allowed to heal during this night journey that offers a temporary respite in the poem before profits are realized, and the entire cycle of accumulation recommences. "Tender hands" that otherwise might "spasm" on an assembly line instead gesture toward the porosity of gender distinctions, turning the word "boy" into a verb. The "hollow" of sores fill with music and light. "My destiny's not a nation," the speaker declares, and it is unclear whether it is a person or a commodity speaking. In either case, the line describes a world where capitalist value production is not bound to any single nation and where it becomes possible to imagine alternative and more expansive forms of collective life beyond a structure of nationally segmented competitive exploitation.

In this temporary reparative vision of a night drive through the interstices of the machinery of accumulation, the speaker's dreams of the free movement of objects give way to a vision of freeing collective human capacities from their violent translation into the abstract value of "labour power raw" (Lai 65):

> to walk to truck to haunt
> these night routes
>
> in the hollow parts
> of anything that moves
>
> (Lai 83)

"[T]o truck" turns a commodity back into a process. Whether understood in terms of material deprivation, need, loss, or desire, what is "hollow" is not only compelled to move, the poem suggests, but a kind of temporal caesura where the speaker can imagine a future that isn't dominated by the rhythms of capitalist production.

These stanzas return readers to the poem's earlier description of a "ghost girl" whose impossible identification with whiteness and wealth quickly shifts from an experience of melancholic loss to anger.[9] What haunts these "night routes," then, are not just travelers momentarily liberated from the gravitational pull of market compulsions but also products that represent the afterlives of the workers who make them.

Gathering together scattered references to the history of US military interventions abroad, the poem concludes with a description of an Iraq War protest staged "against all the vietnams in the world" (Lai 84). This line revises an anti-imperialist slogan from Ernesto "Che" Guevara's 1967 article, "Message to the Tricontinental," in which the Argentine revolutionary famously implores his audience to "create two, three, many Vietnams". The poem situates the 2003 US military invasion of Iraq within a longer imperial chronology that

[9] The "ghost girl" also exists "in the hollow parts/of anything that moves," evoking what Anne Cheng calls the spectral presence of racial others "lost to the heart of the nation" (Cheng 10).

primes readers to interpret "all the vietnams in the world" as a potential reference both to supply chains developed during the 1955–75 war and to the subsequent postwar transformation of Vietnam as an export-oriented manufacturing hub for transnational corporations like Nike.[10] "As machines repetitive wilt spirit / as bones dig mass racial graves" (Lai 58) the poet writes. These lines establish a striking parallel between the capacity of industrial production and the violence of war to transform persons into things—into automatons or reanimated skeletal remains engaged in a grisly and similarly repetitive form of labor. Refusing to naturalize the trajectory of national capitalist development as a solution to histories of imperial domination, the poem's call to write against "all the vietnams in the world" reimagines the terms of a twenty-first-century anti-imperialist politics and poetics beyond the spatial container of the nation and the boundaries of Asiatic racial form.

[10] As Deborah Cowen notes, "the World Bank is currently financing a massive logistics plan in Vietnam. The plan took shape at the behest of Nike, which employed two hundred thousand workers and produced ninety-four million pairs of shoes in the country in 2010. The company began lobbying the government to invest in infrastructure in order to strengthen their supply chain" (Cowen 60).

5

"Where From, Where To Are Faces of Here": Race as Seriality in Ed Roberson's "Sit In What City We're In"

As Brent Hayes Edwards argues in a special issue of the journal *Callaloo* devoted to the poetry of Ed Roberson, "critical interpretation has been slow to come to terms with Roberson's accomplishment" (Edwards 621) even forty years after the publication of the poet's first collection *When Thy King Is a Boy*. Born in 1939, Roberson is the author of eight volumes of poetry. His writings have long been a part of what Aldon Lynn Nielsen calls a literary tradition of "black experiment" (Nielsen 165), relegated to the margins of critical accounts of Black post–Second World War literature and existing beyond the boundaries of a narrowly defined Black vernacular orality.

Instead of explicitly addressing the imbrication of racial group formation and capitalist processes, this chapter focuses on an epochal transition in postwar US history where a series of civil rights movement legislative victories working to end de jure racial segregation immediately throw the meaning and material context of ideals of formal equality and equal citizenship into question. In the language I have been developing over the course of this study, this is a moment where limited acts of state and institutional recognition of historical injustice both ignore movement demands for a reorganization of the postwar US economy and define racial justice more narrowly as racial incorporation into a "democracy of goods"—or "Piece Logic" in the words of poet and critic Erica Hunt. Roberson's 2006 collection, entitled *City Eclogue*, explores this spatial logic of racial incorporation in an unnamed city where a combination of racist practices and ostensibly race-neutral market mechanisms systematically reproduce an extensively surveilled and racially segregated urban space that speakers must navigate.

My reading of Roberson builds on Edwards's description of the poet as "one of the foremost practitioners of serial poetics" (626). By "serial poetics,"

Edwards suggests both the poet's use of serial poetic forms—which emphasize the non-narrative, paratactic combination of repeated particles of language—and seriality as a way of thematizing these forms to illuminate aspects of contemporary Black life and history that might elude more traditional narrative strategies. In *City Eclogue*, Roberson's serial poetics becomes an instrument for historical investigation and speculation about the postwar spatial architecture of the US racial order.

Written sometime in 2001, Roberson's poem "Sit In What City We're In" (26–32) dramatically reimagines a wave of protests following the morning of Monday, February 1, 1960, when four students from the all-Black North Carolina Agricultural and Technical College enter a Woolworth's store in downtown Greensboro. After remaining seated until closing after being refused service at a segregated lunch counter, the four men modeled a protest tactic that touched off a wave of similar protests across the South. Situated against the backdrop of the Montgomery bus boycott and an intensification of nonviolent protest in Southern cities, these sit-ins differed from these other forms of civil disobedience by emphasizing the presence of protestors in social space, rather than their absence.[1] The initial Greensboro protestors scripted their side of verbal exchanges with wait staff and scrupulously projected middle-class respectability, through dress and demeanor, to a national audience.

I read Roberson's poem as a challenge to what Leigh Raiford and Renee C. Romano call the "consensus memory" (Romano and Raiford xv) established by dominant state-sanctioned histories of the civil rights movement. In such narratives, the movement's successes buttress a narrative of American exceptionalism, "the vitality of America's legal and political institutions" (Romano and Raiford xvii), and the "colorblind" character of the nation's founding ideals.

Instead, the poet reimagines the scene of the sit-ins as a moment where the promise of formal equality seems to systematically produce atomized and identical citizen-subjects frozen in racially segregated space and time. To reflect on the ambiguity of this moment does not gainsay movement victories but instead works to unsettle dominant ways of narrating the stakes and historical trajectory of civil rights movement struggles that confine its transformative potential safely to the past.

1 "While boycotters or strikers made their point through concerted absences," Rebekah Kowel argues, "sit-inners exerted pressure by insistent presence, occupying spaces from which they were usually prohibited. Sit-inners put themselves center stage instead of removing themselves from the scene" (Kowal 136).

The poet's use of overlapping syntax plays with structures of "multiple seriality" (Edwards 634) where repeated images and phrases can maintain their distinctiveness while forming new units of meaning across linebreaks. In interviews, Roberson has traced the inspiration for his use of these techniques back to an early work-study summer job listening to a radio at "the Pymatuning Dam, a game preserve and research station in Pennsylvania" (Crown and Roberson 655):

> One evening I was left in charge of the station, and I was playing with the radio in the main lab. We were out in the middle of nowhere, and you get all these overlapping radio signals, and I picked up Canada. So I was getting someone in Canada who was talking about the Mendelssohn Violin Concerto, somebody someplace else talking, and the voices just kept overlapping and fading out in and over each other, and then the voices sounded like a chorus as the concerto started up. So that's how I got the idea for a structure of voices inside the sentences, of the overlap of stations coming in and out, in and out of focus, and someone sitting there hearing them all.
>
> (Crown and Roberson)

In *City Eclogue*, Roberson deploys this technique to capture the overlapping lives of inhabitants in a city undergoing rapid historical change. The technique allows the poet to focus on the slippery syntactical joints and relays between sometimes antagonistic voices and perspectives without depicting the space of the city and its inhabitants as absolutely disconnected.

Scholars of Black experimental poetry, such as Edwards, Nathaniel Mackey, and Fred Moten, have offered various readings of the significance of Roberson's use of serial forms that focus on how they mimic an array of musical techniques and structures. Mackey, in particular, has developed a sweeping theory of Black literary and musical invention that understands racialization as the interplay between combinatory possibilities and serial social constraints.

As Joseph Conte reminds us, serial poetic forms are constructed out of the combinatory arrangement of a set of repeated linguistic units. It is a poetic form crucially defined by how it differs from the developmental trajectory of the poetic sequence:

> The discontinuity of [serial] elements—or their resistance to a determinate order—distinguishes the series from the thematic continuity, narrative progression, or meditative insistence that often characterizes the sequence. At the same time, the series does not aspire to the encompassment of the epic; nor

> does it allow for the reduction of its materials to the isolated perfection of the single lyric. The series demands neither summation nor exclusion. It is instead a combinative form whose arrangements admit of a variegated set of materials. (Conte 21)

As permutable particles of meaning multiply the possible associative links between fragments of text, the circularity or recursivity of the form provides readers with an experience of the "constitutive dialectic between the urge to expansion and exploration, on the one hand, and the confrontation of boundaries, gaps, limits, on the other" (Edwards 629).

In "Sit In What City We're In," the recursivity of serial poetic form becomes a vehicle for critically reflecting on the persistence of segregation and the post–civil rights era spatial reproduction of race as a kind of bounded serial collective identity. The poem reimagines the scene of the sit-ins as a fragmented relational space in which the speaker struggles to discover the principle that might connect all of the incongruous perspectives that make up the scene. The poem's spare pronominal language of parts and wholes maintains a grammatical equivalence between subjects while delaying the quick attribution of racial identity to anyone situated within the space of protest. This momentary suspension of time allows the speaker to examine the spatial configuration of bodies and faces disordered by a breach in the era's color line.

What emerges in this frozen moment is a centrifugal vision of a city, nation, and planet as part of an ever-expanding "intuited totality of serial form" (Edwards 628). In the absence of a recognition of this totality and the exploration of a potential alternative ground of collective life, the poem pursues an elusive principle of relation capable of connecting the otherwise disparate perspectives dramatized in the poem. Here the promise of desegregation is dramatized as the possibility of unimpeded movement through a city but also as an emancipatory vision of the city's relational form freed from racial domination. The poem moves outward into space while also repeatedly returning to an ambiguous moment of impossible recognition in the face of violent attempts to maintain a racist social order. It is a moment where, in the poet's words, "we are so / fused in communication we happen at once" (Roberson, *City Eclogue* 31)—with the "we" describing both a racially representative serial subject of civil disobedience and a risky appeal to the defenders of segregation.[2]

[2] Though *City Eclogue* was published in 2006, Roberson explains in an interview that he wrote the poem "around March 2001" (Crown and Roberson).

Preoccupied with what cultural geographer David Delaney calls the "racialization of space and the spatialization of race" (Delaney 8), the poem registers how the protest tactic of the sit-ins themselves are a portable serial form both spreading rapidly across similar commercial spaces and quickly captured and disseminated in a series of iconic civil rights movement photographs. By reading and rereading the racial meaning of the seriality of the "face" in civil rights movement photography, the poem poses fundamental questions about what Leigh Raiford, in a study of the significance of photography for contemporary Black social movements, calls "memory as a mode of criticism" (17). For Raiford, this *critical Black memory* functions both as "a mode of historical interpretation and political critique that has functioned as an important resource for framing African American social movement and political identities" (Raiford 16). At the same time, the "fecund irony of the 'movement photograph'" (Raiford 7) is that it is both tactically effective and an "aporetic strategy, rife with ambivalences" (Raiford 7). Such photographs helped to coordinate resistance across space and time while also facilitating the subsequent "transformation of history into nostalgia through the cooptation, depoliticization, and commodification of the movements themselves" (Raiford 16).

By representing the outcome of the sit-ins as fundamentally uncertain even long after civil rights movement legislative victories, Roberson's poem delays the absorption of movement struggles into subsequent narratives of inevitable political victory. The poem, like the protests themselves, endeavors to disorder the logic of spatial segregation, or what Elizabeth Abel calls the racial sign system of the Jim Crow South, by representing identities in desegregated space as almost arbitrarily positional and increasingly difficult to racially categorize.[3]

The poet reconfigures the sit-ins in space and in time: spatially, by tracking how mirrors behind a lunch counter seem to create an infinite regress of reflected faces, and temporally, by reconnecting the figure of the city to images of nature and cyclical geological processes. The poem's frieze-like, non-narrative, formal

[3] "By confining the civil rights struggle to the South, to bowdlerized heroes, to a single halcyon decade, and to limited, noneconomic objectives," civil rights historian Jacquelyn Dowd Hall has argued, contemporary conservative narratives of civil rights struggles have isolated the "classical phase" of the movement, from approximately 1954 to 1964, and prevented "one of the most remarkable mass movements in American history from speaking effectively to the challenges of our time" (Hall 5). Echoing recent developments in civil rights historiography which explore site-specific memorials to the movement and the movement's relatively understudied spatial politics, the poem's formal strategies seem to comment reflexively upon what Owen Dwyer calls the "high degree of indeterminacy of the movement's contemporary meaning" (Dwyer 668).

organization is a poetic mapping of the era's five-and-dime stores and their mirrored lunch counters. Here, protestors would sit in the whites-only section of these counters and remain there with their backs to frequently violent crowds of segregationists. Stylistically, Roberson's interruptive, choreographic use of spacing and lineation similarly multiplies ways of reading particular linguistic figures typically situated at the ends of lines—embedding them in larger units of meaning, transforming grammatical subjects into objects and vice versa.

These formal patterns mimic the proliferation of images of protestors, reflected in mirrors, often placed behind lunch counters, across a widely disseminated print, photographic, and television documentary record that was crucial to civil rights movement strategy. As Elizabeth Abel argues, the sit-ins were "sites of intensive and self-conscious signifying activity" (Abel 252), meant to provoke a "crisis of racial legibility" (Abel 252). The poem seems to exacerbate or dilate this crisis by showing how a breach in the color line fragments the scene beyond recognition.

This poem is particularly interested in representing a history of struggles over social space where segregative "spatial configurations are not incidental to power relations such as those predicated on race, but are integral to them" (Delaney 1998, 14):

> This means, first, that such relations are what they are because of how they are spatialized. The long struggle against racial segregation demonstrates that the spatiality of racism was a central component of the social structure of racial hierarchy, that efforts to transform or maintain these relations entailed the reconfiguration or reinforcing of these geographies, *and* that participants were very much aware of this.
>
> (Delaney 1998, 7)

In attempting to reconfigure the "experiential meaning that law inscribes on the physical world" (Delaney 14), civil rights activists challenged claims of local and state sovereignty, which were routinely used to preserve racial segregation from federal judicial intervention. Of course, the movement ultimately succeeded in pressuring the federal government to pass the Civil Rights Act of 1964, overturning the "separate but equal" doctrine enshrined in law in 1896 by *Plessy vs. Ferguson*, ultimately expanding the *Brown vs. Board of Education* decision to integrate public schools, and mandating the desegregation of all public facilities and workplaces.

Elsewhere in *City Eclogue*, in a poem titled "The Open" (Roberson, *City Eclogue* 63–9), Roberson offers a poetics statement that could describe the author's peculiar method of historical reconstruction. By studying "the fine segregations / taken as a core from our society" (Roberson, *City Eclogue* 68), the poems in *City Eclogue* illuminate the segregated spatial form of the city, pictured as the layering of geological strata:

> ... the fine segregations
> taken as a core from our society,
>
> reads like the streets, the history
> of mine shafts, mills   moments before blowing
>
> the chamber, core layers of color   line counting off
> under the pressure.
>
> (Roberson, *City Eclogue* 68)

The urgency of the poet's project of historical investigation is here articulated in explicitly spatial terms, as the momentary opening of a space or pressurized "chamber" (Roberson, *City Eclogue* 68) within an oppressive history that threatens to revert back to ossified "core layers of color" (Roberson, *City Eclogue* 68). The metaphorics of drilling into and mining "the fine segregations" (Roberson, *City Eclogue* 68) also registers the poet's struggle both to illuminate a history of spatial segregation and to connect that history to an era marked by waves of urban riots.

Attempts to restore the fundamentally relational character of social space in "Sit In What City We're In" repeatedly fracture into a jagged field of irreconcilable visual perspectives that ultimately fails to cohere into a dominant narrative of inevitable racial progress.[4] The speaker of the poem cannot construct a narrative progression, or bridge, from the space and time of the protests to the present in which the story of the protests is retold. The speaker is unable to maintain the requisite historical distance from which to "remember," or memorialize, an ongoing struggle that seems condemned to continually restart.[5]

Underscoring the arbitrariness of performing and enforcing the era's conventions governing interracial interaction in social space, the speaker of the poem recalls how segregation has rendered the spatial form of the city so difficult to navigate that nearly every aspect of their memories of urban space

4 My use of the phrase "relational space" is broadly informed by the contemporary "relational turn" in the study of human geography. For a concise summary and critique of relational models of social space, see Jones.

5 For an extended study of the persistence and deepening of urban racial segregation in the post–civil rights era, see Massey and Denton.

requires explanation, including "how many steps we took / to cross one of our streets" (Roberson, *City Eclogue* 26):

Someone may want
to know one day how many steps we took
                    to cross one of our streets,
to know there were hundreds
in one city streets in one direction
                    and as many
as could fit between the land's contours
crossing those,
                    our hive grid as plumb
as circles flanked into the insect
hexagonal,
                    our stone our steel.

(Roberson, *City Eclogue* 26)

The quoted passage draws an implicit comparison between the lives of city inhabitants, who must traverse the space of the city, and the city's spatial form as an aggregate of identical streets. The reader confronts a series of line breaks and spaces, which transform the grammatical objects of phrases, such as "city" in the fifth line of the poem, into the grammatical subject of subsequent lines, "city streets in one direction." The sudden transformation of subjects into objects and vice versa is echoed by the ambiguity of who or what is "crossing those"—what Roberson elsewhere dubs "the municipal legged insect / of streets" (Roberson 1970, 44). Initially, the multiplicity of individuals who constitute a "we" compared to a collective organism of the city itself likened to the honeycomb structure of a beehive. The material form of the city is here seemingly made of the same collective substance shared by the lives of its racially segregated inhabitants.

The hope that the city remains "our stone our steel" attempts to counteract both a denial of Black labor's role in constructing the space of the city and attempts to treat the spatial form of Jim Crow as unalterable and not a product of collective action. Here the poem anticipates later stanzas where segregation defines a seemingly ubiquitous condition of serial separation condensed in the figure of the sovereign citizen. Here the poet renarrates the civil rights movement not as a citizenship claim on what Fred Moten calls "sovereignty's violent democratization" (Moten, "Notes on Passage (The New International of Sovereign Feelings)" 66) but as an insurgent attempt to embody the emergence of foreclosed collective possibilities.

Race as Seriality

In the absence of such possibilities, the city is represented as a machine for reproducing atomized, anonymous, and interchangeable urban citizen-subjects that I want to read as an instance of what Jean-Paul Sartre calls "serial" social collectives. Elaborated in a later work entitled *The Critique of Dialectical Reason* focused on developing a "grammar" of group formation and collective action, Sartre's insights into serial collective identities can help us to read how Roberson's poem traces how sit-in protestors seem to continually gather and disperse into the atomized spatial form of the city—or disappear into the anonymity of formally equivalent national citizen-subjects. For Sartre, various kinds of social collectivities can be distinguished by their degrees of social organization. The philosopher counterposes the active, self-determining activity of a "fused group" (Sartre, *Crit. Dialect. Reason. Vol. One* 345), oriented toward a specific purpose, with passive, objectified, or "practico-inert" social collectivities conceived as *series*—a formulation that suggests the recurrence, substitutability, and contiguity of individuals in social space.

For Sartre, a "fused group" (Sartre, *Crit. Dialect. Reason. Vol. One* 345) emerges from serial social relations by committing itself to a common project (examples of the "fused group" in the *Critique* range from organized book swaps to contending economic classes).[6] Sartre is not so much interested in the specific social or political objectives of these groups but in elaborating a general structural grammar of group formation, dissolution, and bureaucratization. In this late work, the philosopher identifies racial oppression, exploitation, and segregation as essentially "serial" phenomena—a term that Sartre defines as a social relationship between individuals paradoxically predicated on nonreciprocity and structurally equivalent forms of isolation or deprivation, or on what the philosopher describes as mutual nonrecognition.

Roberson's civil rights protestors constitute a Sartrean "fused group" by reacting to forms of common oppression and marginalization in racially segregated urban space—a group whose principle of solidarity is not a shared

[6] Fredric Jameson has called the opposition between serial social relations and the "fused group" as the "central conceptual antithesis between two fundamental forms of collective existence" in Sartre's *Critique*, "between the side-by-side indifference and anonymity of the serial agglomeration and the tightly knit interrelationship of the group-in-fusion. This is an antithesis that is not merely a classificatory one, for as a principle of social dynamics and an empirical fact of social history, the group-in-fusion emerges from seriality as a reaction against it, its subsequent development and fate governed by the danger of its dissolution back into seriality again" (Jameson xxvi).

racial identity but, at least initially, a negative unity imposed on its members by segregated social relations.

If, as Brent Hayes Edwards argues, Roberson's career is exemplary of Black serial poetics, then my reading focuses on how the poet's use of serial forms tracks the "mix of ongoingness and constraint" (Edwards 2010, 629) faced by civil rights protestors who seem to anticipate their own potential historical museumification. In a social space where politicized group formation is continually at risk of decomposing into what Sartre calls the "practico-inert" character of reified serial identities vulnerable to political neutralization, Roberson identifies an underlying relational "grammar" of racial group formation as both the subject and the object of antiracist social transformation.

Although white protestors began to participate in sit-ins as the tactic spread, the poem's second stanza describes how a host of racist social taboos lend additional coherence to an emergent mass subject of protest forced to count "what steps aside the southern streets required" (Roberson 2006, 26) and prohibited from meeting the gaze of white citizens "face / to face" (Roberson 2006, 26) without the threat of violence. The speaker's increasingly equivocal use of pronouns represents the protestors as an undifferentiated mass of individuals whose differences have been temporarily suppressed for purposes of collective protest:

> Others may want more
> to know what steps aside the southern streets required
>   to flow at last free to clear,
> to know how those kept out
> set foot inside, sat down, and how
>   the mirrors around the lunch counter
> reflected the face
> to face—the cross-mirrored depth reached
>   infinitely back into either—
> the one pouring the bowl over the head of
> the one sitting in
>   at that counter.
>
> (Roberson 2006, 26–7)

The pronominal language of the poem tracks the molecular aggregation of individual perspectives into relational wholes and the disaggregation of the latter back into scenes of casual violence presented, for example, through the interlinked figures of "the one pouring the bowl over the head of / the one sitting in / at that counter" (Roberson 2006, 27). The poem reveals how "those kept out" defy a legal sanction that refuses the excluded a place to settle. For the remainder of the poem, the speaker struggles to read and reread the relationship between political equality and the mutual recognition of difference and injustice, from the fleeting symmetry of a moment of a "face / to face" (Roberson 2006, 26) encounter mutilated by segregationist animosity.

In an analysis of photographs of the sit-in protests from 1960 to 1963, Abel discerns an unresolved tension between "the facelessness of the abstract citizen" and later demands for the recognition of "embodied difference" (Abel 273):

> That principled effacement of embodied differences from the conception of citizenship has a less attractive underside, however, in the facelessness of the abstract citizen. The principle of formal equivalence that dispels the burden of difference from the political realm also obscures the enduring burden of difference in the social realm, a burden that contradicts the abstract form of citizenship and calls out for recognition. That call and its social implications are registered through a different set of faces that reverse the path from the embodied subject's expressive registers to representational systems (linguistic, economic, political) that evacuate the body.
>
> (Abel 273)

Abel's analysis of the systems of exchange and equivalence reveals a departicularizing political logic at work in a politics of racial integration predicated upon the figure of the abstract citizen. Abel's attention to what is left out of various systems of political representation can help us to read the poem's juxtaposition of the "facelessness of the abstract citizen" and the embodied particularity of specific faces. The poem's disjointed, heavily enjambed syntax indicates where unassimilable particularity might interrupt the circulation or exchange of equivalent terms. "The flesh form of the city," Roberson writes elsewhere in *City Eclogue*, "doesn't move / in the same time as the city's material / Forms move into era and monument" (2006, 42). For the speaker of "Sit In What City We're In," racial segregation has seeped into the very "material / Forms" of the city. The poem instead attends to "the flesh form of the city"—a peculiar phrase that imagines the inhabitants of the city as a single organism. Or to put it differently, the first two stanzas evoke urban space and segregated social relations as equally object-like and petrified. The poem restores life to these inert forms and restores the city's links to the natural world by reimagining space in alternative relational terms that seem to cross over the boundary separating the speaker's present from the struggles of a previous era.

As the title of Roberson's book suggests, nearly every poem in *City Eclogue* employs the figure of the city, which is repeatedly linked to natural cyclical processes, from the earth's rotation to its water cycle. "In my own poems I try to show our social nature," Roberson explains, "in and as the growth of our cities and city culture.... Restoring this larger earth to urban poetry, embedding city life within a living Nature focuses on an interrelation that should keep us sensitized to exploitative relationships which could cut us off, cut us out of life" (Roberson, "'We Must Be Careful'" 5).

Registering how a breach in the color line alters the spatial form of the city, the poem resituates civil rights historiography in relation to a hybrid urban/geophysical spatiality instead of allowing it to remain at the scale of a strictly southern or national phenomenon. The poem thus imagines alternative forms of social belonging implied by the figure of the city and later the planet. As Nikhil Pal Singh argues, the "distinctively dialectical discourse of race and nation" has constituted "a relentlessly 'negative dialectic,' in which Black intellectuals and activists recognized that racial belonging operates at scales that are both smaller and larger than the nation-state" (44).

A distinctive formal feature of Roberson's poetry is the syntactical lineated "break" or intralinear spacing, which are what poet and critic Fred Moten calls the "break" or "cut," slippery terms that refer to repetition or a sudden transition in a musical performance, and to interracial contact or conflict more generally—the "encountering time of the caesura" (Moten, *In the Break: The Aesthetics of the Black Radical Tradition* 71). Beyond movement photographs, however, I read the poem as not simply a snapshot of spatial relations at a single moment in time but instead as a dynamic exploration of a temporalized rhythmic spacing that dramatizes the active formation of a collective agent out of serial individuals and the decomposition and dispersal of this agent back into seriality. In my reading, what Moten calls the "cut" or "break" in contemporary Black cultural production is a useful entry point into reading the formal features of Roberson's modular, overlapping syntax as mapping the deep serial structure of contemporary racial group formation.[7]

The poem's distinctive use of lineation or spacing, which interrupts the syntax of specific phrases and subsequently aggregates these phrases into larger, overlapping units of meaning, links a series of visual perspectives that have seemed to fragment and recombine under the impact of white supremacist violence. These syntactical "breaks" register different ways of partitioning social space across the poem's three sections. As a further elaboration of "what steps

[7] Peter Quartermain, *Disjunctive Poetics: from Gertrude Stein and Louis Zukofsky to Susan Howe.*

aside the southern streets required," the speaker recognizes in the space of the sit-ins another disjunctive "break" between stillness and movement, a kind of wavelike interval between the bodies of protestors, determined not to move aside, and the virtual mobility of their mirror reflections:

> this regression this seen stepped
> back into nothing both ways
> From which all those versions of the once felt sovereign
> self locked together in the mirror's
> march from deep caves of long alike march back
> into the necessary together
> living we are
> reflected in the face to face we are
> a nation facing ourselves our back turned
> on ourselves how
> that reflection sat in demonstration
> of each faces
> mirror reflecting into mirror generates
> a street cobbled of the heads of
> our one
> long likeness
> the infinite regressions.
>
> (Roberson, *City Eclogue* 27)

These "versions" of the scene's participants, through a kind of optical illusion, seem to march simultaneously into the scene and away from it and are susceptible to visual, political, and psychic "regression" back into the violence of racially partitioned social space. Yet the poet's use of the term "regression" also describes the *mise en abyme* of "mirror reflecting into mirror," tapering off into "nothing both ways"—an emptiness or a false depth that marks the nonrelational limits of "the once felt sovereign / self" (Roberson 2006, 27)—a formulation that reveals how such a self, conceived as the locus of an isolated particularity, becomes indistinguishable from the figure of the sovereign, abstract citizen.

The Body without Perspective

Here I want to read the poem's treatment of the intricate racial dialectics of the gaze in relation to a tradition of Black existential phenomenology that includes contemporary scholarship by theorists like Naomi Zack and Lewis Gordon. In particular, the permutations of the specular "face to face" relation that structure Roberson's poem echo Fanon's meditations on the phenomenology of anti-Black racism in *Black Skin, White Masks*, in particular Fanon's introduction of race into the Hegelian dialectic of "Lord and Bondsman" and the reciprocal reification of the Sartrean gaze, or "look."[8] Roberson's protestors' confrontation with the possibility or impossibility of mutual recognition between two "equal" subjects parallels Fanon's revision of Hegelian and Sartrean dialectics to account for the brutal racial Manichaeism and historical durability of the white/Black divide.[9] Anti-Black racism, Gordon argues, has skewed the existential structure of interpersonal recognition by representing the Black body as a "body without a perspective" (Gordon 102)—a body that throughout Roberson's poem is homogenized by both the Jim Crow social order and the abstract figure of the national citizen. "Being ultimately regarded by black and antiblack racists as a body without a perspective," Gordon further argues, "the black body is invited to live in such a way that there is no distinction between *a* particular black body and *black bodies*. Every black person becomes a limb of an enormous black body: THE BLACK BODY" (Gordon 105).

For the speaker of Roberson's poem, the segregated "body without perspective" becomes a kind of vanishing point for a multiplicity of perspectives that have been curtailed and profoundly distorted by the era's racial codes:

> In the glass, the face
> observed, changes the looking at that face, cancels both
>   their gaze to transparence, opens
> around it a window containing right here
> around us; and in that window these
>   same
> —in the lapped frame of this one moment—

[8] Sartre describes the existential confrontation of two subjects, who attempt to reduce each other to the status of objects, as a relation "which is without parts, given at one stroke, inside of which there unfolds a spatiality which is not *my* spatiality" (Sartre, *Being and Nothingness* 342). "If the Other-as-object is defined in connection with the world as the object which sees what I see," Sartre argues, "then my fundamental connection with the Other-as-subject must be able to be referred back to my permanent possibility of *being seen* by the Other. It is in and through the revelation of my being-as-object for the Other that I must be able to apprehend the presence of his being-as-subject" (Sartre, *Being and Nothingness* 344–5). As Ato Sekyi-Otu observes, "Manicheism, violence, the reduction of the human being to a thing by the look and action of another human being; or the condemnation of the Other to the status of a dreaded or spurned 'surplus' entity: these and other characteristic figures in Sartre's account of being-for-others reappear in Fanon's representation of the racial drama of the 'colonial context' " (Sekyi-Otu 66).

[9] For a brief summary of Fanon's reimagining of Hegelian and Sartrean dialectics, see Gibson. For an extended discussion of Fanon's reconceptualization of Hegelian recognition, see Marriott 354–63.

are the other one's
        world we see into in ours.

(Roberson, *City Eclogue* 29)

In the poem, a transitory perspectival subject is formed, stitched together through crisscrossing lines of sight, and periodically coalescing into a "we" who marks the vanishing point of a segregated "nation facing ourselves our back turned / on ourselves" (Roberson, *City Eclogue* 27). Segregated urban space is here defined by complex relations between embodied perspectives rather than imagined as an empty container in which social relations are simply added.[10] In other words, the poem's representation of this space also marks the emergence of a collective "transparence" in which the conflict between equality and particularity is reimagined in terms of spatial adjacency. Yet the poem's overlapping syntax continues to unsettle what remains "sovereign" and stubbornly self-identical in such a space—a single definitive perspective on or "version" of the scene of the protest. What the poem represents as "sovereign," a sense of national belonging predicated on the production of "versions" of formally equivalent citizen-subjects sequestered in "deep caves of long alike" (Roberson, *City Eclogue* 27), is continually disrupted by varieties of particularity that skew the reciprocal recognition of formal equality. Such sovereign selves are incompatible with the poem's vision of "necessary together / living" (Roberson, *City Eclogue* 27), which can recognize and honor particularity while engaged in an ongoing attempt to reimagine the ground of collective life beyond the abstract form of national citizenship.

As in previous stanzas, the "break" that transforms the grammatical objects of phrases into the subjects of new phrases, and vice versa, also functions as a metaphor for the protestors' resistance to racial objectification. For example, the refrain-like repetition of "we are" (Roberson, *City Eclogue* 27) functions both as a halting attempt at collective self-description asserted in the "necessary together / living we are" (Roberson, *City Eclogue* 27) and as the grammatical subject of the next phrase "we are / reflected in the face to face we are" (Roberson, *City Eclogue* 27). By weaving together what each "sovereign self" glimpses from its fixed position within the scene, the grammatical mobility of the "we are"

[10] Describing the emergence of a notion of "relational space," as opposed to the idea of Cartesian or Euclidean space, in recent theories of cultural geography, Jonathan Murdoch writes: "The relational making of space is both a consensual and contested process. 'Consensual' because relations are usually made out of agreements or alignments between two or more entities; 'contested' because the construction of one set of relations may involve both the exclusion of some entities (and their relations) as well as the forcible enrolment of others" (Murdoch 20).

traces the expanding outline of an omniperspectival subject emerging from the fragmentary views that constitute the poem.

When the "we are" appears for the last time in this quoted passage as the divided subject of "a nation facing ourselves our back turned / on ourselves" (Roberson, *City Eclogue* 27), the poem establishes the sit-in as itself a kind of virtual space of political "reflection" on the racial exclusivity of the space of the nation. The momentary tableau formed by the "face / to face" (Roberson, *City Eclogue* 26) encounter between protestors and segregationists gives way to an unsettling, asymmetrical image of a contorted national subject, which marks the uneasy coexistence of multiple forms of ideological "reflection" implied by national belonging; a "demonstration" (Roberson, *City Eclogue* 27) of the particularity of "each face" (Roberson, *City Eclogue* 27) morphs into "a street cobbled of the heads of / our one / long likeness" (Roberson, *City Eclogue* 27). Although the sit-ins momentarily allow a "demonstration" of the particularity of "each face," the discordance between equality and particularity is represented as insoluble, as endless and abyssal as what "mirror reflecting into mirror generates" (Roberson, *City Eclogue* 27). The poem here uses the city to problematize the promise of formal equality as fundamentally compatible with racially segregated social relations. The poem's ambivalent treatment of resemblance as a guarantor of racial inclusion suggests that "infinite regressions" (Roberson, *City Eclogue* 27) constitute the material form of ideals of equality that do not, after all, either fundamentally end spatial segregation or recognize the extent to which the history of the nation has been defined by racist violence.

The latter half of the poem could thus be read as an ambivalent registration of the limits of ideals of abstract equality and of how urban space both reflects and produces endless "versions" of mass sovereign individuality. Thus protestors' attempts to "face their actions" (Roberson, *City Eclogue* 29) and risk the unpredictability of white segregationist response to an interruption of the racial status quo dramatically reconfigures the "face to face" relation:

> In the glass, the face
> observed, changes the looking at that face, cancels both
>   their gaze to transparence, opens
> around it a window containing right here
> around us;   and in that window these
>   same
> —in the lapped frame of this one moment—
> are the other one's
>   world we see into in ours.
>
> (Roberson, *City Eclogue* 29)

As a metaphor for literary mimesis and the color line, the mirror's alternating transparency and opacity dramatize the interruption of the visual logic of communal self-recognition that has until then composed the scene. Such mirrors, after all, typically reflected white customers' "membership in a virtual community of their peers" (Abel 257).

In the absence of alternative reflected images, the mirror and, by implication, Jim Crow spatial codes become an impassable barrier. The shift from "mirror to window glass to thin air" (Roberson, *City Eclogue* 31) marks the increasing attenuation of what separates the protestors from their political antagonists and the weakening of uniform serial identities premised on reciprocal *nonrecognition*. Similarly, the meaning of "transparence" (Roberson, *City Eclogue* 29) in the poem refers to a literal object in the scene and indicates the possibility of recognizing the "lapped" (Roberson, *City Eclogue* 29) or overlapping serial logic of formal equality and spatial segregation in "one frame" (Roberson, *City Eclogue* 29)—an "elemental moment" (Roberson, *City Eclogue* 29) that nevertheless allows for spatial differentiation between the scene's participants. The lack of agreement in "both / their gaze" (Roberson, *City Eclogue* 29) suggests that the individuals in the scene share a single "gaze" despite their drastically unequal positioning in segregated space. "Transparence" here evokes both the possibility of reciprocal recognition across the color line and a description of protestors glimpsing their own mirrored reflections in which "the face / observed, changes the looking at that face" (Roberson, *City Eclogue* 29). Although the speaker's invocation of the "face" functions as a metonym for forms of particularity that resist being subsumed into social logics that establish equivalence between subjects, particularity can become an object of recognition precisely because of its spatialization. Difference here is represented not as an isolable attribute of specific bodies or perspectives but a merger of worlds, where "the other one's / world we see into in ours" (Roberson 2006, 29). Here the protests hold out the promise of altering the self-perception of every participant in the scene:

> You can't smash the mirror   there but it break here.
> And in it you see   that you can't see
>   your own back,
> your angel of the unfamiliar, of that not like
> your face... See.
>
> (Roberson, *City Eclogue* 30)

Here the poem begins to represent relational "integration" by turning away from the terrain of the nation as an aggregation of sovereign subjects.[11]

The speaker's vision of a racially integrated collective subject might simply represent a solipsistic fantasy of the multiplication of a single face through the fantasmatic "mirror" of representation. In the seventh stanza of the poem, however, the speaker imagines a kind of political wish to occupy a "godlike" (Roberson, *City Eclogue* 31) perspective on the scene capable of imagining the relational coherence of a world where every perspective is unfamiliar:

> From mirror to window   glass   to thin air
> between   and finally, us with no you nor I
>   but being
> —with all our world—   inside the other;
> but there only in   our each part yet having
>   no displacement of the other,
> just as each wishes the self not lost, shared
> being in common in each other   being
>   as different as
> night and day still   of one spin.
>
> (Roberson, *City Eclogue* 30–1)

Thus the poem's vision of the emancipatory promise of this relational space represented not as a form of passive subjection to the other or an ontologized asymmetry in the structure of being but instead as the product of a political intervention that temporarily balances difference and similarity as mutually defining spaces inflected each "inside the other" (Roberson, *City Eclogue*

[11] The poem invokes the figure of the "face" in terms which echo the ethical thought of Emmanuel Levinas. For Levinas, the figure of the "face" embodies a kind of prediscursive otherness which interrupts any phenomenological account of consciousness as self-sufficient: "the abstractness of the face is a visitation and a coming which *disturbs* immanence without settling into the horizons of the World. Its abstraction is not obtained by a logical process starting from the substance of beings and going from the individual to the general. On the contrary, it goes toward those beings but does not compromise itself with them, withdraws from them, ab-solves itself. Its wonder is due to the *elsewhere* from which it comes and into which it already withdraws" (Levinas 60).

As an ethical social relation founded upon the recognition of the prerational "abstractness of the face," produced by a confrontation of the "face to face" (Levinas 2001, 81), the otherness of the "face" is continually threatened by an appropriative gaze which violently asserts a mimetic identity between the "individual" and the "general." As Jill Robbins explains in an account of Levinasian modes of literary interpretation, the "face" can ultimately transform this objectifying gaze into "generosity and language, forms of nonadequation" (Robbins 6) which describe the primary "*non*totalizing modes of relating to the other" (Robbins 6). "For Levinas ethics in the most general sense," Robbins argues, "is this putting into question of self-sufficiency, the interruption *of* self—described variously as an obligation, an imperative, an imposition, a responsibility—that arises in the encounter with the face of the other (*le visage d'Autrui*)" (Robbins 23).

31). What the speaker calls "spin" (Roberson, *City Eclogue* 31) figured as the migratory terrestrial boundary dividing day from night describes these relational configurations as temporal rather than simply spatial structures. The counterposing of "spin," or circulation, to stillness, also characterizes the sit-in as a tactic. As Susan Leigh Foster has argued, the "static, tensile posture of the protestors" (399) stands in stark contrast to the flow of bodies through commercial space.

Although my reading has thus far emphasized Roberson's non-narrative mapping of the spatial politics of the sit-ins, the poem's final stanzas reveal how the geometry of (non)recognition gives way to historical repetition. The space of the sit-ins collapses into the cyclical "lapped frame of this one moment" (Roberson 2006, 29):

> A here and not-here division of things,
> where the future is in the same
>   place as the past, is
> maybe one of the African
> masquerades of time   like these facing mirrors
>   in which time is making faces
> at you from the elemental
> moment,   the faced and yet to be
>   faced
> in one frame where from, where to are faces of here.
> Where a few in the crowd at that lunch counter
>   face their actions.
>
> (Roberson, *City Eclogue* 29)

The protestors at the lunch counter "face their actions" by orienting themselves toward the possibility of social transformation while preparing for violent resistance. The phrase also implies that protest has opened a "break" in the existing racial order where serialized "faces of here" might finally be brought into "one frame"—a moment of historical decision that can only be made collectively.

This stanza, however, shows how increasingly difficult it is for the speaker to either exit the scene or consolidate a contemplative historical vantage external to the moment of the sit-ins from which to construct a narrative of inevitable emancipation. Both the speaker and the protestors confront not only the serial constraint of segregated space but also a segregated historical time in which "the future is in the same / place as the past" (Roberson 2006, 29). In this stanza, the "face to face" comes to symbolize the apparent permanence of racial segregation, which turns out to be fundamentally compatible with the notion of formal equality and the perpetual renewal of political resistance to segregated social relations.

Suggesting the interchangeability of "future" and "past" in African ritual performances, the poet likens the "faces of here" poised at the threshold of historical change to ambiguous ritual masks that may be mocking the very possibility of escaping from a kind of prison of historical repetition. Yet here, the poem makes use of a kind of centrifugal momentum generated by this cyclical pattern to situate the protests in progressively broader contexts. As James Snead observes, in a study of the significance of cyclicity for Black expressive forms, such repetition affords the possibility of reimagining historical time in terms of the "periodic regeneration of biological and agricultural systems… often in homage to an original generative instance or act" (212):

> Cosmogony, the origins and stability of things, hence prevails because it recurs, not because the world continues to develop from the archetypal moment. Periodic ceremonies are ways in which black culture comes to terms with its perception of repetition, precisely by highlighting that perception.
>
> (212)

Snead points out that the complex forms of repetition that pattern Black expressive culture can suggest a return to mythic or historical roots, a resolution of opposing forces or ideas, and possibilities of regeneration and rebirth. Like a musical "cut" which for Snead "insists on the repetitive nature of the music, by abruptly skipping back to another beginning which we have already heard" (216), Roberson's poem draws on the momentum of "spin," turning "infinite regressions" (Roberson 2006, 27) into an occasion move outward into space beyond the borders of the city.

The appearance of Christian imagery in the poem's later stanzas begins to alter the narrative temporalities of religious allegories that powerfully shaped this movement with deep roots in Black liberation theology. The speaker's seemingly omniscient vantage is ultimately folded back into a position within the scene among the protestors, where "To know ourselves as a god would know us / would make us gods / of ourselves" (Roberson 2006, 31). Already the collective pronoun implies that the speaker has at least in part become one of "us," standing inside and outside of the scene. In other words, what the speaker recognizes or "knows" is the dissolution of Jim Crow and the revelation of a hidden principle of relationality that could reveal the city as a collective creation. Yet the speaker's, and by extension, the reader's, "godlike simply knowing" (Roberson 2006, 31) remains present only as a momentary glimpse of unrealized collective possibilities:

Here, in the glass of the city,
a godlike simply knowing doesn't determine
                                        what built
rafts of citizen draughts where the street runs
up the walk to the door.

(Roberson 2006, 31)

The speaker must here acknowledge that "simply knowing" (Roberson 2006, 31) can't intervene in the construction of "rafts of citizen draughts" (Roberson 2006, 31), an ambiguous phrase that suggests the reproduction of identical "versions" of citizen-subjects from out of a fungible mass of city inhabitants. These lines also gesture toward images of water throughout the poem as a figure for collectivity and the reparative abundance of the non-human natural world erupting into urban space at moments of political contestation. As the *Oxford English Dictionary* reminds us, a "draught" can refer to displaced water along with "the withdrawing, detachment, or selection of certain persons, animals, or things from a larger body for some special duty or purpose; the party so drawn off or selected; *spec.* in military use." "Citizen draughts" (Roberson, *City Eclogue* 31) could potentially allude to the Vietnam war draft, white segregationist citizens' councils "welded together by common dedication to the principles of white supremacy" (McMillen 116), or the sit-in protestors themselves as an organized group.

Here the poet evolves a pastoral, lyric vocabulary that is nevertheless suffused with a history of racist state violence:

The oceans, themselves one,   catch their image
                                        hosed by riot cops down the gutter into
The sphere surface
river

                                        looked into   reflects
                                        one face.

(Roberson, *City Eclogue* 27–8)

Like the possibility of mixed or composite perspectives and identities across a fixed color line, the "elemental" (Roberson, *City Eclogue* 29) forms that water assumes circulate throughout the poem's urban spaces. Here the water recalls both the decision of Birmingham police officers, under orders from notorious police official and staunch segregationist Theophilus Eugene "Bull" Connor, to turn fire hoses on civil rights protestors, and how such brutal tactics galvanized national public opinion against Jim Crow. The stanza also suggests that the aggressive police response has further fused the protestors together, who recognize their "one face" (Roberson, *City Eclogue* 28) in response to external threats.

From droplets of water and the "sphere surface / of this river" (Roberson, *City Eclogue* 31) to the shape of the planet, the poem's attention to spherical forms present in nature begins to insist upon the alignment of political and natural processes of circulation, of "spin." Although the "ocean teased apart / to its each drop" (Roberson, *City Eclogue* 31) can serve as a metaphor for racial division, the metaphor also allows the speaker to place "each drop" (Roberson, *City Eclogue* 31) back into circulation. In other words, the poem returns to the figure of isolated individuals engaged in acts of political resistance whose outcome is unclear, and the desperation of these acts before they become exemplary or are attributed to heroic individuals:

Someone is riding a bus, too tired
for everything except what is right;
a god has his back against the wall
of a church in Birmingham;
the marchers take to the streets.
Someone may want to know
what city we're in
that curves glowing over the edge
into an earth.

(Roberson, *City Eclogue* 30)

The speaker's minimal description of these two anonymous figures and their gestures of refusal do not render them any less recognizable as civil rights icons Rosa Parks and Martin Luther King Jr.—the former refusing to comply with segregated transportation laws and subsequently triggering the Montgomery bus boycott in 1955, and the latter perhaps delivering a sermon at the Sixteenth Street Baptist Church before its bombing in 1963 by the Ku Klux Klan.

Yet the speaker's refusal to name these figures dramatizes the poem's persistent concern with imagining segregation not through historical personages but in terms of racialized mobility and containment, or in other words of the opposition, between stasis and "spin." The "someone" who names potential addressees of the speaker's historical reconstruction becomes Parks herself, "riding a bus, too tired / for everything except what is right" (Roberson, *City Eclogue* 30)—a scene of moral exhaustion at having to move aside for white passengers. What I have read as the speaker's "godlike simply knowing" (Roberson, *City Eclogue* 31) becomes an implicit invocation of King, with "his back against the wall / of a church in Birmingham" (Roberson, *City Eclogue* 32). Here the resistance to these political acts is dramatized through bodies whose movements are controlled or constrained by racial codes, which seem to have seeped into a world of objects—a bus, a wall, the spatial form of the city. The poem depicts a body that refuses to move, and that can subsequently only continue to circulate endlessly through the city without ever arriving at a destination. The same poem also describes a moving body constrained, bumping up against the "wall" of a racially partitioned present in which a "godlike simply knowing" (Roberson, *City Eclogue* 31) cannot guarantee the emergence of a desegregated future.

In a final turn, the poet contrasts the definiteness of the proper name of Birmingham with the indefiniteness of "curves glowing over the edge/into an earth" (Roberson, *City Eclogue* 32). Indefiniteness itself becomes a luminous quality of relation at the borders between the human and non-human natural world—transforming the "infinite regressions" (Roberson, *City Eclogue* 27) of a receding dream of future justice into the faint light of a social whole momentarily visible on "faces of here" (Roberson, *City Eclogue* 29).

Coda: The Affordances of Racial Form

By continually putting into question the referent of race as a contested social form, "Sit In What City We Are In" presents a moment of struggle over the object of state, institutional, and intersubjective recognition. Protestors' demands for an end to segregation, however, give way to an experience of historical repetition over the course of the poem. In my reading, such demands for equal citizenship are forced to confront the "Piece Logic" that poet and critic Erica Hunt understands as the price of racial incorporation into a "Democracy of Goods."

Roberson's *City Eclogue* represents a spatial logic of incorporation where political movements and forms of coordinated activity emerge from and lapse back into a spatially dispersed serial condition. The poet represents the titular city as a spatial archive of the history of Jim Crow that is rapidly transformed by projects of urban renewal and gentrification that displace Black city residents from their homes and progressively reshape the "flesh form of the city" (Roberson 42). In one grim passage, the liquidation of personified "living" (Roberson 2006, 57) housing stock renders Black sanitation workers a kind of waste product of the economy, driven by an economic logic seemingly impervious to political transformation. "When the city tore down like shooting/all the houses living on our street," the poet writes, "we couldn't even get the job/of hauling/away/our dead" (Roberson 57).

Elsewhere in the collection, the poet describes how this economic geography of racial poverty and precarity continues to be maintained by "That powerful level of segregationists/the civil rights movement never reached" (Roberson 45):

That powerful level of segregationists
the civil rights movement never reached

never guilty or active agent within
the necessarily narrow focus needed to pin

never guilty of any more obvious
than wanting things this way,

the great weigh of wealth's want
that moves other men's hands

and feet and leaves its own clean,
the weight that never touches

anything but is carried
into the place it is always preparing

for itself above all movements.
into presidencies, oligarchies. These.

(Roberson 45)

Here "That powerful level of segregationists" come to be associated not only with the "obvious" defenders of Jim Crow but with the guardians of an economic order that could continue to reproduce an unequal, segregated society through the distribution of "the great weigh of wealth's want." The subtle shifts in diction here from "wanting" to "want," and from "weigh" to "weight," indicate how the will of "That powerful level of segregationists," a state–capital nexus of "presidencies" and "oligarchies," continues to produce material deprivation "that moves other men's hands/and feet and leaves its own clean."

In "Sit In What City We're In," a moment of thwarted recognition haunted by a vision of reciprocity forces the speaker of the poem to adopt a series of ever more expansive contextual frames to situate the stakes of political contention—connecting the site of the sit-ins to vaster human and non-human spaces and temporalities. The poet imaginatively translates varieties of social separation into a vision of entangled histories that models what I want to call, after political theorist Michael Dawson, a poetics of "linked fate" (Dawson 77). While Dawson develops the concept of "linked fate" to describe aggregate Black political behavior and racial group solidarity that need not be premised upon the assertion of group homogeneity, *City Eclogue* arguably extends the concept to the city itself as a figure of unrealized collective possibility across deep social divisions.[1]

The production of a rights-bearing subject of state recognition dispersed through the "hive" (Roberson 26) structure of the city does not only hinder but also enable coordinated action at increasing spatial scales. The poets who are the subject of this study register how capitalist processes do not progressively eliminate racial animus over time but instead powerfully shape a range of

[1] Other theorists have applied the concept of "linked fate" to a range of other racial, ethnic, gendered, and national populations. See for example Simien; Sanchez and Masuoka.

different socio-spatial configurations that racial positioning might take. These poems trace the complex and combinatory postwar configurations of *racial form* as a changing relational structure mirrored in images of a "democracy of goods," disposable "surplus" populations, a colonial and capitalist history of measure; a network of "factory girls" assembled and disassembled through global supply chains; or the "practico-inert" spatial form of a city and its serial collective inhabitants.

Even when poems do not explicitly address the relationship between capitalism and comparative racialization, contemporary Asian North American and Black experimental poetry reimagine race as a social form in ways that radically reframe contemporary discourses of identity and "identity politics." Representing identity as a serial social form that both limits and enables action, poet and critic Nathaniel Mackey has developed a sweeping theory of Black musical and literary tradition defined by a recursive shuttling between historically specific racial constraints and aesthetic and social possibilities. As perhaps one of the most influential theorists and practitioners of a Black experimental poetics, Mackey has consistently invested the combinatory expressive possibilities of serial poetic, musical, and literary forms with a special political significance. For the poet, the repeated racial experience of "failed advance" (Mackey, "Preface" xiv) against "limits we find ourselves up against again and again, limits we'd get beyond if we could" (Mackey, "Preface" xiv) becomes the condition of possibility for improvisation with limited materials like commercial melodies or textual fragments.[2] It is a movement that reimagines Blackness as a form of serial collectivity that does not suggest a fixed or fluid identity so much as a relational field generated through the pursuit of such possibilities. "Individual expression

2 Mackey's fiction and poetry consistently celebrate how contemporary Black music, and in particular open-ended improvisatory reconfigurations of musical standards, model a serial poetics that explores a "sense of disquiet and susceptibility to endless revisitation and variation" (Mackey, *Paracritical Hinge: Essays, Talks, Notes, Interviews* 337). The poet's ongoing epistolary novel series, entitled *From A Broken Bottle Traces of Perfume Still Emanate*, for example, is constructed out of an intricate weave of cross-cultural allusions and occasionally featuring libretti, lecture notes, and diagrams, the series primarily consists of an epistolary exchange between the multi-instrumentalist N. and a mysterious interlocutor named "Angel Of Dust," whose letters are not reproduced in text. N. uses his letters to "The Angel of Dust" chronicles the performances of an imagined group of avant-garde jazz musicians, the "Molimo m'Atet," of which he is a founding member. While readers are kept guessing as to whether the anonymity or pseudonymity of the "Angel of Dust" names an imagined muse, an addiction, or perhaps Mackey himself, the combination of the particulate metaphor of dust with the implicit animating power of "angel" provides a compact description of the novels' assemblage of figures out of permutable textual building blocks.

both reflects and redefines the collective, realigns, refracts it," Mackey contends. "Thus it is that Lester Young was in the habit of calling his saxophone's keys his people" (Mackey, *Discrepant Engagement: Dissonance, Cross-Culturality and Experimental Writing* 303):

> A desperate accent or inflection runs through seriality's recourse to repetition, an apprehension of limits we find ourselves up against again and again, limits we'd get beyond if we could. This qualifies the promise of advance and possibility the form otherwise proffers, the feeling for search it's conducive to complicated by senses of constraint. Circularity, a figure for wholeness, also connotes boundedness. Recursiveness can mark a sense of deprivation fostered by failed advance, a sense of alarm and insufficiency pacing a dark, even desperate measure, but this dark accent or inflection issues from a large appetite, or even a utopic appetite or, better—invoking Duke Ellington's neologism—a blutopic appetite. Seriality's mix of utopic ongoingness and recursive constraint is blutopic.
>
> (Mackey, "Preface" xiv)

This "recursive constraint" is also a principle of poetic composition and musical improvisation that is "blutopic" precisely because its non-teleological vision of "ongoingness" responds to but cannot overcome a repeated experience of "failed advance."[3]

My account of racial form is reducible neither to a repertoire of specific formal or technical poetic strategies, however, nor to poems that explicitly address the historical imbrication of capitalism and racial group formation. By staying attentive to "the historical force of aesthetic form and the formal mediation of social relations" (Lye, "The Afro-Asian Analogy" 1735), reading for racial form offers an alternative to dominant forms of poetic interpretation premised upon New Critical and Post–New Critical assumptions about how poetic formal strategies possess an intrinsic political valence or aesthetic value. The fact that the same formal strategies can signify in radically divergent ways allows readers to track how the meaning of racial form, or its "affordances" in

[3] Mackey understands a post-nationalist Black experimental poetics as elaborating a dynamic, improvisational structure in the face of a set of broadly shared social constraints. "Individual expression both reflects and redefines the collective, realigns, refracts it. Thus it is that Lester Young was in the habit of calling his saxophone's keys his people" (Mackey, *Discrepant Engagement: Dissonance, Cross-Culturality and Experimental Writing* 303). Lester Young's stretched definition of "his people" figure musical instruments themselves as a utopian or perhaps bluetopian process of transforming constraint into combinatory aesthetic and political possibilities.

the language of New Formalist criticism, might alter dramatically even over the course of a single poem.

I want to now turn to two poems, by John Yau and June Jordan, that both expose and deliberately frustrate readerly attempts to construe race as a legible, "transparent" subject of recognition. These works instead attempt to exit the hermeneutic circle produced by the protocols of "racialized reading" (Reed 7) that configure race as the "self-confirming ground of its own *raison d'etre*," as Kimberly Benston writes, "enfolding origin and end in a quest that has always already arrived at its destination" (Benston 285). Trapped in the serial recurrence of "failed advance," these poems refuse to construct a transparent "I" and respond to racial interpellation by instead affirming what I want to call the opacity of racial form.

Fluent in Coercive Mimeticism: John Yau

Perhaps no poet besides Theresa Hak Kyung Cha has so powerfully shaped the course of Asian American experimental writing than the poet and art critic John Yau. Born in 1950 in Massachusetts to Shanghainese immigrant parents, Yau is the author of over fifty published works of poetry, prose, and art criticism. The author's poems have often attempted to address the experience of racialization at the same time that they draw inspiration from European avant-garde art and writing, as well as contemporary twentieth-century painting.

From the poet's earliest collections of poems—the 1976 *Crossing Canal Street*, 1983 *Corpse and Mirror*, and 1992 long serial poem *Edificio Sayonara*—Yau has persistently frequently made use of combinatory serial poetic forms—from villanelles to humorous non-narrative chains of association created through puns, homonyms, anagrams, rhymes, and word-substitutions. Generated in part through the use of avant-garde surrealist literary techniques and Oulipian procedural writing, Yau's writing has consistently explored "neo-surrealist dramatic monologue[s]" (Leong 512) that feature speakers whose alternately mechanical and ludic "voice" is assembled through combinatory textual cutups of pulp detective, horror, and science fiction.

This formal strategy develops a sharp satirical edge in poems that parody the language of Orientalist stereotypes and the legacy of yellowface film and performance traditions.[4] As Joseph Jeon observes, the "often befuddling

[4] For an extended reading of "Genghis Chan" series, see Wang 205–43.

objecthood of avant-garde objects—be they books, films, or sculptures," becomes for the poet "a means of investigating the foreignness of racialized bodies" (Jeon 3). In poetic series like "Genghis Chan: Private Eye" (Yau, *Adventures in Monochrome* 25–77), Asiatic racial form is presented as a mask—a grotesque, unsettling, darkly humorous, and almost sculptural object of racial projection that speaks in these poems through a series of villainous or servile "Yellow Peril" personae—from the cringing and servile detective Charlie Chan to Fu Manchu, the diabolical Chinese "devil doctor" at the center of a series of popular novels by British fiction writer Sax Rohmer.[5]

In the author's late works, however, this formal strategy takes on an increasingly tragic inflection—registering the limits not only of parody but of the extent to which racial form and the terms of racial interpellation can be resignified. Yau's "Ing Grish," a poem from a 2005 collection of the same title produced with visual artist Thomas Nozkowski, is organized around a series of autobiographical reflections on the poet's chronic inability to perform a legible version of a Chinese racial identity for poetry audiences, and in particular on an incident where the poet is chastised for being unable to speak or read Chinese by a white poet and translator who does.

As a parodic reference to an implied non-native Asian speaker's rendering of the word "English," the collection features a number of different poems where speakers attempt to puzzle out the appropriate cultural signifiers, forms of linguistic competence, and political beliefs associated with the Asiatic racial form of Chineseness. As Dorothy Wang has argued, Yau consistently plays with the fact that the "Mishearing, misrecognition, and misstatement often characterize the non-native speaker's relationship to English" (235)—while taking that relationship as a condition of possibility of linguistic experimentation opened up by the non-native Asian speaker's "Weird English" (Ch'ien). The poem's polemical stanzas that repeatedly insist that the speaker simultaneously does and does not understand either English or Chinese give way to an elegy for the author's late parents whose specific and unrepeatable lives can only be superficially understood through the fact of their fluency in a native language.

As a series of responses to an implied question of whether the author knows or does not a particular language, the speaker of "Ing Grish" displays a sly and strategically fluctuating sense of their own linguistic competence and powers of

[5] On Fu Manchu's seminal role in defining yellow peril discourse and British and American white fantasies of "reverse colonization" (Seshagiri 171) see Seshagiri.

comprehension when confronting how English is entangled in the imperial and settler colonial history of the United States:

> I do not know Ing Grish, but I will study it down to its
> black and broken bones.
> I do not know Ing Gwish, but I speak dung and dungaree,
> satrap and claptrap.
> Today I speak barbecue and canoe.
> Today I speak running dog and yellow dog.
> I do not know Spin Gloss, but I hear humdrum and humdinger,
> bugaboo and jigaboo.
>
> (Yau and Nozkowski 62)

The question of language proficiency in the poem euphemizes Orientalist fantasies and encodes the implicit threat of racial and sexual violence within slurs—from "jigbaoo" to "chink" (Yau and Nozkowski 65)and "gook" (Yau and Nozkowski 65). The speaker subjects the "black and broken bones" of English to forensic investigation while satirizing the impulse to believe that processes of ascriptive racialization might be countered through more accurate forms of ethnic self-identification. "I do not know Chinese because during the Vietnam War/I was called a gook instead of a chink," Yau writes, "and realized/that I had managed to change my spots without meaning to" (Yau and Nozkowski 65). Here the misidentification of the speaker's ethnic identity reveals how Asian racialization doesn't depend on language proficiency at all but differences in physical appearance.

The speaker's conclusion that they must, as a result, "not know Chinese," can be read as a confession of failure at being unable to translate the involuntary nature of racial identification into the voluntary decision to acquire a different language and "change my spots without meaning to." "I do know English," Yau writes elsewhere in the poem, "because I remember what 'Made in Japan' meant/ when I was a child" (Yau and Nozkowski 64). What the speaker knows, in this case, is not simply proper English grammar and pronunciation but a postwar history of anti-Asian racial hatred in which the postwar Japanese manufacturing sector posed a competitive threat to the livelihoods of US workers in a rapidly deindustrializing economy.[6]

[6] For a history of the impact of the "Buy American" campaigns of the 1980s, intended to support the US auto industry against the competitive threat of Japanese imported automobiles, on anti-Asian racial animus, see Frank. The "black and broken bones" of English broadly refers to this history, marked by the 1982 murder of Vincent Chin, a Chinese American man beaten to death by two white Detroit auto workers in the midst of the trade wars between Japan and the United States in the 1970s–80s.

These opening stanzas prime readers to interpret language proficiency as evidence of racial belonging in the poem and the degree of assimilation to the worlds conjured up by, for example, "barbecue and canoe." Or conversely, knowing the "language" of "running dog and yellow dog" positions the speaker between a US anti-Chinese epithet and a derisive term used to describe individual and state supporters of Western imperialism within a Maoist political lexicon (zǒugǒu). Implied Asian American speaker is represented in the poem as a fundamentally disloyal and racially inauthentic subject whose intergenerational diasporic trajectory renders them foreign to both the United States and China. The speaker is simultaneously racially unassimilable and culturally hyperassimilated—the puppet of distant alien powers.

Unlike the author's earlier works that have been widely celebrated for exploiting the generative possibilities of miscommunication and mistranslation, the speaker's playful evasions quickly turn to anguish at how repeated attempts to clarify what languages they do and do not speak only further confirms their racial inauthenticity. The pairing of "dung and dungaree," and "satrap and claptrap," establishes a repeated pattern throughout the poem where sonic echoes suggest a non-native speaker's attempts puzzle through subtle differences between similar-sounding words. The procedure disorders English to mimic Asian languages as gibberish or "claptrap." "I no speak Chinee, Chanel, or Cheyenne" (Yau and Nozkowski 62) Yau writes, cobbling together an alliterative chain of signifiers which suggest a crisis of racial intelligibility and their uncertain position in the United States:

> I do not know Ang Grish, but I can tell you that my last name
> consists of three letters, and that technically all of them are vowels.
>
> I do not know Um Glish, but I do know how to eat with two sticks.
>
> Oh but I do know English because my father's mother was English
> and because my father was born in New York in 1921
> and was able to return to America in 1949
> and become a citizen.
>
> I no speak Chinee, Chanel, or Cheyenne.
>
> I do know English because I am able to tell others
> that I am not who they think I am.
> I do not know Chinese because my mother said that I refused to learn it

> from the moment I was born, and that my refusal
> was one of the greatest sorrows of her life,
> the other being the birth of my brother.
>
> (Yau and Nozkowski 62–3)

The speaker's failed attempts to explain to others and to themselves how to pronounce a foreign surname, along with their comically precocious refusal to learn Chinese from birth, confirms their vexed status as both an insider and outsider. A consonant, in the surname "Yau," for example, turns out to be a vowel. Describing chopsticks as "two sticks" momentarily adopts an outsider's perspective on these implements. In each stanza, the speaker emphasizes how appearances are misleading in ways that only speed the translation of entangled histories of racial exclusion, changing cultural practices, and personal choices into a discourse of inherent racial characteristics. The speaker somehow inherits the English language due to the mixed-race ancestry of the speaker's father rather than a series of voluntary immigration decisions.

The speaker's inability to perform a prescripted racial role dramatizes a peculiar response to what Rey Chow calls "coercive mimeticism" (107), a demand for "the ethnic person… to come to resemble what is recognizably ethnic" (107):

> [C]oercive mimeticism [represents] a process (identitarian, existential, cultural, or textual) in which those who are marginal to mainstream Western culture are expected, by way of what Albert Memmi calls 'the mark of the plural,' to resemble and replicate the very banal preconceptions that have been appended to them, a process in which they are expected to objectify themselves in accordance with the already seen and thus to authenticate the familiar imagings of them as ethnics.
>
> (107)

For Chow, coercive mimeticism describes the imperative to perform projected roles which are "prescripted, pre-read, and pre-viewed in their utterances, attitudes, gestures, writings, behaviors, and psychologies" (116). "And, if it is difficult for the ethnic to become a perfect imitation of the white man," Chow writes in terms that we could apply to the speaker of "Ing Grish," "it is even more difficult for her to become a perfect imitation of herself" (116).

Yau's poem is centrally organized around a contentious exchange between Yau and the translator, editor, and poet Eliot Weinberger that illustrates the continuing impact of "coercive mimeticism" on the production and reception of Asian American literary works. In response to Yau's critical review of Weinberger's racially exclusionary editorial curation of an anthology of US postwar experimental poetry, *American Poetry Since 1950: Innovators and Outsiders* (Weinberger, *American Poetry Since 1950: Innovators and Outsiders, an Anthology*), Weinberger accuses the poet of racial opportunism.[7] "Yau, a poet and Soho art critic," Weinberger writes, "has created a remarkable new persona for himself: that of the angry outsider 'person of color' " whose criticisms of notable omissions from the anthology are moot because he has "probably never written a topical social-protest poem in his adult life" (Weinberger, "Letter" 43):

> [B]ecause of the skins we were born into, John can feel free to claim that I "refuse to address" pluralism and multiculturalism, knowing full well that this has been my entire life. I spent years studying Chinese which John barely speaks and cannot read-and have written extensively on Chinese poetry. (Weinberger, "Letter" 43)

In response to the critique of gaps in the anthology's coverage, Weinberger questions the racial representativeness of Yau's aesthetic and political commitments, and in particular, his knowledge of the Chinese language. It is a response that conflates race, culture, and political perspective in ways that confuse the dynamics of racial ascription with voluntary practices. In the language of contemporary sociology, race is translated into a discourse of ethnic culture in a move that structures the pluralist multicultural imaginary Weinberger invokes.[8]

[7] "Let me make this plain: I believe that, in this society, all poets are Others," Weinberger continues, "that any poem can be about anything the writer desires; and that differences among poets must be drawn along aesthetic lines" (Weinberger, "Letter" 43–4). The exchange anticipates contemporary debates over race and appropriation techniques utilized by contemporary Conceptual writers. "Racial identity isn't something you put on and take off, like a shirt or shoes" (Yau, "'Purity' and the 'Avant-Garde'"), Yau writes over two decades later, reiterating the language of his response to Weinberger almost verbatim in a critique of Conceptual writers' embrace of a "post-identity" poetics that reveals the continued racialization of the category of avant-garde experimental writing.

[8] For an overview of how sociologists have theorized race and ethnicity as distinct but sometimes overlapping categories of analysis, see Cornell and Hartmann. For an account of how contemporary Asian American literature and politics have been shaped by the pervasive "morphing of race into ethnicity in public discourses about national belonging, social difference, economic inequality, and global competitiveness" (Koshy 156), see Koshy. "The recent shift from racial to ethnic senses of U.S. belonging," Koshy continues, "reinforced by the culturalist bias of institutionalized multiculturalism, the accommodation of new immigrants, and the resurgence of white ethnicity, shows how the new discourse of ethnicity in a transnational context obscures the operations of race and class" (Koshy 156). On the "culturalization of politics and the resultant depoliticization of anti-racism" (Lentin 390) from the 1980s onward in the United States and the United Kingdom, see Lentin.

Leaving aside the question of the organization of Weinberger's anthology, these authors display radically different understandings of the meaning of race in this brief exchange. Yau's reply highlights the involuntary nature of racialization. "Mr. Weinberger characterizes me as having 'created a remarkable new persona… that of the angry outsider "person of color,"'" the poet writes, "One's color is neither something you can put on and take off, like a coat, nor an ideology you announce one moment and ignore at another" (Yau, "Letter" 44). Yau is positioned as an unrepresentative and inauthentic racial subject without the requisite epistemic authority to stage a critique of racial exclusion. Such inauthenticity is not simply the product of Yau's interest in the work of white avant-garde artistic and literary figures like Andy Warhol and John Ashbery, but also in my reading symptomatic of the contemporary racial positioning of Asian Americans as "imperfect, because contaminated, copies of their culture" (Chow 124). "Because many of them no longer have the claim to ethnic authority through the possession of ethnic languages," Chow points out, "Asian Americans are perhaps the paradigmatic case of a coercive mimeticism that physically keeps them in their place" (Chow 125).

Over twenty years later, "Ing Grish" revisits the exchange with Weinberger and draws a series of tragicomic conclusions about the consequences of failing to successfully mimic Asiatic racial form:

> Because I do not know Chinese I have been told that means
> I am not Chinese by a man who translates from the Spanish.
> He said that he had studied Chinese and was therefore closer
> To being Chinese than I could ever be. No one publicly disagreed with him,
> Which, according to the rules of English, means he is right.
> I do know English and I know that knowing it means
> that I don't always believe it.
> The fact that I disagree with the man who translates from the Spanish
> is further proof that I am not Chinese because all the Chinese
> living in America are hardworking and earnest
> and would never disagree with someone who is right.
> This proves I even know how to behave in English.
> […]
> The authority on poetry announced that I discovered that I was Chinese
> When it was to my advantage to do so.
> (Yau and Nozkowski 63–4)

While these stanzas satirize the premise that one can slip in and out of a racial group due to language proficiency, ideological disagreements, and codes of behavior, the speaker neither embraces a "colorblind" universalism nor constructs a "transparent" and affirmative ethnocultural identity in response to this mimetic failure. Such failure becomes over the course of the poem a willed refusal to abide by the "rules" of racial interpellation that conflate racial positioning with cultural practices, forms of knowledge, codes of behavior, and heterogeneous political beliefs.

The speaker reflects on how a system of racially typed work, and an intragroup division of immigrant labor, renders language proficiency a materially consequential adaptive response to conditions beyond the speaker's control:

> My father was afraid that if I did not speak English properly
> I would be condemned to work as a waiter in a Chinese restaurant.
> My mother, however, said that this was impossible because
> I didn't speak Cantonese, because the only language
> waiters in Chinese restaurants know how to speak was Cantonese.
>
> (Yau and Nozkowski 64)

"Ing Grish" is the peculiar language produced by a diasporic rupture of intergenerational continuity and the speaker's thwarted sense of racial belonging. Mishearing his English grandmother's confession of being a descendent of the Huguenots as a claim that he is a "descendent of the Argonauts" (Yau and Nozkowski 64), the speaker struggles to translate the seemingly idiosyncratic experiences of his extended family, and their strained relations, into a form recognizable not only to outsiders but to himself as well:

> I do not know Chinese even though my parents conversed in it every day.
> I do know English because I had to ask the nurses not to put my mother
> in a straitjacket, and reassure them that I would be willing to stay with her
> until the doctor came the next morning.
> I do know English because I left the room when the doctor told me
> I had no business being there.
> [...]
> I do not know English because when father said that he would
> like to see me dead, I was never sure quite what he meant.
>
> (Yau and Nozkowski 64–5)

"Ing Grish" ends by describing an experience of racial illegibility in which "Anguish is a language everyone can speak," the poet writes, "but no one listens to it" (Yau and Nozkowski 64). It is precisely through "listening" to this "language," however, that the speaker is able to partially free the untranslatable particularity of his parents' immigrant lives from the demands of coercive mimeticism:

> I do not know either English or Chinese and, because of that,
> I did not put a gravestone at the head of my parents' graves
> as I felt no language mirrored the ones they spoke.
>
> (Yau and Nozkowski 65)

Here only death seems to arrest the speaker's impulse to offer further textual permutations that have, over the course of the poem, exposed the serial structure of racial constraint. Leaving graves unmarked memorializes an experience of shared non-belonging that in the poem restores both a sense of intergenerational continuity and the troubled inheritance of fluency in the opacity of "no language." Reckoning with how easily the existential particularity of such lives can be ignored and overwritten, the speaker momentarily stops trying to answer an implied question that is not a question at all but a demand to adopt the grammar of Asiatic racial form.

June Jordan and the Opacity of Racial Form

Published over thirty-five years before "Ing Grish," poet and essayist June Jordan's poem "Toward a Personal Semantics," published in the 1971 collection *Some Changes*, begins with a speaker questioning whether an interlocutor's words are trustworthy. As the title of the poem suggests, this uncertainty raises broader questions about how to determine the semantic content of speech acts and, as I will later argue, the semantic referent of race as a signifier. At the beginning of this compact poem, the speaker questions how statements of fact might refer to a politically contested context of utterance in part shaped by the force of performative speech acts:

> if I do take somebody's word on
> it means I don't know and you have to
> believe if you just don't know
>
> how do I dare to stand as
> still as I am still standing
>
> arrows create me
> but I am no wish
> after all the plunging
> myself is no sanctuary

birds feed and fly inside me shattering
the sullen spell of any
accidental
eyeless storm to twist and sting
the tree of my remaining
like the wind.

(Nielsen and Ramey, *Every Goodbye Ain't Gone: An Anthology of Innovative Poetry by African Americans*, 137)

The opening conditional, "if I do," can be read either as the acceptance of "somebody's word" or as speculation about the consequences of not doing so. In either case, the interrogative that frames the remainder of the poem describes the price of refusing to accept that "word" as a neutral act of description and refusing to "believe if you just don't know."

The speaker's refusal to believe in this "word" distances the speaker from this rhetorical situation, exposing language as contested intersubjective terrain and seems to occasion a turbulent, solitary process of self-questioning and self-definition that warps the syntax of the poem. The fact that "arrows create me" implies that the "me" is a product of both the interpellative force of "somebody's word" and a struggle to alter the meaning of that "word."

Neither a "wish" nor "sanctuary," the speaker refuses to idealize a "me" that is here represented as the troubled object of contending projections. That "me" both absorbs the psychically "shattering" force of those "arrows" but also seems to come into existence as a specific kind of oppositional subject. The speaker's initial act of daring "to stand" momentarily reproduces the outlines of this subject only to expose how it is not whole, but hollow. The poem describes the collapse of this imposed "I" into a kind of mordant pun—an "eyeless storm" with no calm center.

Featured in her second book, "Toward a Personal Semantics" seems to contrast sharply with poems that more explicitly address race, gender, and sexuality. As part of a series of scattered early career poems that seem to explore the expressive limits of a "Personal Semantics," these poems have long puzzled critics expecting the more unambiguous political assertions contained in the widely anthologized "Poem About My Rights," for example.[9]

[9] See for example Hayden Carruth's 1977 *New York Times* review of Jordan's selected poems, *Things We Do In The Dark*. Carruth finds the abstraction and absence of racial reference in poems like "Toward a Personal Semantics" baffling. "One section of her book is called, for instance, 'Towards a Personal Semantics,' and it contains many poems of this sort, exactly the ones that baffle me," Carruth argues. "They are full of polysyllabic abstractions, images pulled out of nowhere, themes that appear and disappear and never quite define themselves."

The political ambiguity of Jordan's 1971 poem arguably highlights the stakes of ongoing post-1960s poetic debates over the representational status of the autobiographical speaking subject, or the lyric "I," as a long-standing boundary marker between a US mainstream, "expressive" poetics and an experimental or avant-garde "other tradition" (Perloff 104). In a recent anthology of contemporary Black experimental poetry, *What I Say: Innovative Poetry by Black Writers in America,* Jordan's poem is framed as an example of how Black experimental poetry constitutes a taxonomic challenge to what editors Lauri Ramey and Aldon Lynn Nielsen call "the long-standing argument that Black poets in America were busy 'telling their own stories' while white poets pursued a more experimental course" (Nielsen and Ramey, *What I Say: Innovative Poetry by Black Writers in America* xv). Because critics have typically not categorized Jordan as an experimental poet, her presence in Nielsen and Ramey's anthology is intended to question "the common view both inside and outside the academy… that the 70s marked an era in which L=A=N=G=U=A=G=E poetries arose to contest official verse culture" while "postwar black poetry presumably followed a separate course" (Nielsen and Ramey, *What I Say: Innovative Poetry by Black Writers in America* xiv).

The dominant narratives of postwar US poetry have long cast the divide between mainstream and experimental poetry in terms of a distinction between normative versus non-normative syntax. Because assessments of normative language use are, of course, context-dependent, it is a taxonomic division historically freighted with contested racial meaning. Framed in alternately opposed or complementary terms, the difference between what was broadly characterized as a mainstream and experimental poetics by the 1990s had congealed around a distinction between a "politics of form" and a "poetics of identity."[10] Despite the fact that these bodies of writing are sometimes overlapping, the concept of identity as a basic unit of analysis has been subsequently threaded through a number of oppositions that continue to broadly organize the study of postwar US poetry: lyric and anti-lyric impulses, expression and construction, voice and textuality, and difficulty and accessibility.

These antinomies of postwar poetics have generally associated experimentation with a set of disjunctive or defamiliarizing formal strategies that denaturalize the lyric subject, "ideologies of expression" (Dworkin xliii), and identity more

[10] For more on the history of this opposition and its relationship to New Left and Post–New Left political movements, see Chen and Kreiner.

broadly as a linguistic convention and ascriptive social form. New Critical and post–New Critical discourses of formal abstraction often presuppose a racial opposition between fixed and fluid subjects, where formal innovation, aesthetic agency, and political universality are frequently understood in terms of rendering speaking subjects socially unlocatable.

Conversely, contemporary racially marked poetic traditions have been broadly framed in terms of the expression of identities and the reclamation of marginalized voices. Jordan's poem raises the question, however, of whether race, as what Evelyn Brooks Higginbotham has called a "metalanguage" (Higginbotham 255), is reducible to the concept of identity in the first place and what sorts of social forms it might otherwise assume. By representing the speaking subject not as a fixed social location or "identity," but instead as an inflection point between constraint and possibility, Jordan's poem can help us to rethink race as a politically contested signifier, comparative social form, and context for poetic experimentation.

The poem helps us to reframe race beyond the idiom or "container" of identity and to reflexively interrogate the parameters of racial representation within contemporary poetic works where explicit racial reference may be absent. As a shifting articulation of relations between subjects, structures, and formative processes, racial form functions as a kind of hinge concept in my reading that mediates between race understood as a structure of domination on the one hand, and as an affirmative subject of liberation, group solidarity, and shared history on the other.[11]

Still

The final image of "the tree of my remaining" returns us to the two senses of "still," tracing the mutation of the word from adjective to adverb, subtly altering the meaning of a subject fixed and immobilized by "somebody's word" to a willed commitment to "remaining." The poem concludes by offering a complex simile—"the tree of my remaining / like the wind"—that raises the question

[11] Lye's characterizes racial form as a kind of historically shifting relation between "archives of racial representation" (Lye, "Racial Form" 96) and "archives of ethnic self-expression" (Lye, "Racial Form" 96)—a move that highlights a fundamental definitional ambiguity of the concept of race itself that frequently collapses a basic sociological distinction between race and ethnicity in popular discourse. I read racial form as a kind of hinge concept that mediates between principles and practices of hierarchical social differentiation on the one hand, and a range of historically specific responses to racial positioning on the other.

of whether the speaker identifies with the enduring solidity of the form of the tree or with the seeming formlessness of wind. It seems that the speaker's commitment to "remaining" only momentarily assumes a visible material form—rooted yet also capable of movement. Perseverance is here not rooted in embodiment, however, but a will to "dare" that seems to draw energy from the external forces assailing the body. Poised between a noun and verb, the gerund "remaining" then comes to identify its own constancy with the very elemental forces that deprive the speaker of a stable enunciative position and fixed social location. The commitment to "remaining" is not an "accidental" result of external determination, nor does it simply assert the fiction of a completely non-relational subject.

It is this willed commitment, the poet insists, that transforms the lived experience of inhabiting a social location from ascriptive fixity to a resolute endurance—from "still" to "still." The movement from the former to the latter sense of "still," and back again, traces the circulation of a figure that only exists in motion—the wind. If the speaker assumes the form of a static and discrete subject, the poem implies, they will be continually battered by experience. The "tree of my remaining / like the wind" could be read then as registering the speaker's repeated attempts to undo a kind of defensive psychic rigidification in the face of a "shattering" traumatic experience and what I have been describing as a loss of epistemic "standing."

The speaker's hesitation at accepting "somebody's word" arguably dramatizes an important distinction between two fundamentally different kinds of language use: what philosopher of language J. L. Austin has called the symbolic action of a "performative utterance" (27) versus a descriptive "constative utterance" (47) that declares some set of facts or conditions to be the case. For Austin, performative utterances are a linguistic speech act, such as making a promise or offering a warning, in which "the issuing of the utterance is the performing of an action" (6). A constative utterance, on the other hand, is a form of descriptive language that can be assessed as either "true or false" (Austin 54). Whether performative speech acts "misfire" (Austin 25), Austin contends, can be attributed to "varieties of infelicity" (19) that include performing utterances under duress or having verbal acts misunderstood. Such acts are, strictly speaking, neither true nor false but can either fail or succeed.[12]

[12] Austin has also controversially suggested that language used by actors on a stage or contained within a poem can be considered infelicitous in assessing any performative utterance. Such language is "hollow or void" because it is "parasitic upon its normal use" (Austin 22). "[T]he constative utterance is true or false," Austin maintains, "and the performative is happy or unhappy" (Austin 54)

The speaker's difficulty in determining whether to believe or disbelieve "somebody's word" highlights the entanglement of these two types of speech acts. Readers do not know whether the speaker is evaluating an interlocutor's performative or constative utterance, and, as Jacques Derrida has famously argued, neither the meaning nor the context of speech acts can be fixed.[13] The poem suggests that there is a high price to be paid for daring "to stand" apart from the unnamed interlocutor's epistemic authority to determine what counts as assertion or description. The play of assertion and description throughout the poem casts this intersubjective communicative situation in intrapsychic terms, where the empirical givenness of the speaker's sense of "I" and "me" as an object of description comes into a torsional relation with a shattered and reconstructed subject of assertion.

We might read this simultaneously fluid, yet insistent, commitment to endure as an instance of more explicit defiant responses to racial marginalization and gender and sexual subordination in Jordan's other poems. But what I argue constitutes one experimental impulse of the poem is its registration of how the very "shape" of identity, and what Gillian White has called "the expressive and humanistic subject that the word 'lyric' metonymizes" (White 17), can never become a stable object of recognition. Instead, what the speaker "expresses" is not an identity but a process of constrained self-fashioning in the absence of intersubjective reciprocity. The increasingly compressed imagistic logic of the poem dramatizes the speaker's attempt to strike a balance between a will to defend themselves from external threats and a desire to remain receptive to a non-human natural order of trees, birds, and wind.[14]

Jordan's poem traces the "shape" of endurance, reimagining the will to "dare" not only as a form of resistance but also as a commitment to the agential possibilities of "remaining" receptive to changing external conditions. In other words, the poem challenges the interpretive presupposition that in racially marked literature, "agency derives its shape from identity rather than action itself being constitutive of identity" (McNay 164). The poem describes a field of action that is inevitably shaped by the "constraint" of identity itself as a bounded social form imposed upon a speaker whose capacity for action continually breaches the contours of this container.

[13] See Derrida.

[14] We can situate Jordan's poem within a tradition of Black environmental writing and Black ecopoetics that dramatically reimagines the non-human natural world as both a space of a renewal and a symbolic geography profoundly shaped and scarred by racial history. On Black poetry and the environmental imagination, see Dungy; Postmentier.

"Toward a Personal Semantics" ultimately provides a suggestive, compact model for how to read racial form as describing not only a set of social constraints but also how such constraints condition a range of specific agential possibilities. The question, "how do I dare to stand as / still as I am still standing," dramatizes the play between a description of an already existing state of affairs and a kind of performative assertion, where a commitment to "remaining" becomes a background condition for further action. The speaker confronts not only the interpellative "word" of others but the history of their own previous choices. Jordan does not associate agential capacity with a deracinated, universal lyric speaking subject, however, but with a socially embedded set of political and imaginative possibilities for intervention. In my reading, the poem elaborates a "grammar" of situated action that potentially applies across multiple contexts and communicative situations.

If we read the poem as describing a compressed phenomenology of racialization, or Fred Moten has described as a Black "subjectivity structure born in objection" (*In the Break: The Aesthetics of the Black Radical Tradition* 13), the speaker's response to racial objectification ultimately refuses to reproduce the figure of an absolutely self-sufficient, "transparent" subject as its emancipatory horizon.[15] The speaker of "Towards a Personal Semantics" could be read as refusing what I want to call a "poetics of recognition" governed by the imperative to not only perform a legible social identity but to reproduce the very social form of identity itself.[16] As the language of the poem shifts from the human to the non-human natural world, the poem associates survival not only with refusal but with attunement to the elemental power of lyric or postlyric "world-making" (Culler 8) under severe social constraint.[17]

15 Denise Ferreira da Silva has characterized this subject as a racially unmarked "transparent 'I' " (xxiv) central to Enlightenment and post-Enlightenment European thought. For Da Silva it is a subject that historically been negatively defined in relation to the "affectable 'I' " (196) of non-European racial subjects understood as especially susceptible to environmental influences and therefore incapable of independent rational action and judgment.

16 For an overview of the intellectual genealogy of terms like "identity" and "identity politics" in contemporary popular and scholarly discourse, see Marie Moran, *Identity and Capitalism*; Philip Gleason, "Identifying Identity: A Semantic History"; and Frederick Cooper and Rogers Brubaker, "Beyond Identity".

17 I borrow the term "postlyric" (Reed 97) from the work of Anthony Reed. "The ideology of the stable voice, typified by a certain critical hermeneutics of 'the' lyric," Reed writes, "is one backdrop against which black experimental writing works" (97). Such a postlyric Black experimental poetics accomplishes this by "confronting readers with a subject that does not easily reduce to an appropriable object of knowledge" while "it suspends the presumption of speaking *for* by making visible the literary production of 'speech' " (98).

Jordan would dilate the poem's gnomic declarations in a much longer prose poem, written from 1958 to 1973, entitled "Fragments from a Parable," published in *New Days: Poems of Exile and Return* (1974). Begun during what the poet called the "civil rights decade," "Fragments from a Parable" was published after the shorter version of the poem appeared in *Some Changes*. The later work offers significantly more context for some of the language in "Towards a Personal Semantics" while continuing to rely on the earlier poem's highly associative, non-narrative style.[18] "Somebody's word" is here reframed as the word of God changing Saul to Paul on the road to Damascus, or as the suffocating patriarchal "word" of a violent and domineering West Indian immigrant father looking to insulate his family from external threats but instead imprisoning the speaker within a "syntax of stone" (Jordan 66).[19]

Although a more thorough close reading of "Fragments of a Parable" is beyond the scope of this conclusion, the racial form of Blackness represented in the poem emerges from the interplay of fluidity and "arrest"—the latter word evokes police violence but also the reduction of Black life to inert, fungible matter:

> My name is me. I am what you call black. (Only I am still. Arrest me. Arrest me any one or thing. If you arrest me I am yours. I am yours ready for murder or am I yours ready to expose any closed vein. Which is not important. Am I matter to you? Does it? You will try when. But now I am never under arrest.
>
> (Jordan 60)

"Black" is a word that belongs only partially to the speaker—a word that seems to "lie on the borderline between oneself and the other" (Bakhtin 293). The speaker is crucially aware of the fact that, as Mikhail Bakhtin points out about the socially embedded and contested nature of the meaning of any linguistic signifier, "The word in language is half someone else's" (Bakhtin 293). We might reread the earlier poem in light of this passage from the latter one, where the speaker does not counter her ascriptive racial positioning by asserting an idealizable, whole,

[18] Jordan, June, and Archive of Recorded Poetry and Literature *June Jordan Reading Her Poems with Comment in the Recording Laboratory*, 1973, Audio, Retrieved from the Library of Congress, <www.loc.gov/item/94838932/>.

[19] Jordan's poetry, essays, and nonfiction memoir *Soldier: A Poet's Childhood* has persistently politicized the "private" domain of family relations as a space where the possibility of constituting a "personal semantics" is consistently preempted by a set of inherited meanings reinforced not only through a racist social order but also through the insular and patriarchal social form of the family. As Richard Flynn has argued, Jordan's persistent interest in rendering the complexity of childhood experience presents "a decidedly unsentimental view of the child as a soldier-poet who wrests power over a literally paternal language" (Flynn 161).

"transparent" identity, but instead by moving "between / beyond / beneath / illusions" (Jordan 60) into a space that might be better characterized in terms of what Edouard Glissant has called "the right to opacity" (Glissant 189).

What survives the shattering violence of external forces in the poem, and what escapes confinement within a family fatally shaped by a father's "delusion" (Jordan 64), is a simultaneously shattered and self-shattering subject that breaks free from the hold not only of implied authorities but also from the congealed "syntax" (Jordan 66) of the speaker's own prior actions. "I am one of those suffering frozen to the perpetual corrosion of me" (Jordan 60) Jordan writes—a condition that both limits and enables further action in a space whose very continued existence comes to signify "aggressively resisting" (Jordan 60).

This brief but suggestive passage from Jordan's later poem draws attention to the convergence of two conceptions of form. First, form describes what Raymond Williams has called the "generative moments" (190) where the "shape" of historical pressures and constraints register in the very formal patterns and formative processes that literary works encode—in "the poem first 'heard' as a rhythm without words, the dramatic scene first 'visualized' as a specific movement or grouping, the narrative sequence first 'grasped' as a moving shape inside the body" (190).

Second, the passage invokes the racial forms of what the poet Douglas Kearney, writing over four decades later, has satirically dubbed, after Bertolt Brecht, "Negrotesque gestus" (Kearney 62). "*Gestus/gest* are Brechtian theatrical techniques," Kearney writes, "indicating 'the mimetic and gestural expression of the social relationships prevailing between people of a given period'" (62). Such gestures map a repeated experience of social constraints that convey "the 'gist' of larger structures of power and domination" (Kearney 62). At the same time, *gestus/gest* refers to a repertoire of aesthetic strategies for Kearney—a racialized kinesics that both registers the force of such constraints and attempts to transform them into expressive possibilities: the shake, shimmy, shuffle, stagger, and stutter. In Jordan's poem, the speaker's claim that "I am never under arrest" is not an assertion of the fundamental indeterminacy of identity but what could instead be read as a repeatable gesture in an unrepeatable itinerary—as the mobile *gestus* of stillness itself, of "still."

Reading Jordan's two poems together encourages us to develop a more capacious conception of form that not only includes aesthetic techniques but also race understood as a complex, historically shifting amalgam of patterns of experience and social organization operating above and below the molar threshold of "identity." In this case, racial form is shaped not only by the organization of state violence, or by the heteropatriarchal family as a stifling container of the speaker's childhood experiences constructed to protect them from anti-Black racism, but crucially by how all of these structures are interarticulated.

While most of the works I've examined in this study map the historical imbrication of racial group formation and capitalist processes, the works by Roberson, Yau, and Jordan that I have selected interrogate how acts of state and institutional recognition help to construct normative racial subjects. The legibility of such subjects is governed by a dominant "grammar" of racial reference, I contend, that translates the complex dynamism of racial form into a language of objects and objectlike identities. These works deploy a range of experimental formal strategies to resist reducing relational structures and historical worlds to the transhistorical attributes of isolable "identities" that mirror key features of the commodity form.

Across these poems, however, survival and social transformation are not premised on simply refusing to assert a "transparent" subject of racial representation in response to racial interpellation and shared oppression. By mapping hidden material interconnections between populations, and the relays that gather together what Edouard Glissant calls "the expanse of the world" (55), these works imagine the potential shapes that solidarity can take across difference. The opacity of racial form is not empty space, after all, but a field of relational possibilities illegible to the prevailing terms of racial order.

Works Cited

Abbott, Steve, editor. *Left Write! Edited Transcripts of 1981 Left Write Conference*. Left Write Conference, 1982.

Abel, Elizabeth. *Signs of the Times: The Visual Politics of Jim Crow*. University of California Press, 2010.

Acemoglu, Daron, and Alexander Wolitzky. "The Economics of Labor Coercion." *Econometrica*, vol. 79, no. 2, pp. 555–600.

Ad Hoc Committee On The Triple Revolution. "The Triple Revolution." *Liberation*, no. April, 1964, pp. 9–16.

Alcala, Rosa. *MyOTHER TONGUE*. Futurepoem Books, 2017.

Alcoff, Linda. *Visible Identities: Race, Gender, and the Self*. Oxford University Press, 2005.

Alkhatib, Ali, et al. "Examining Crowd Work and Gig Work Through The Historical Lens of Piecework." *CHI '17: Proceedings of the 2017 CHI Conference on Human Factors in Computing Systems*, 2017, pp. 4599–616.

Altieri, Charles. "Without Consequence Is No Politics: A Response to Jerome McGann." *Politics and Poetic Value*, edited by Robert Von Hallberg, University of Chicago Press Journals, 1988, pp. 301–7.

Anderson, Benedict. *Imagined Communities: Reflections on the Origin and Spread of Nationalism*. Verso, 2016.

Anderson, Benedict. *The Spectre of Comparisons: Nationalism, Southeast Asia, and the World*. Verso, 1998.

Appadurai, Arjun. *Modernity At Large: Cultural Dimensions of Globalization*. University of Minnesota Press, 1996.

Armstrong, Meg. "'The Effects of Blackness': Gender, Race, and the Sublime in Aesthetic Theories of Burke and Kant." *The Journal of Aesthetics and Art Criticism*, vol. 54, no. 3, 1996, pp. 213–36.

Arruzza, Cinzia. "A Queer Union between Marxism and Feminism?" *Dangerous Liaisons: The Marriages and Divorces of Marxism and Feminism*, Merlin Press, 2013, pp. 115–28.

Atanasoski, Neda, and Kalinda Vora. *Surrogate Humanity: Race, Robots, and the Politics of Technological Futures*. Duke University Press, 2019.

Austin, J. L. *How To Do Things With Words*. Oxford University Press, 1962.

Avilez, GerShun. *Radical Aesthetics and Modern Black Nationalism*. University of Illinois Press, 2016.

Bakhtin, Mikhail. *The Dialogic Imagination: Four Essays*. Edited by Michael Holquist, Translated by Michael Holquist and Caryl Emerson, University of Texas Press, 1983.

Baldwin, Kate A. *The Racial Imaginary of the Cold War Kitchen: From Sokol'niki Park to Chicago's South Side*. Dartmouth College Press, 2016.

Banaji, Jairus. *Theory As History: Essays on Modes of Production and Exploitation*. Haymarket Books, 2011.

Bannerji, Himani. *The Dark Side of the Nation: Essays on Multiculturalism, Nationalism, and Gender*. Canadian Scholars Press, 2000.

Baraka, Amiri. *Hard Facts*. Second, People's War, 1972.

Baraka, Amiri. "Nationalism, Self-Determination, and Socialist Revolution." *The Black Nation*, vol. 2, no. 1, 1982, pp. 4–10.

Baraka, Amiri. *S O S: Poems 1961-2013*. Grove Press, 2016.

Baraka, Amiri. *The Autobiography of Leroi Jones*. Larence Hill Books, 1997.

Barth, Fredrik. *Ethnic Groups and Boundaries: The Social Organization of Culture Difference*. Waveland Press, 1998.

Baudry, Jean-Louis. "Ideological Effects of the Basic Cinematographic Apparatus." *Film Quarterly*, vol. 28, no. 2, pp. 39–47.

Becker, Gary. *The Economics of Discrimination*. University of Chicago Press, 1971.

Benanav, Aaron. *Automation and the Future of Work*. Verso, 2020.

Benston, Kimberly W. *Performing Blackness: Enactments of African-American Modernism*. Routledge, 2000.

Berk, Sarah Fenstermaker. *The Gender Factory: The Apportionment of Work in American Households*. Plenum Press, 1985.

Bernes, Jasper. *The Work of Art in the Age of Deindustrialization*. Stanford University Press, 2019.

Bernstein, Charles. *A Poetics*. 1992, p. 240, doi:vswRL.

Bernstein, Charles. *The Politics of Poetic Form: Poetry and Public Policy*. Roof Books, 1989.

Bhandar, Brenna. *Colonial Lives of Property: Law, Land, and Racial Regimes of Ownership*. Duke University Press, 2018.

Blasing, Mutlu. *Politics and Form in Postmodern Poetry: O'Hara, Bishop, Ashbery, and Merrill*. Cambridge University Press, 2009.

Blauner, Bob. *Still the Big News:* Temple University Press, 2001.

Boggs, James. *Pages From A Black Radical's Notebook: A James Boggs Reader*. Edited by Stephen M. Ward, Wayne State University Press, 2011.

Boggs, James. *Racism and the Class Struggle*. Monthly Review Press, 1970.

Bonacich, Edna. "A Theory of Middleman Minorities." *American Sociological Review*, vol. 38, no. 5, 1973, pp. 583–94.

Borzutzky, Daniel. *Memories of My Overdevelopment*. Kenning Editions, 2015.

Bracey J.H. Jr., et al. "SOS/Calling All Black People: A Black Arts Movement Reader." *SOS/Calling All Black People: A Black Arts Movement Reader*, 2014.

Bradway, Tyler. "Introduction: The Promise of Experimental Writing." *College Literature*, vol. 46, no. 1, pp. 1–31.

Bray, Joe, et al., editors. *The Routledge Companion to Experimental Literature*. Routledge, 2012.

Brenner, Robert. *The Economics of Global Turbulence: The Advanced Capitalist Economies from Long Boom to Long Downturn, 1945-2005*. Verso, 2006.

Brooks, Gwendolyn. *Blacks*. Third World Press, 1987.

Brown, Bill. "Reification, Reanimation, and the American Uncanny." *Critical Inquiry*, vol. 32, no. 2, pp. 175–207, doi:https://doi.org/10.1086/500700.

Brown, Scott. *Fighting for US: Maulana Karenga, the US Organization, and Black Cultural Nationalism*. NYU Press, 2005.

Buell, Lawrence. "Transcendentalist Catalogue Rhetoric: Vision Versus Form." *American Literature*, vol. 40, no. 3, 1968, pp. 325–39, doi:10.2307/2923769.

Burger, Peter. *Theory of the Avant-Garde*. Translated by Michael Shaw, University of Minnesota Press, 1984.

Burt, Stephanie. *Close Calls With Nonsense: Reading New Poetry*. Graywolf, 2009.

Callahan, Allen Dwight. "Perspectives for a Study of African American Religion: From the Valley of Dry Bones." *Nova Religio: The Journal of Alternative and Emergent Religions*, vol. 7, no. 1, 2003, pp. 44–59.

Carastathis, Anna. *Intersectionality: Origins, Contestations, Horizons*. University of Nebraska Press, 2016.

Carruth, Hayden. "Politics and Love." *The New York Times*, 9 Oct. 1977.

Ch'ien, Evelyn Nien-Ming. *Weird English*. Harvard University Press, 2005.

Cha, Theresa Hak Kyung. *Dictee*. Second Edi, University of California Press, 2009.

Cha, Theresa Hak Kyung. *Exilée and Temps Morts: Selected Works*. Edited by Constance M. Lewallen, University of California Press, 2009.

Chávez, John R. "Aliens in Their Native Lands: The Persistence of Internal Colonial Theory." *Journal of World History*, vol. 22, no. 4, 2011, pp. 785–809.

Chen, Christopher, and Timothy Kreiner. "The Politics of Form and Poetics of Identity in Postwar American Poetry." *The Routledge Companion to Literature and Economics*, edited by Michelle Chihara and Matt Seybold, Routledge, 2018, pp. 27–40.

Cheng, Anne Anlin. "Ornamentalism: A Feminist Theory for the Yellow Woman." *Critical Inquiry*, vol. 44, no. 3, pp. 415–46, doi:https://doi.org/10.1086/696921.

Cheng, Anne Anlin. *The Melancholy of Race: Psychoanalysis, Assimilation, and Hidden Grief*. Revised Ed, Oxford University Press, 2001.

Chow, Rey. *The Protestant Ethnic and the Spirit of Capitalism*. Columbia University Press, 2002.

Clark-Oates, Angela, et al. *Understanding the Life Narratives of Immigrants through Naming Practices*. Feb. 2016, doi:10.4324/9781315693347.

Clune, Michael W. *American Literature and the Free Market, 1945–2000*. Cambridge University Press, 2015, doi:1107680654.

Cohen, Lizabeth. "A Consumers' Republic: The Politics of Mass Consumption in Postwar America." *Journal of Consumer Research*, 2004, doi:10.1086/383439.

Coleman, Robin Means. *African American Viewers and the Black Situation Comedy: Situating Racial Humor*. Routledge, 2000.

Conte, Joseph. *Unending Design*. Cornell University Press, 1991.

Cooke, Marvel. "The Bronx Slave Market." *New York Compass*, 1950.

Cooper, Melinda. *Family Values: Between Neoliberalism and the New Social Conservatism*. Zone Books, 2017.

Cooper, Esther V. *The Negro Woman Domestics in Relation to Trade Unionism*. Fisk University, 1940.

Cornell, Stephen E., and Douglas Hartmann. *Ethnicity and Race: Making Identities in a Changing World*. Pine Forge Press, 2006.

Cowen, Deborah. *The Deadly Life of Logistics: Mapping Violence in Global Trade*. University of Minnesota Press, 2014.

Cowie, Jefferson. *Stayin Alive: The 1970s and the Last Days of the Working Class*. The New Press, 2012.

Crawford, Margo Natalie. *Black Post-Blackness: The Black Arts Movement and Twenty-First-Century Aesthetics*. University of Illinois Press, 2017.

Crown, Kathleen, and Ed Roberson. "'Down Break Drum': An Interview with Ed Roberson (Part 1)." *Callaloo*, vol. 33, no. 3, pp. 651–82.

Culler, Jonathan. *Theory of the Lyric*. Harvard University Press, 2017.

da Silva, Denise Ferreira. *Toward a Global Idea of Race*. University of Minnesota Press, 2007.

Davis, Angela. "The Approaching Obsolescence of Housework: A Working-Class Perspective." *Women, Race, & Class*, Vintage, 1983, pp. 222–44.

Davis, Mike. *Planet of Slums*. Verso, 2007.

Dawson, Michael. *Behind the Mule: Race and Class in African-American Politics*. Princeton University Press, 1995.

Day, Iyko. *Alien Capital: Asian Racialization and the Logic of Settler Colonial Capitalism*. Duke University Press, 2016.

"Decimate, V." *OED Online*, Oxford University Press, 2020.

Delaney, David. *Race, Place, and the Law, 1836-1948*. University of Texas Press, 1998.

Denning, Michael. "Wageless Life." *New Left Review*, no. 66, pp. 79–97.

Derrida, Jacques. "Signature Event Context." *Limited Inc*, Northwestern University Press, 1988, pp. 1–24.

Disorders, National Advisory Commission on Civil. *The Kerner Report*. Princeton University Press, 2016.

Du Bois, W. E. B. *Black Reconstruction in America, 1860-1880*. Free Press, 1998.

Dubey, Madhu. *Signs and Cities: Black Literary Postmodernism*. The University of Chicago Press, 2003.

Dungy, Camille T. *Black Nature: Four Centuries of African American Nature Poetry*. University of Georgia Press, 2009.

"Dura Mater, N." *OED Online*, Oxford University Press, 2016.

Dworkin, Craig. "The Fate of Echo." *Against Expression: An Anthology of Conceptual Writing*, edited by Craig Dworkin and Kenneth Goldsmith, Northwestern University Press, 2011, pp. xxiii–liv.

Dwyer, Owen J. "Interpreting the Civil Rights Movement: Place, Memory, and Conflict." *The Professional Geographer*, vol. 52, no. 4, 2000, pp. 660–71.

Edmond, Jacob. *Make It the Same: Poetry in the Age of Global Media*. Columbia University Press, 2019.

Edwards, Brent Hayes. "Black Serial Poetics: An Introduction to Ed Roberson." *Callaloo*, vol. 33, no. 3, 2010, pp. 621–37.

Elbaum, Max. *Revolution in the Air: Sixties Radicals Turn to Lenin, Mao and Che*. Verso, 2018.

Elson, Diane, and Ruth Pearson. "`Nimble Fingers Make Cheap Workers': An Analysis of Women's Employment in Third World Export Manufacturing." *Feminist Review*, no. 7, pp. 87–107.

Eng, David, and Shinhee Han. "A Dialogue on Racial Melancholia." *Psychoanalytic Dialogues*, vol. 10, no. 4, 2000, pp. 667–700.

Eng, David, and Walter Kazanjian, editors. *Loss: The Politics of Mourning*. University of California Press, 2002.

Ewen, Stuart, and Elizabeth Ewen. *Typecasting: On the Arts and Sciences of Human Inequality*. Seven Stories Press, 2008.

Federici, Silvia. *Revolution at Point Zero*. PM Press, 2012.

Felski, Rita. *The Limits of Critique*. University of Chicago Press, 2015.

Ferguson, Roderick A. *Aberrations In Black: Toward A Queer Of Color Critique*. University of Minnesota Press, 2003.

Ferguson, Roderick A. *The Reorder of Things: The University and Its Pedagogies of Minority Difference*. University of Minnesota Press, 2012.

Ferguson, Roderick A., and Grace Kyungwon Hong, editors. *Strange Affinities: The Gender and Sexual Politics of Comparative Racialization*. Duke University Press, 2011.

Ferguson, Susan, and David McNally. "Precarious Migrants: Gender, Race and the Social Reproduction of a Global Working Class." *Socialist Register 2015*, Monthly Review Press, 2014, pp. 1–23.

Fields, Barbara J., and Karen E. Fields. *Racecraft: The Soul of Inequality in American Life*. Verso, 2014.

FitzGerald, David Scott. *Culling the Masses*. Harvard University Press, 2014.

Flynn, Richard. "'Affirmative Acts': Language, Childhood, and Power in June Jordan's Cross-Writing." *Children's Literature*, vol. 30, 2002, pp. 159–85.

Foster, Susan Leigh. "Choreographies of Protest." *Theatre Journal*, vol. 55, no. 3, 2003, pp. 395–412.

Fox, Cybelle. *Three Worlds of Relief: Race, Immigration, and the American Welfare State from the Progressive Era to the New Deal*. Princeton University Press, 2012.

Frank, Dana. "Demons in the Parking Lot: Auto Workers, Buy American Campaigns, and the 'Japanese Threat' in the 1980s." *Amerasia Journal*, vol. 28, no. 3, 2002, pp. 33–50.

Frazier, E. Franklin. *Black Bourgeoisie*. The Free Press, 1957.

Fred Moten. "The Case of Blackness." *Criticism*, vol. 50, no. 2, 2009, pp. 177–218, doi:10.1353/crt.0.0062.

Freud, Sigmund. "Mourning and Melancholia." *The Standard Edition of the Complete Psychological Works of Sigmund Freud Volume XIV (1914-1916): On the History of the Psycho Analytic Movement, Papers on Metapsychology, and Other Works*, edited by James Strachey, Hogarth Press, 2964.

Friedan, Betty. *The Feminine Mystique*. Dell Books, 1964.

Galbraith, John Kenneth. *The Affluent Society*. Mariner Books, 1998.

Gates Jr., Henry Louis. *Figures in Black: Words, Signs, and the "Racial" Self*. Oxford University Press, 1989.

Geary, Daniel. *Beyond Civil Rights: The Moynihan Report and Its Legacy*. University of Pennsylvania Press, 2015.

Gibson, Nigel. "Dialectical Impasses: Turning the Table on Hegel and the Black." *Parallax*, vol. 8, no. 2, 2002, pp. 30–45.

Gikandi, Simon. "Race and the Idea of the Aesthetic." *Michigan Quarterly Review*, vol. 40, no. 2, 2001, pp. 318–50.

Gilmore, Ruth Wilson. *Golden Gulag: Prisons, Surplus, Crisis, and Opposition in Globalizing California*. University of California Press, 2007.

Gilroy, Paul. *The Black Atlantic: Modernity and Double-Consciousness*. Harvard University Press, 1993.

Gimenez, Martha. "The Dialectics of Waged and Unwaged Work: Waged Work, Domestic Labor, and Household Survival in the United States." *Work Without Wages: Comparative Studies of Domestic Labor and Self-Employment*, SUNY Press, 1990, pp. 25–46.

Glazer, Nona. "Servants to Capital: Unpaid Domestic Labor and Paid Work." *Work Without Wages: Comparative Studies of Domestic Labor and Self-Employment*, edited by Jane L. Collins and Martha E. Gimenez, SUNY Press, 1990, pp. 142–67.

Glenn, Evelyn Nakano. *Forced To Care: Coercion and Caregiving in America*. Harvard University Press, 2012.

Glenn, Evelyn Nakano. "From Servitude to Service Work: Historical Continuities in the Racial Division of Paid Reproductive Labor." *Signs*, vol. 18, The University of Chicago Press, pp. 1–43, doi:10.2307/3174725. Accessed 9 Mar. 2018.

Glickman, Lawrence B. *Buying Power: A History of Consumer Activism in America*. 978-0226298672, 2009.

Glissant, Édouard. *Poetics of Relation*. Translated by Betsy Wing, University of Michigan Press, 1997.

Goings, Kenneth W. *Mammy and Uncle Mose: Black Collectibles and American Stereotyping*. Indiana University Press, 1994.

Goldsmith, Kenneth. "Conceptualism, Identity Politics & Globalization: A Response." *Poetry Foundation Harriet Blog*, 2009, https://www.poetryfoundation.org/harriet/2009/07/conceptualism-identity-politics-globalization-a-response.

Gompers, Samuel, and Herman Gutstadt. *Meat vs. Rice: American Manhood Against Asiatic Coolieism, Which Shall Survive?* Asian Exclusion League, 1908.

Gordon, Lewis. *Bad Faith and Antiblack Racism*. Humanity Books, 1995.

Gramsci, Antonio. *Selections From The Prison Notebooks*. Translated by Quintin Hoare and Geoffrey Nowell Smith Smith, International Publishers Co, 1971.

Guevara, Ernesto Che. *Che Guevara Reader: Writings on Politics & Revolution*. Edited by David Deutschmann, Ocean Press, 2003, pp. 350–64.

Gutierrez, Ramon A. "Internal Colonialism: An American Theory of Race." *Du Bois Review*, vol. 1, no. 2, 2002, pp. 281–95.

Hackworth, Jason. *The Neoliberal City*. Cornell University Press, 2007.

Hall, Jacquelyn Dowd. "The Long Civil Rights Movement and the Political Uses of the Past." *The Journal of American History*, vol. 91, no. 4, 2005, pp. 235–71.

Hall, Stuart. *The Fateful Triangle: Race, Ethnicity, Nation*. Edited by Kobena Mercer, Harvard University Press, 2017.

Hardt, Michael, and Antonio Negri. *Multitude: War and Democracy in the Age of Empire*. Penguin Books, 2005.

Harper, Phillip Brian. *Abstractionist Aesthetics: Artistic Form and Social Critique in African American Culture*. New York University Press, 2015.

Harraway, Donna. "A Manifesto for Cyborgs: Socialist Feminism in the 1980s." *Simians, Cyborgs, and Women: The Reinvention of Nature*, Routledge, 1996, pp. 149–82.

Harris, Cheryl. "Whiteness As Property." *Harvard Law Review*, vol. 106, no. 8, 1993, pp. 1707–91.

Hartman, Saidiya V. *Scenes of Subjection: Terror, Slavery, and Self-Making in Nineteenth-Century America*. Oxford University Press.

Hartman, Saidiya V. "Venus in Two Acts." *Small Axe*, vol. 12, no. 2, 2008, pp. 1–14.

Harvey, David. *A Brief History of Neoliberalism*. Oxford University Press, 2005.

Harvey, David. "Neoliberalism and the City." *Studies in Social Justice*, vol. 1, no. 1, pp. 2–13.

Hayden, Tom. *Rebellion in Newark: Official Violence and Ghetto Response*. Vintage Books, 1967.

Hayot, Eric. *The Hypothetical Mandarin: Sympathy, Modernity, and Chinese Pain*. Oxford University Press, 2009.

Hejinian, Lyn. *The Language of Inquiry*. University of California Press, 2000.

Higginbotham, Evelyn Brooks. "The Metalanguage of Race." *Signs: Journal of Women in Culture and Society*, vol. 17, no. 2, pp. 251–74.

Hing, Bill Ong. *Making and Remaking Asian America Through Immigration Policy: 1850-1990*. Stanford University Press, 1993.

Ho, Fred and Bill V. Mullen. *Afro Asia*.

Hochschild, Arlie. *The Second Shift: Working Families and the Revolution at Home*. Penguin Books, 2012.

Honey, Michael K. *To the Promised Land: Martin Luther King and the Fight for Economic Justice*. W. W. Norton & Company, 2019.

Hong, Grace. "Existentially Surplus: Women of Color Feminism and the New Crises of Capitalism." *GLQ: A Journal of Lesbian and Gay Studies*, vol. 18, no. 1, 2011, pp. 87–106.

HoSang, Daniel Martinez. "A Wider Type of Freedom." *Antiracism Inc.: Why the Way We Talk about Racial Justice Matters*, edited by Felice Blake et al., Punctum Books, 2019, pp. 57–79.

HoSang, Daniel Martinez, and Natalia Molina. "Introduction: Toward a Relational Consciousness of Race." *Relational Formations of Race: Theory, Method, and Practice*, edited by Natalia Molina et al., University of California Press, 2019, pp. 1–18.

Hudson, Peter James. "Racial Capitalism and the Dark Proletariat." *Boston Review*, 2018 http://bostonreview.net/forum/remake-world-slavery-racial-capitalism-and-justice/peter-james-hudson-racial-capitalism-and.

Hunt, Erica. "Notes For An Oppositional Poetics." *The Politics of Poetic Form*, Roof Books, 1989, pp. 197–212.

Hunt, Erica. *Piece Logic*. Carolina Wren Press, 2002.

Hunter, Tera. *To 'Joy My Freedom: Southern Black Women's Lives and Labors after the Civil War*. Harvard University Press, 1998.

Jackson, John P. *Social Scientists for Social Justice: Making the Case against Segregation*. NYU Press, 2005.

Jackson, Virginia, and Yopie Prins, editors. *The Lyric Theory Reader: A Critical Anthology*. Johns Hopkins University Press, 2016.

Jaeggi, Rahel, and Nancy Fraser. *Capitalism: A Conversation in Critical Theory*. Polity, 2018.

Jameson, Fredric. "Foreword." *Critique of Dialectical Reason, Volume One*, edited by Jonathan Ree, Verso, 2004, pp. xiii–xxxiii.

Jancovich, Mark. *The Cultural Politics of the New Criticism*. Cambridge University Press, 1993.

Jenkins, Destin. *The Bonds of Inequality: Debt and the Making of the American City*. University of Chicago Press, 2021.

Jennison, Ruth, and Julian Murphet, editors. *Communism and Poetry: Writing Against Capital*. 2019.

Jeon, Joseph Jonghyun. *Racial Things, Racial Forms: Objecthood in Avant-Garde Asian American Poetry*. University of Iowa Press, 2012.

Jessop, Bob. "Fordism and Post-Fordism: A Critical Reformulation." *Pathways to Regionalism and Industrial Development*, edited by Allen J. Scott and Michael J. Storper, Routledge, 1992, pp. 43–65.

Johnson, Cedric. *Revolutionaries to Race Leaders: Black Power and the Making of African American Politics*. University of Minnesota Press, 2007.

Johnson, Walter. *River of Dark Dreams: Slavery and Empire in the Cotton Kingdom*. Belknap Press, 2017.

Jones, Claudia. "An End to the Neglect of the Problems of Negro Women." *Claudia Jones: Beyond Containment*, edited by Carole Boyce Davies, Ayebia Clarke Publishing Limited, 2011, pp. 74–86.

Jones, Jacqueline. *Labor of Love, Labor of Sorrow*. Basic Books, 2010.

Jones, Martin. "Phase Space: Geography, Relational Thinking, and Beyond." *Progress in Human Geography*, vol. 33, no. 4, 2009, pp. 487–506.

Jordan, June. *Naming Our Destiny: New and Selected Poems*. Basic Books, 1993.

Jun, Helen Heran. *Race for Citizenship: Black Orientalism and Asian Uplift from Pre-Emancipation to Neoliberal America*. NYU Press, 2011.

Kant, Immanuel. *Critique of the Power of Judgment*. Translated by Paul Guyter and Eric Matthews, Cambridge University Press, 2001.

Kaufman, Robert. "Red Kant, or the Persistence of the Third 'Critique' in Adorno and Jameson." *Critical Inquiry*, vol. 26, no. 4, pp. 682–724.

Kearney, Douglas. *Mess And Mess And*. Noemi Press, 2015.

Keller, Lynn. *Thinking Poetry: Readings in Contemporary Women's Exploratory Poetics*. University of Iowa Press, 2009.

Kelley, Robin D. G., and Jordan T. Camp. "Black Radicalism, Marxism, and Collective Memory: An Interview with Robin D. G. Kelley." *American Quarterly*, vol. 65, no. 1, 2013, pp. 215–30.

Kelley, Robin D. G., and Betsy Esch. "Black Like Mao: Red China and Black Revolution." *Souls: Critical Journal of Black Politics & Culture*, vol. 1, no. 4, 1999, pp. 6–41.

Kim, Claire Jean. "The Racial Triangulation of Asian Americans." *Politics & Society*, vol. 27, no. 1, pp. 105–38.

Kim, Daniel. *Writing Manhood in Black and Yellow: Ralph Ellison, Frank Chin, and the Literary Politics of Identity*. Stanford University Press, 2005.

Kim, Elaine, et al. *Writing Self, Writing Nation: A Collection of Essays on Dictee by Theresa Hak Kyung Cha*. Edited by Norma Alarcon and Elaine Kim, Third Woman Press, 1994.

Kim, Myung Mi. *Civil Bound*. Omnidawn, 2019.

Kim, Myung Mi. *Commons*. University of California Press, 2002.

Kim, Myung Mi. "Convolutions: The Precision, The Wild." *American Poets in the 21st Century: The New Poetics*, edited by Claudia Rankine and Lisa Sewell, Wesleyan University Press, 2007, p. 251.

Kim, Myung Mi. *Dura*. Nightboat Books, 1998.

Kim, Myung Mi. *The Bounty*. Chax Press, 2000.

Kim, Myung Mi. *Under Flag*. Kelsey Street Press, 1991.

King Jr., Martin Luther. *All Labor Has Dignity*. Beacon Press, 2012.

King Jr., Martin Luther. "The Other America." *Grosse Pointe Historical Society*.

King Jr., Martin Luther. *Where Do We Go From Here: Chaos or Community?* Beacon Press, 2010.

King, Tiffany Lethabo. "Black 'Feminisms' and Pessimism: Abolishing Moynihan's Negro Family." *Theory & Event*, vol. 21, no. 1, 2018, pp. 68–87.

Kinnahan, Linda A. "'Bodies Written Off': Economies of Race and Gender in the Visual/Verbal Collaborative Clash of Erica Hunt's and Alison Saar's Arcade." *We Who Love to Be Astonished: Experimental Women's Writing and Performance Poetics*, edited by Laura Hinton and Cynthia Hogue, University of Alabama Press, 2002, pp. 165–78.

Kluger, Richard. *Simple Justice: The History of Brown v. Board of Education and Black America's Struggle for Equality*. Vintage, 2004.

Koshy, Susan. "Morphing Race into Ethnicity: Asian Americans and Critical Transformations of Whiteness." *Boundary 2*, vol. 28, no. 1, 2001, pp. 153–94.

Koshy, Susan. "Why the Humanities Matter for Race Studies Today." *PMLA*, vol. 123, no. 5, 2008, pp. 1542–49.

Kowal, Rebekah J. "Staging the Greensboro Sit-Ins." *TDR/The Drama Review*, vol. 48, no. 4, 2004, pp. 135–54.

Kramnick, Jonathan, and Anahid Nersessian. "Form and Explanation." *Critical Inquiry*, no. 43, pp. 650–69.

Lai, Larissa. *Automaton Biographies*. Arsenal Pulp Press, 2009.

Laurent, Sylvie. *King and the Other America: The Poor People's Campaign and the Quest for Economic Equality*. University of California Press, 2019.

Le Blanc, Paul, and Michael Yates. "Appendix: A Freedom Budget For All Americans." *A Freedom Budget for All Americans: Recapturing the Promise of the Civil Rights Movement in the Struggle for Economic Justice Today*, Monthly Review Press, 2013, pp. 242–50.

Leach, William R. "Transformations in a Culture of Consumption: Women and Department Stores, 1890-1925." *The Journal of American History*, vol. 71, no. 2, 1984, pp. 319–42.

Lee, Ching Kwan. *Gender and the South China Miracle*. University of California Press, 1998.

Lee, Christopher J., et al. "Introduction: Between a Moment and an Era: The Origins and Afterlives of Bandung." *Making a World after Empire: The Bandung Moment and Its Political Afterlives*, Ohio University Press, Cleveland, Ohio, 2019, pp. 1–42.

Lee, Erika. "The 'Yellow Peril' and Asian Exclusion in the Americas." *Pacific Historical Review*, vol. 76, no. 4, 2007, pp. 537–62.

Lee, Julia H. *Interracial Encounters: Reciprocal Representations in African and Asian American Literatures, 1896-1937*. NYU Press, 2011.

Lee, Rachel C., and Sau-Ling Cynthia Wong, editors. *Asian America.Net: Ethnicity, Nationalism, and Cyberspace*. Routledge, 2003.

Lee, Robert G. *Orientals: Asian Americans in Popular Culture*. Temple University Press, 1999.

Leighton, Angela. *On Form: Poetry, Aestheticism, and the Legacy of a Word*. Oxford University Press, 2007.

Lentin, Alana. "Replacing 'Race', Historicizing 'Culture' in Multiculturalism." *Patterns of Prejudice*, vol. 39, no. 4, 2005, pp. 379–96.

Leong, Michael. "Conceptualisms in Crisis: The Fate of Late Conceptual Poetry." *Journal of Modern Literature*, vol. 41, no. 3, 2018, pp. 109–31.

Leong, Michael. "Neo-Surrealism's Forked Tongue: Reflections on the Dramatic Monologue, Politics, and Community in the Recent Poetry of Will Alexander and John Yau." *Contemporary Literature*, vol. 55, no. 3, pp. 501–33.

Lesjak, Carolyn. "A Democracy of Forms: Levine, Latour, and the New Formalism." *Historical Materialism*, 2019, https://www.historicalmaterialism.org/book-review/democracy-forms-levine-latour-and-new-formalism.

Levinas, Emmanuel. *Emmanuel Levinas: Basic Philosophical Writings*. Edited by Adriaan T. Peperzak et al., Indiana University Press, 1996.

Levine, Caroline. *Forms: Whole, Rhythm, Hierarchy, Network*. Princeton University Press, 2017.

Levinson, Marc. *The Box: How the Shipping Container Made the World Smaller and the World Economy Bigger*. Princeton University Press, 2016.

Lew, Walter, editor. *Premonitions: The Kaya Anthology of New Asian North American Poetry*. Kaya Press, 1995.

Lewis, Oscar. *Five Families: Mexican Case Studies in the Culture of Poverty*. New American Library, 1959.

Liu, Warren. "Making Common the Commons: Myung Mi Kim's Ideal Subject." *American Poets in the 21st Century: The New Poetics*, edited by Claudia Rankine and Lisa Sewell, Wesleyan University Press, 2007, pp. 252–66.

Lloyd, David. *Under Representation: The Racial Regime of Aesthetics*. Fordham University Press, 2018.

Locke, John. *Second Treatise of Government*. Edited by C.B. Macpherson, Hackett Publishing Company, Inc., 1980.

LoLordo, Nicholas. "Identity Poetics? Or, The Norton Anthology of Modern and Contemporary Poetry." *Postmodern Culture*, vol. 15, no. 1, 2004.

Lopez, Ian Haney. *White by Law: The Legal Construction of Race*. NYU Press, 2006.

Lowe, Lisa. *Immigrant Acts: On Asian American Cultural Politics*. Duke University Press, 1996.

Lukacs, Georg. *History and Class Consciousness: Studies in Marxist Dialectics*. The MIT Press, 1972.

Lye, Colleen. *America's Asia: Racial Form and American Literature, 1893-1945*. Princeton University Press, 2004.

Lye, Colleen. "Racial Form." *Representations*, no. 104, pp. 92–101.

Lye, Colleen. "The Afro-Asian Analogy." *PMLA*, vol. 123, no. 5, pp. 1732–36.

Mackey, Nathaniel. *Discrepant Engagement: Dissonance, Cross-Culturality and Experimental Writing*. Cambridge University Press, 2009.

Mackey, Nathaniel. *Paracritical Hinge: Essays, Talks, Notes, Interviews*. University of Wisconsin Press, 2005.

Mackey, Nathaniel. "Preface." *Splay Anthem*, New Directions, 2006, pp. ix–vxi.

Marchand, Roland. *Advertising the American Dream*. University of California Press, 1985.

Marcus, Sharon, and Stephen Best. "Surface Reading: An Introduction." *Representations*, vol. 108, no. 1, pp. 1–21.

Marriott, David. "Signs Taken For Signifiers: Language Writing, Fetishism, and Disavowal." *Assembling Alternatives: Reading Postmodern Poetries Transnationally*, Wesleyan University Press, 2003, pp. 338–46.

Marriott, David. *Whither Fanon?: Studies in the Blackness of Being*. Stanford University Press, 2018.

Marx, Karl. *Capital: A Critique of Political Economy. Vol.1*. 1978, pp. 1–1138.

Marx, Karl. "Grundrisse." *Statewide Agricultural Land Use Baseline 2015*, vol. 1, 1993, doi:10.1017/CBO9781107415324.004.

Marx, Karl. *The German Ideology*. Prometheus Books, 1998.

Massey, Douglas S., and Nancy A. Denton. *American Apartheid: Segregation and the Making of the Underclass*. Harvard University Press, 1993.

Mathes, Carter. *Imagine the Sound: Experimental African American Literature after Civil Rights*. University of Minnesota Press, 2015.

Maxwell, Angie. *The Indicted South: Public Criticism, Southern Inferiority, and the Politics of Whiteness*. University of North Carolina Press, 2014.

May, Elaine Tyler. *Homeward Bound: American Families in the Cold War Era*. Basic Books, 1988.

McCaffrey, Stephen. *The Politics of the Referent*, no. 7, 1977, pp. 60–107, http://publish.uwo.ca/~fdavey/home.htm.

McCall, Linda. "The Complexity of Intersectionality." *Signs*, vol. 30, no. 3, 2005, pp. 1771–800.

McGovern, Charles F. *Sold American: Consumption and Citizenship, 1890-1945*. University of North Carolina Press, 2006.

McGurl, Mark. *The Program Era: Postwar Fiction and the Rise of Creative Writing*. Harvard University Press, 2011.

McIntyre, Michael. "Race, Surplus Population and the Marxist Theory of Imperialism." *Antipode*, vol. 43, no. 5, 2011, pp. 1489–515.

McKittrick, Katherine. "Mathematics Black Life." *The Black Scholar*, vol. 44, no. 2, pp. 16–28.

McMillen, Neil R. *The Citizens' Council: Organized Resistance to the Second Reconstruction, 1954-64*. University of Illinois Press, 1994.

McNally, David. *Monsters of the Market: Zombies, Vampires and Global Capitalism*. Haymarket Books, 2012.

McNay, Lois. *Against Recognition*. Polity, 2008.

Melamed, Jodi. "Racial Capitalism." *Critical Ethnic Studies*, vol. 1, no. 1, 2015, pp. 76–85.

Melamed, Jodi. *Represent and Destroy: Rationalizing Violence in the New Racial Capitalism*. University of Minnesota Press, 2011.

Mezzadra, Sandro, and Brett Nielson. *Border as Method, or, the Multiplication of Labor*. Duke University Press, 2013.

Mignolo, Walter. *The Darker Side of the Renaissance: Literacy, Territoriality, & Colonization*. University of Michigan Press, 2003.

Mitropoulos, Angela. *Contract & Contagion: From Biopolitics to Oikonomia*. Minor Compositions, 2012.

Mitropoulos, Angela. "Oikonomia." *Philosophy Today*, vol. 63, no. 4, 2019, pp. 1025–36.

Morrison, Yedda, and Myung Mi Kim. "Generosity as Method: Excerpts from a Conversation with Myung Mi Kim." *Tripwire: A Journal of Poetics*, no. 1, 2000, pp. 75–85.

Moten, Fred. *In the Break: The Aesthetics of the Black Radical Tradition*. University of Minnesota Press, 2003.

Moten, Fred. "Notes on Passage (The New International of Sovereign Feelings)." *Palimpsest: A Journal on Women, Gender, and the Black International*, vol. 3, no. 1, 2014, pp. 51–74, doi:10.1353/pal.2014.0010.

Moten, Fred, and Charles Henry Rowell. "'Words Don't Go There': An Interview With Fred Moten." *Callalloo*, vol. 27, no. 4, 2004, pp. 953–66.

Moynihan, Daniel Patrick. *The Negro Family: The Case For National Action*.

Mullen, Harryette. *Recyclopedia: Trimmings, S*PeRM**K*T, and Muse & Drudge*. Graywolf, 2006.

Mullen, Harryette. *The Cracks Between What We Are and What We Are Supposed to Be: Essays and Interviews*. University of Alabama Press, 2012.

Mumford, Kevin. *Newark: A History of Race, Rights, and Riots in America*. NYU Press, 2007.

Murdoch, Jon. *Post-Structuralist Geography: A Guide to Relational Space*. SAGE Publications.

Naples, Nancy A. "The 'New Consensus' on the Gendered 'Social Contract': The 1987-1988 U.S. Congressional Hearings on Welfare Reform." *Signs*, vol. 22, no. 4, pp. 907–45.

Neal, Larry. "The Black Arts Movement." *Drama Review*, no. 12, 1968, pp. 29–39.

Ngai, Mae. *Impossible Subjects: Illegal Aliens and the Making of Modern America*. Princeton University Press, 2014.

Ngai, Mae M. *Impossible Subjects: Illegal Aliens and the Making of Modern America*. Princeton University Press, 2014.

Ngai, Pun. "Becoming Dagongmei: Politics of Identities and Differences." *Made in China: Women Factory Workers in a Global Workplace*, Duke University Press, 2005, pp. 109–32.

Nielsen, Aldon Lynn. *Black Chant: Languages of African-American Postmodernism*. Cambridge University Press, 1997.

Nielsen, Aldon Lynn, and Lauri Ramey, editors. *Every Goodbye Ain't Gone: An Anthology of Innovative Poetry by African Americans*. The University of Alabama Press, 2006.

Nielsen, Aldon Lynn, and Lauri Ramey, editors. *What I Say: Innovative Poetry by Black Writers in America*. University of Alabama Press, 2015.

Nopper, Tamara K. "The 1992 Los Angeles Riots and the Asian American Abandonment Narrative as Political Fiction." *CR: The New Centennial Review*, vol. 6, no. 2, pp. 73–110.

O'Neill, Dave M., and June E. O'Neill. *The Declining Importance of Race and Gender in the Labor Market*. Rowman and Littlefield, 2012.

Okihiro, Gary Y. *Margins and Mainstreams: Asians in American History and Culture*. University of Washington, 2014.

Omi, Michael, and Howard Winant. *Racial Formation in the United States*. Third, Routledge, 2014.

Palumbo-Liu, David. *Asian/American: Historical Crossings of a Racial Frontier*. Stanford University Press, 1999.

Park, Josephine. *Apparitions of Asia: Modernist Form and Asian American Poetics*. Oxford University Press, 2014.

Patterson, Orlando. *Slavery and Social Death: A Comparative Study*. Harvard University Press, 1982.

Peck, Janice. "Why We Shouldn't Be Bored By The Political Economy Versus Cultural Studies Debate." *Cultural Critique*, vol. 64, no. 1, 2006, pp. 92–125.

Perloff, Marjorie. "Whose New American Poetry? Anthologizing in the Nineties." *Diacritics*, vol. 26, no. 3/4, pp. 104–23.

Pietz, William. "Fetishism and Materialism: The Limits of Theory in Marx." *Fetishism as Cultural Discourse*, edited by Emily Apter and William Pietz, Cornell University Press.

Pilgrim, David. *Understanding Jim Crow: Using Racist Memorabilia to Teach Tolerance and Promote Social Justice*. PM Press, 2015.

Polanyi, Michael. *Personal Knowledge: Towards a Post-Critical Philosophy*. University of Chicago Press, 2015.

Pon, Gordon. "IMPORTING THE ASIAN MODEL MINORITY DISCOURSE INTO CANADA: Implications for Social Work and Education." *Canadian Social Work Review*, vol. 17, no. 2, 2000, pp. 277–91.

Postmentier, Sonya. *Cultivation and Catastrophe: The Lyric Ecology of Modern Black Literature*. Johns Hopkins University Press, 2017.

Postone, Moishe. *Time, Labor, and Social Domination: A Reinterpretation of Marx's Critical Theory*. Cambridge University Press, 1996.

Pritchett, Wendell E. "Which Urban Crisis?: Regionalism, Race, and Urban Policy, 1960—1974." *Journal of Urban History*, vol. 34, no. 2, 2008, pp. 266–86.

Radhakrishnan, R. "Ethnic Identity and Post-Structuralist Differance." *Cultural Critique*, no. 6, pp. 199–220.

Raighford, Leigh. *Imprisoned in a Luminous Glare: Photography and the African American Freedom Struggle*. University of North Carolina Press, 2013.

Ralph, Michael, and Maya Singhal. "Racial Capitalism." *Theory and Society*, vol. 48, no. 6, 2019, pp. 851–81.

Ramey, Lauri. *A History of African American Poetry*. Cambridge University Press, 2019.

Reed, Anthony. *Freedom Time: The Poetics and Politics of Black Experimental Writing*. Johns Hopkins University Press, 2016.

Rehmann, Jan. *Theories of Ideology*. Haymarket Books, 2014.

Remarks by President Trump, Vice President Pence, and Members of the Coronavirus Task Force in Press Briefing. 2020.

Robbins, Jill. *Altered Reading: Levinas and Literature*. University of Chicago Press, 1999.

Roberson, Ed. *City Eclogue*. Atelos, 2006.

Roberson, Ed. "'We Must Be Careful.'" *Black Nature: Four Centuries of African American Nature Poetry*, edited by Camille T. Dungy, University of Georgia Press, 2009, pp. 3–5.

Roberson, Ed. *When Thy King Is A Boy*. University of Pittsburgh Press, 1970.

Robinson, Cedric J. *Black Marxism: The Making of the Black Radical Tradition*. University of North Carolina Press, 2000.

Robinson, Josh. *Adorno's Poetics of Form*. 2019.

Roh, David S., et al., editors. *Techno-Orientalism: Imagining Asia in Speculative* Fiction, *History, and Media*. Rutgers University Press, 2015.

Romano, Renee Christine, and Leigh Raiford, editors. *The Civil Rights Movement in American Memory*. University of Georgia Press, 2006.

Ronda, Margaret. "'Not/One': The Poetics of the Multitude in Great Recession-Era America." *Class and the Making of American Literature: Created Unequal*, edited by Andrew Lawson, Routledge, 2014, pp. 245–64.

Rosenthal, Caitlin. "Capitalism When Labor Was Capital: Slavery, Power, and Price in Antebellum America." *Capitalism: A Journal of History and Economics*, vol. 1, no. 2, 2020, pp. 296–337.

Rothstein, Richard. *The Color of Law: A Forgotten History of How Our Government Segregated America*. Liveright, 2017.

Rubin, Jr., Louis D., editor. *I'll Take My Stand: The South and the Agrarian Tradition*. Louisiana State University Press, 2006.

Ryan, William. *Blaming the Victim*. Vintage, 1976.

Ryan, William. "The New Genteel Racism." *The Crisis*, no. 72, pp. 623–31.

Safa, Helen I. "Runaway Shops and Female Employment: The Search for Cheap Labor." *Signs: Journal of Women in Culture and Society*, vol. 7, no. 2, pp. 418–33.

San Juan, Jr., E. "Marxism and the Race/Class Problematic: A Re-Articulation." *Cultural Logic*, 2003, https://clogic.eserver.org/2003/sanjuan.

Sanchez, Gabriel R., and Natalie Masuoka. "Brown-Utility Heuristic? The Presence and Contributing Factors of Latino Linked Fate." *Hispanic Journal of Behavioral Sciences*, vol. 32, no. 4, 2010, pp. 519–31.

Sanchez, George J. "Face the Nation: Race, Immigration, and the Rise of Nativism in Late Twentieth Century America." *The International Migration Review*, vol. 31, no. 4, pp. 1009–30.

Sartre, Jean-Paul. *Being and Nothingness*. Translated by Hazel E. Barnes, Methuen, 1993.

Sartre, Jean-Paul. *Critique of Dialectical Reason, Volume One*. Edited by Jonathan Ree, Translated by Alan Sheridan-Smith, Verso, 2004.

Sassatelli, Roberta. *Consumer Culture: History, Theory, and Politics*. SAGE Publications, 2007.

Scarry, Elaine. *The Body In Pain: The Making and Unmaking of the World*. Oxford University Press, 1987.

Schling, Hannah. "Gender, Temporality, and the Reproduction of Labour Power." *Social History Online*, no. 14, 2014, pp. 41–61.

Schulten, Susan. *Mapping the Nation: History and Cartography in Nineteenth-Century America*. University of Chicago Press, 2012.

Schultz, Kathy Lou. "Rock and a Hard Place: Erica Hunt and the Poetics of African-American Postmodernity." *How2*, 2000.

Sekyi-Otu, Ato. *Fanon's Dialectic of Experience*. Harvard University Press, 1997.

Seshagiri, Urmila. "Modernity's (Yellow) Perils: Dr. Fu-Manchu and English Race Paranoia." *Cultural Critique*, no. 62, pp. 162–94.

Sexton, Jared. "Proprieties of Coalition: Blacks, Asians, and the Politics of Policing." *Critical Sociology*, vol. 36, no. 1, pp. 87–108.

Sharpe, Christina. *In The Wake: On Blackness and Being*. Duke University Press, 2016.

Shaw, Lytle. *Fieldworks: From Place to Site in Postwar Poetics*. 2013.

Shepherd, Reginald, editor. *Lyric Postmodernisms: An Anthology of Contemporary Innovative Poetries*. Counterpath, 2008.

Shockley, Evie. *Renegade Poetics: Black Aesthetics and Formal Innovation in African American Poetry*. 2011.

Silliman, Ron. "Poetry and the Politics of the Subject." *Socialist Review*, no. 18, 1988, pp. 62–8.

Simien, Evelyn M. "Race, Gender, and Linked Fate." *Journal of Black Studies*, vol. 35, no. 5, 2005, pp. 529–50.

Singh, Nikhil Pal. *Black Is a Country: Race and the Unfinished Struggle for Democracy*. Harvard University Press, 2005.

Smith, Adam. *Wealth of Nations*. Edited by Kathryn Sutherland, Oxford University Press, 1998.

Smith, Jason E. "Nowhere to Go: Automation, Then and Now." *Brooklyn Rail*, 2017, https://brooklynrail.org/2017/03/field-notes/Nowhere-to-Go.

Smith, Jason E. "Nowhere to Go: Automation, Then and Now Part Two." *Brooklyn Rail*, 2017.

Smith, Rachel Greenwald. "Six Propositions on Compromise Aesthetics." *The Account*, 2014, https://theaccountmagazine.com/article/six-propositions-on-compromise-aesthetics.

Snead, James. "Repetition as a Figure of Black Culture." *Critical Essays on American Literature Series - African-American Literary Criticism, 1773-2000*, edited by Hazel Arnett Ervin, Twayne Publishers, 1999, pp. 206–22.

So, Christine. *Economic Citizens: A Narrative of Asian American Visibility*. Temple University Press.

Steen, Shannon, and Heike Raphael-Hernandez, editors. *AfroAsian Encounters: Culture, History, Politics*. New York University Press, 2006.

Swenson, Cole, and David St. John, editors. *American Hybrid: A Norton Anthology of New Poetry*. W. W. Norton & Company, 2009.

Tadiar, Neferti X. M. "Decolonization, 'Race,' and Remaindered Life Under Empire." *Qui Parle: Critical Humanities and Social Sciences*, vol. 23, no. 2, pp. 135–60.

Taylor, Keeanga-Yamahtta. *How We Get Free: Black Feminism and the Combahee River Collective*. Haymarket Books, 2017.

Taylor, Paul. *Race: A Philosophical Introduction*. Polity, 2013.
"The Combahee River Collective Statement." *How We Get Free: Black Feminism and the Combahee River Collective*, Haymarket Books, 2017, pp. 15–28.
The International Wages For Housework Campaign.
Tronti, Mario. "La Fabbrica e La Società." *Quaderni Rossi*, no. 2, 1962, pp. 1–31.
Trotter, JW, and MB Katz. "The 'Underclass' Debate: Views from History." … *Debate: Views*…, 1993.
Tuma, Keith, editor. *Rainbow Darkness: An Anthology of African American Poetry*. Miami University Press, 2005.
Turner, Patricia. *Ceramic Uncles & Celluloid Mammies: Black Images and Their Influence on Culture*. University of Virginia Press, 2002.
Tyner, James. "Population Geography I: Surplus Populations." *Progress in Human Geography*, vol. 37, no. 5, 2013, pp. 701–11.
Villegas, Sonia, and Larissa Lai. "On Reading and Writing: An Interview with Larissa Lai." *Canada And Beyond: A Journal of Canadian and Literary and Cultural Studies*, vol. 4, no. 1–2, 2014, pp. 117–27.
Vogel, Lise. *Marxism and the Oppression of Women: Toward a Unitary Theory*. Haymarket Books, 2014.
Wacquant, Loic. *Punishing the Poor:* Duke University Press, 2009.
Wang, Dorothy. "Race and the Poetic Avant-Garde." *Boston Review*, Apr. 2015, bostonreview.net/blog/boston-review-race-and-poetic-avant-garde.
Wang, Dorothy. *Thinking Its Presence: Form, Race, and Subjectivity in Contemporary Asian American Poetry*. Stanford University Press, 2013.
Weinberger, Eliot, editor. *American Poetry Since 1950: Innovators and Outsiders, an Anthology*. Marsilio Publishers, 1993.
Weinberger, Eliot, editor. "Letter." *American Poetry Review*, pp. 43–4.
Westerman, Richard. *Lukács's Phenomenology of Capitalism: Reification Revalued*. Palgrave Macmillan, 2018.
White, Gillian. *Lyric Shame: The "Lyric" Subject of Contemporary American Poetry*. Harvard University Press, 2014.
Wilderson, Frank. *Red, White & Black: Cinema and the Structure of U.S. Antagonisms*. Duke University Press, 2010.
Wilderson, Frank. "The Prison Slave as Hegemony's (Silent) Scandal." *Social Justice*, vol. 30, no. 2, 2003, pp. 18–27.
Williams, Eric. *Capitalism and Slavery*. University of North Carolina Press, 1994.
Williams, Raymond. *Marxism and Literature*. Oxford University Press, 1978.
Williams, Tyrone. "A=B=L=A=C=K=W=O=M=A=N Poetics: Erica Hunt's Prose Poetry." *On: Contemporary Practice*, no. 2, 2009, pp. 145–54.
Wilson, William Julius. "The Truly Disadvantaged: The Inner City, the Underclass and Public Policy." *Educational Studies*, 2012, doi:10.2307/3323400.
Wimmer, Andreas. *Ethnic Boundary Making: Institutions, Power, Networks*. Oxford University Press, 2013.

Wolfe, Patrick. *Traces of History: Elementary Structures of Race*. Verso, 2016.

Woodard, Komozi. "Introduction." *A Guide to the Microfilm Edition of The Black Power Movement*, edited by John H. Bracey Jr. et al., University Publications of America, 2001.

Wright, Melissa W. *Disposable Women and Other Myths of Global Capitalism*. Routledge, 2006.

Yao, Steven G. *Foreign Accents: Chinese American Verse from Exclusion to Postethnicity*. Oxford University Press, 2010.

Yates, Michael, and Paul Le Blanc. *A Freedom Budget for All Americans: Recapturing the Promise of the Civil Rights Movement in the Struggle for Economic Justice Today*. Monthly Review Press, 2013.

Yau, John. *Adventures in Monochrome*. Copper Canyon Press, 2012.

Yau, John. "Letter." *American Poetry Review*, p. 44.

Yau, John. "'Purity' and the 'Avant-Garde.'" *Boston Review*, 2015.

Yau, John, and Thomas Nozkowski. *Ing Grish*. Saturnalia Books, 2005.

Young, Iris Marion. "Beyond the Unhappy Marriage: A Critique of the Dual Systems Theory." *Women and Revolution: A Discussion of the Unhappy Marriage of Marxism and Feminism*, edited by Lydia Sargent, South End Press, 1981, pp. 43–70.

Young, Kevin. *Bunk*. Graywolf, 2018.

Yu, Timothy. *Race and the Avant-Garde: Experimental and Asian American Poetry Since 1965*. Stanford University Press, 2009.

Zhou, Xiaojing. "'What Story What Story What Sound': The Nomadic Poetics of Myung Mi Kim's 'Dura.'" *College Literature*, vol. 34, no. 4, pp. 63–91.

Index

www.ingramcontent.com/pod-product-compliance
Lightning Source LLC
Chambersburg PA
CBHW070531100726
47907CB00004B/1067

* 9 7 8 1 3 5 0 2 7 8 8 0 6 *